CHRIST BECOMING

CHRIST BECOMING

The Lives of Jesus
& His Path to the Christ

Channeled by
Reverend Penny Donovan

—————————————————————

Edited by Peter Santos

Sacred Garden Fellowship, Inc.
Albany, New York

CHRIST BECOMING: The Lives of Jesus & His Path to the Christ

Edited by Peter Santos.

Cover image: *Jesus Goes Up Alone to a Mountain to Pray* by James Tissot.

Published by Sacred Garden Fellowship, Inc.
Albany, NY
www.sacredgardenfellowship.org

ISBN-13: 978-1932746075

Acknowledgements

This book would not have been possible without the support and efforts of many in the Sacred Garden Fellowship (SGF) community who have helped sustain and promote SGF's mission over the years, including many who were instrumental in recording and preserving these wonderful teachings. We also offer deep, loving gratitude to the nonphysical teachers, guides, and angels who have been there every step of the way, challenging us and offering opportunities for both the organization and the community to grow spiritually, and guiding us ever forward on the path to Truth. And finally, many thanks to the reader who has been drawn to these lessons and is now joined on the path of advancing themselves toward awakening the Christ within, that which Jesus himself displayed through the manner in which he lived.

Table of Contents

Preface

In October of 1987, my life changed very drastically one Sunday. I went to church, as I had done for twenty-three years. As I went into my office to get my Bible and get ready to go up on the podium, I felt very light-headed and dizzy and I thought, "Well, I ate dinner early. Maybe I just need some food." The feeling kind of passed as I went out on the podium.

I remember saying to the congregation, "Before I give my talk, we have a meditation." The last thing I remember was the meditation. The next thing I knew I was standing at the lectern with everyone standing up and applauding! I didn't know what had happened. The people were saying, "It was wonderful! A teacher came."

It was during the next few days that the teacher revealed himself to me as being the Archangel Gabriel. He said, "I will teach you things and if you will follow and do them, they will change your life for the better."

That was the beginning of the twelve years during which he channeled through me, teaching truths and providing spiritual guidance. His teachings were simple, loving. I watched the people in my congregation change, evolve, and grow.

He was challenged many times by me and others, and never did he lose his temper. He never was anything but loving and kind, and he never failed to have an answer to any question that was given to him. He was a very powerful, loving force in my life and in the lives of the people who came to hear him over the years.

People have often asked me what it was like to channel Gabriel and how I felt after he left us for good in 1999. For a long time, it was difficult to put into words the feelings I had of the channeling and his leaving. I awoke one morning and the words were there and I share them now with you.

Gabriel was an energy, a divine energy, that overtook my consciousness and my body from an indefinable Source. He was not greater than I, but he was more powerful and strong-willed with an intent of absolute love and goodness. He overrode my fears and caused me to be so still that I seemed to disappear. I was aware of him, bound and consumed in the love of him. My surrender was complete and only in retrospect do I realize how totally I trusted him. Once I surrendered, I never entertained the idea of stopping.

When it was over, I felt an emptiness inside, an emptiness that rises to the surface now and then as a great longing for something lost before time began. Yet at other times the mere memory of him brings a comfort beyond words. It will never be again, yet it will never be totally gone. Gabriel left something of himself that will be with me always, beyond Earth or Heaven; an addition to the fabric that is my true self, a gift more pure than mind can comprehend. And so it is.

Reverend Penny Donovan

Introduction

One of the most influential spiritual teachers of all time, Jesus has been the subject of countless books that attempt to explain the historical, political, religious, metaphysical, and spiritual aspects of the man born Yeshua ben Joseph over 2,000 years ago. The Bible, the largest selling book in history, endeavors to provide the truth about the man and his life, but the human fingerprints of its numerous translators and often partisan structure under which the translations were completed contaminated some of the original messages and lessons. While the Bible holds certain truths, we must be careful to understand the background and context of the stories it contains, for if we truly knew the man, Jesus, we would know why he came to teach us so many years ago.

Jesus lived many, many lives, as we all do. He spent lifetimes moving through particular states of consciousness that served to prepare him for each incarnation that followed, eventually culminating in the man who lived an earthly life as the Christ.

Born into an Essene community with all of its strict rules, Jesus eventually returned after years of travel and study to challenge its precepts and to show people that the freedom they sought was to be found within, not through archaic Essene regulations or through overthrowing the Romans. This was difficult for people to accept at the time, as they were being persecuted and were looking for a Savior, but his skills as an orator, healer, miracle-worker, and most of all, as a teacher of truths that resonated within, helped him naturally gain a following and produce the lasting impact that we see today.

Much of what is written in the Bible about Jesus' life and the people in it—Mary Magdalene, Mother Mary, Joseph, the disciples, his siblings—became distorted by those who didn't fully understand his teachings and who tried to fit them into the social and political norms of the era, as well as minimize threats to their very lives. When we appreciate the circumstances of the times and understand his teachings through their symbolism and codes, we can recognize the reasons behind his choices and view his whole life in the context that he intended. Indeed, he teaches us that he was just like us, a flesh and blood human being with all the ups and downs of personal experience, but also so much more—divinity in earthly form that we can also express when we embody the profound truth of the Christ.

As you will read in the following pages, Jesus was a divine rebel. He flaunted the rules of his time but had the knowledge, wisdom, charisma, and most importantly, divine truth, to support his words and actions. This truth, often inaccurately conveyed in the Bible and other texts, is clarified within these pages through direct lessons from Archangel Gabriel and Jesus himself, channeled through Rev. Penny Donovan.

Each of the three lectures contained in this book was a day-long seminar attended by dozens of people. Because the teachers had instructed, "Don't interpret what you are transcribing; transcribe it word for word, even if the language is incorrect," the following pages reflect only minor copyediting. So, as directed, the text is word for word from the audio recordings, including seeming inconsistencies in grammar, such as not using a comma when normally appropriate to reflect more rapid speaking and conversely, adding a comma to reflect a substantial pause. And as the seminars were originally recorded on cassette tapes, there are a few brief gaps in the lectures, which are noted in the text. In addition, care was taken to reflect Gabriel's and Jesus' manner of speaking and emphasis on particular words or phrases. Both teachers' frequent pauses and recurrent use of "Now," "And," and "But" at the beginning of sentences are also retained, as well as Gabriel's use of "wise" for the word "way."

Also, while speaking through Rev. Penny's physical form, Gabriel and Jesus sometimes joke around with the group, often to break up the heavy, mental energy of the lesson. And Gabriel occasionally speaks or consults with his playful angel helper, Tinkerbell, who has a better understanding of earthly matters and who delights in joking and finding joy in even the smallest of things. These digressions from the lessons are included to show both teachers' grand and wondrous personalities. In all, the goal was to invite the reader into the feeling of being present at the seminars.

Over the course of twelve years of teaching through Rev. Penny from 1987 to 1999, Gabriel covered a wide spectrum of spiritual truths ranging from the nature of God and who we are as Spirit to our current level of evolvement and spiritual understanding in this physical dimension. He explained how we came to the earth, our purpose for being here, and what we must do to return home to our remembrance of our Spirit within. Through over two hundred fifty lectures on a wide range of topics—including our levels of consciousness, reincarnation, energy, our egos, the power of our thoughts, negative and positive thinking, the life of Jesus, unconditional love, forgiveness, and the purpose of the experiences we go through in our lives—his central theme always centered on living our truth through unconditional love, compassion, forgiveness, and knowing that we are truly the Children of God. The other master teachers channeled by Rev. Penny, including Jesus, taught along similar themes.

Although this book is not a complete compilation of all that these two magnificent teachers shared about Jesus' life through Rev. Penny over the years, it presents the details about how and why he lived, providing an updated context within which to view his life, teachings, the Bible, Christianity, and spiritual growth.

This is not a religious book. Rather, it is a spiritual book that speaks to what is inherent in us all, a divine Spirit that seeks expression through what we see as the physical body. As Gabriel once said, "Religion is man's concept of God; true spirituality is what God knows you to be."

May you be blessed on your journey and expression of truth.

CHRIST BECOMING

The Lives of Jesus
& His Path to the Christ

The Lives & States of Consciousness of Jesus
January 18, 1997

Handout

The Master Jesus as given by Gabriel
January 18, 1997

The following names represent states of consciousness in the human evolution.

<u>Adam</u>: The first physical form to be used by humans that was not part animal or animal-based.

<u>Enoch</u>: "He who walks with God" Consciousness begins to remember some of the spiritual truths and seeks to worship one God. Archangel Metatron assisted this consciousness.

<u>Hermes</u>: Alchemist - tried to bring spirit into matter but was only partially successful because he lacked the love connectedness to do it with purity.

Melchizedek: This consciousness was familiar with Abram (faith in the unseen). The personality manifested became aware that all that is seen is supported by the unseen. It was this consciousness that introduced the ritual of Holy Communion to humankind. He was also a Gentile. Archangel Michael worked with Melchizedek. He was a high priest and a king.

Joseph: Son of Jacob and Rachel. The first forgiveness consciousness that used love rather than vengeance. Joseph represents Light entering darkness (Egypt).

Joshua: Moses' minister. Moses represents spiritual law or conscience. The Joshua consciousness knew how to use the higher laws to obtain physical results. The Jordan river parted for him to take the Israelites across after Moses' death. Also the walls of Jericho crumbled before him as well after seven days of marching blowing trumpets. Joshua conquered all the hill cities and soon had taken control of the Promised Land. Angel Metatron helped Joshua.

Buddha: Born to wealth which he left at the age of twenty-nine to seek the meaning of life. He so totally desired to know God that he refused to allow anything to take his attention that he felt would keep him from his goal. He knew in his mind what he could not take into his heart. He felt that there was more to life than what the physical offered and in that lay the meaning of life.

Jesus: The manifestation of the ideal Son of God – as it was in the beginning and is forever more – without end.

Lives of the Master Jesus

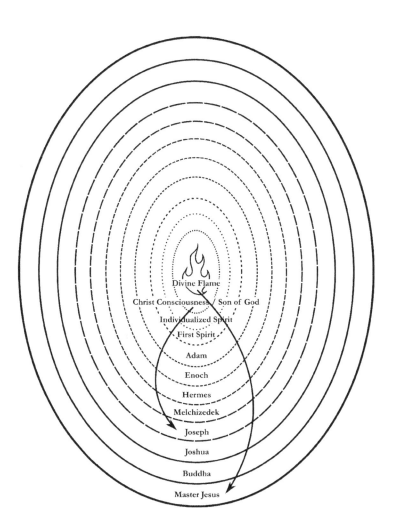

Divine Flame

Christ Consciousness / Son of God

Individualized Spirit

First Spirit

Adam

Enoch

Hermes

Melchizedek

Joseph

Joshua

Buddha

Master Jesus

Lesson

Archangel Gabriel: You are well this day? Some of you traveled through blizzards, climbed the mountain, crossed oceans, aye? Indeed! Ah, we have our beloved blackboard. Good!

This day we are going to learn about the Christ. We are going to learn how that is made manifest in the world of form and why it is necessary for it to be manifest in the world of form. [Gabriel draws on the blackboard] I have been spending time with Rembrandt. (Laughter)

Divine Flame

Divine Flame, Son of God, Christ consciousness, Spirit manifested as an individual entity... [See diagram] Beloved woman, if you would write "Divine Flame," "Christ," and so forth.

Now, you must understand that this is on a level far, far, far, far removed from any sense of earth or any solid physical. The Divine Flame—as some of you know but for those of you who are new to us—is what you term "God." It is all Beingness. It is all Mind. It is all Love. It is that from which springs forth *every* form of life, be it in the Spirit or be it in the physical body; it makes no difference. Everything had its origin in Divine Flame.

Christ Consciousness / Son of God

The very first issue of Divine Flame was the ideal Son of God, you term to be the Christ Consciousness. Now I care not whether you are Gentile, Jew, Christian, Muslim; it makes no difference. Those are human terms.

This is a divine fact and if you care to call it something else, that is your prerogative, but the very first issue from Divine Flame is the Christ.

The Christ is pure love. You have a concept of a *kind* of love, but in your finite minds, you cannot begin to even comprehend the love that is the Christ Consciousness, for it is all encompassing. It sees no wrong. It is totally unaware of any kind of what you perceive to be sin or evil. It sees the purity and the ideal Son of God in every human being *without exception*. It looks upon the saint and looks upon the murderer with the same eyes of love. Do not misunderstand, I am not condoning murder, so please do not read into my words what is not there.

The Christ encompasses all form of life. The Christ loves the flower. The Christ loves the animals, the devas, the mineral world, everything. The Christ does not choose whom or what to love and leave anything out. It is the most total, complete form of love. I would think the closest that you can come to it in your Earth form would be a Mother's love for her child. It is even beyond that. However, we shall leave it there.

God looked upon the Christ Consciousness and He/She/It was deeply pleased. "This is my beloved Son in whom I am well pleased."

Individualized Spirit

Now the next issue from that was the Spirit known as the individualized unit of God or, in other words, you. Now I am not going to get into the creation of angels and so forth because that is not our purpose this day and it would take us far afield. So we are going to stay completely within the human element.

The Spirit manifestation of you at this point was in at total At-one-ment with these two. [Referring to the diagram] It was completely absorbed into an active part of the Christ awareness. It knew it was the Son of God. It knew it was the *only* begotten Son of God. No other creation was given free will. No other creation was given the ability to create beyond their own form. Roses beget roses. Dogs beget dogs. People bring forth after their own kind and then beyond that they create, they use, they discover electricity and they make it into form. You have all manner of form that you have created. So the free will and the creative ability was given *only* unto the Son of God.

First Spirit

Now, because you were given free...unlimited free will with no exception, you created anything you wanted. And at this point... Oh, beloved woman, wouldst thou come forth and write here, "First Spirit." I know not of any other term to use. Now when I say, "First Spirit," I am referring to that aspect of you which was still in complete alignment with the Christ awareness and with Divine Flame, and whose creations were ones of beauty, joy, loveliness, happiness, uplifting, nurturing, life-giving, life-sustaining.

There was no concept of evil, no concept of death, no concept of illness, of lack, of limitation, of anything that was not a *total* awareness of these two: of the Christ and of the Spirit manifestation.

Now, for more time than your minds can comprehend, you lived in that state. For eons and eons of time...there was no time at that point; you were in eternity. You were *aware* of eternity *as* eternity and there was no concept in your mind of a beginning or an ending; it simply *was* and nothing else mattered.

Adam

Now in your creations you came yet another step further away in awareness. Now, beloved woman, would you come forth and write another word? Let me see, what is a good word of your language? Alright. Put "Adam." You know how to spell Adam?

Participant: Yeah, I've got that one. (Laughter)

Gabriel: Good. I can't spell, I can't write yet. I'm learning but I haven't got that down yet. Now we're going to talk about Adam. Not the individual man because there was no such thing as the individual man, "Adam." Beloved woman, would you write over here...would you write "States of consciousness" with an arrow?

Now beloveds, understand that *all* of this is a state of consciousness. It has no other delineation. There is no geographical place. There is no sense of time. It is a complete, absolute sense of consciousness, which, by the way, is totally, absolutely available to you at any time you choose to go there. "Well, easy for you," you say. Well, you wait.

Now, these states of consciousness became as a result of the ever expanding Divine Flame. Now one thing about the Divine Flame—and you must understand and that it ever, ever seeks to become more—it never stops. Everybody thinks creation stopped way back in biblical times. Oh, no. If you look around, you will note that that is not so.

Now the expansion of consciousness began *in you* with the Spirit manifestation. It was at that point that you discovered you could create and you created simply by thinking. You conceived in your mind of an idea and immediately manifested it. There was no time-lapse between the conception and the manifestation.

Now, you think that that is not true with you any longer, but it is as true this moment in your time as it was, if I might use the term, back then because all of these states of consciousness are now. You have not left them behind. They are a present, absolutely complete sense of awareness that is available to you now.

Now, we're going to come to Adam. You all know the story of the Garden of Eden. Adam went into the Garden of Eden, he got lonely, God said, "Alright, I'll give you a help mate," so he took the dust of the earth and Adam's rib and he made Eve. And then a little, slivery snake came along and said, "Hey Babe, you're pretty good looking but you're not too smart. Let me help you." Well, I'll tell you what. None of that is true. Adam represents a state of consciousness in which humankind ceased to use animal bodies to dwell in.

Now, in the Adam consciousness you created solid form. You dallied around with it and became quite enamored with it and until after a bit, you decided that solid form was just...what is it, "the cat's pajamas"? Is that your term? And you concentrated your efforts so completely on form that you began to lose interest in these higher things. However, whenever you cared to manifest upon the earth, you borrowed a body, similar to what I do with Beloved Woman [Rev. Penny]. Only because you had not created a physical form for yourselves, you borrowed bodies of animals. Mostly the great apes...that's how they came to be.

You started out with lesser forms. You even manifested a little bit in the mineral kingdom but found that was extremely limiting since minerals tend to stay in one spot forever. That's why they very rarely have parties. (Laughter) Can't get anybody there.

Now, the thing is that after a bit, this became a little dull. It was no longer fun to manifest as a mineral or something because you couldn't do anything, so you began to borrow animal bodies. Now when I say, "borrow," remember, you created them out of your own thinking, out of your own concept.

When, in your Scripture, it tells you, "God said, go forth and multiply," He didn't mean, "Go forth and have a lot of babies." He meant, "Go forth and create a lot of form," because you are the avenue—one of the avenues— through which Divine Flame becomes more and more and more. So, I know someone's going to get up and ask, "Well, what about this six days of creation? What's all that got to do?" Represents states of consciousness, and you were the vehicles.

When you were out dallying around in the universe, you said, "What do you think would happen if we made a great big round sphere and put life on it? Oh, let's do that. It sounds like a lot of fun." And so you went off creating.

Anyway, the thing is that these are states of consciousness *where you poured your energy.* Energy follows thought, ever. It's an unbreakable rule. When you have a thought, the energy required to manifest that thought in whatever form it is to take is immediately present and immediately begins its work. This is why we've told you so many times, "Watch what you think."

Don't allow yourself the little games of "What if?" because that's exactly what you're creating.

Now, you got tired of fooling around in animal form so you said, "Well, why are we doing...why are we bothering with this? Why don't we make a form that's uniquely ours?" So you experimented and you tried one thing and you tried another and so on and so forth and the best that you came up with was what you've got. (Laughter) Personally, you could have done a little better, but that's alright. (Laughter)

Now because you were used to creating animal form, the first forms you created were hairy and long arms, short legs, and kind of grunted as they walked and so forth. Now remember, you did not have a language then because you had been used to communicating with thought. You didn't have to think of a word or speak a word; you simply thought it and the person to whom you directed the thought received it and made a response and so forth and so on. So there were no language—as you know languages to be today—absolutely none because there was no need.

Because you had no need for a language, you did not create the ability within the forms you created—such as your animal forms, plant life, and so forth—with any kind of a specific language. The creatures developed that themselves, mostly body language with sounds that represented certain things, but this was of *their* own creation rather than yours, born of a necessity to make known.

So, you created a people form. Well, that worked pretty good excepting that in the beginning, you still had the open communication with your Source—Son of God, only begotten of God—and you still, even though the

12

bodies you created were rather primitive, to say the least, you still had the mental and spiritual capability of *tuning in* and becoming aware of a higher form of life and being inspired by it.

Because you were aware of the vastness of the Spirit as compared to the limitation of the body, you very rarely had bodies that lived longer than twenty to twenty-five years of your earth time. By the time a cave person reached the twenty-fifth year, they were old and decrepit and died. And the reason being, because you still had that connectedness.

Now you're sitting there thinking, "You mean to tell me that a cave person was a highly evolved spiritual being?" Yes, and that's why the bodies were not highly evolved because the cave person knew that the bodies were simply a vehicle they used to lumber about and have adventures on the earth plane.

Now, as you did this, you became so enamored with form, it was as though you, little by little—this part up in here, the Christ, the Spirit manifestation—all that began to fade. It became, at best, a form of superstition. You began to believe that it was possible to have an enemy. Now up until this time, you didn't believe there were any enemies. Even the flesh-eating animals were not regarded as enemies because you knew if they captured you and ate you, that was no big deal. You simply created another body and away we went.

However, the allegory of being tossed out of the Garden comes at this point in awareness when Adam began to believe that he—I'll use the term "he"...it was "he/she"—was so complete within themselves that they didn't *need* God. At the risk of sounding Catholic, it was what you would term to be the "original sin."

Now sin simply means...the word "sin" simply means to slide backward or to not go forward. Now you can put any connotation to it that you desire but that's what the word actually means.

Now that meant that you were sliding backward into an animalistic type of thinking, into a kill-or-be-killed world, into a "if I don't eat you, you will eat me," into the belief system that the only life you had was the form you took and beyond that there was, who knew? Nothing, perhaps?

You lost this Christ awareness. You forgot that you were the only begotten Sons of God. Now, we have a lot of symbolism in this. There was no individual person, Adam. That is an allegory. It is symbolic of a human being drifting in consciousness away from its knowledge of its Source.

Eve was not responsible for the fall of Adam. Eve represents the sustaining aspect of the creative aspect of Adam. This is why, symbolically, she is taken from his rib or *be-side* him because one does not exist without the other. What is the good of creating something if there's no sustaining life to keep it alive?

So Adam needed Eve to keep his creations going. Eve needed Adam to create the creations that she kept going. So, symbolically, we have here the nurturing aspect questioning whether or not it wanted to continue to support a life form that was so terribly temporary and seemed to have no spiritual basis behind it.

So, the "let's live forever" theory began to fade away and in its place came a sensuous—represented by the snake—a sensuous idea that the only form was the physical. And the Eve aspect recognized that it could sustain—or would...I wouldn't say could...I would say *would*—sustain it only for a certain length of time.

The difference in the male and female consciousness is this: The male being the creator—the action, the moving part—creates and moves on; the Eve, or the female aspect of it, comes in to sustain that which has been created.

So who is more aware of the creative life? The female, because the female remains with it. The male acts and goes, acts and goes, and so forth and so on. So, the sustaining or the awareness of the form and its continuing life is lesser known to the male, to the action, then it is to the female.

Now because the female is...stuck? [To Tinkerbell] You want me to use the word "stuck"? Alright. Tinkerbell says, "Because the female is *stuck* with maintaining the irrational life forms that males make..." I don't think that goes well. (Laughter) Stuck. [To Tinkerbell] You think you're funny, don't you? She's having a great laugh here.

The nurturing energy is completely aware of the form that has been created *and its purpose.* Now the male creates a form with an idea in mind and then goes on, and if the idea manifests and goes forth, wonderful. And if it doesn't, no matter. We'll go and we'll create another. This is why males frequently like more than one female. It goes back to the idea of creating and moving on, creating and moving on, and I'm not telling you males to go out and find another female. Don't want anything misread here. (Laughter)

Now, the sustaining life force in the Adam consciousness... Because form was what it was, a slow moving, solid, not-quick-to-evolve thing, the female aspect of it became a little disenchanted with it. In other words, it was sustaining something that, to the feminine aspect, had little or no value. Therefore, the question came in, represented by the snake, "Are you sure you know what you're doing?" to the male. Adam…"Of course I do. Why not? I do as I please."

Now, enter here the rational thinking of the female and that being, "Don't you think you ought to look past the moment? Do you not think you need to consider all the aspects of what you're doing? Do you not think that there is a tree of knowledge that would give you a concrete idea of what you are creating?"

So, keep in mind the story of the Garden of Eden came about in a male-dominant society. Females could reproduce. This was a great mystery to the male and it frightened him. Females had great power. Certain times of the month their power was at its greatest and could easily destroy a male. So what did the males have to do? They had to bring the female into a subservient concept, subservient to the male. And so the stories, the myths and so forth, of creation, always blamed the female. It was the female who brought to the consciousness of the male the idea that he'd better *pay attention* to what he was creating. Now, it's that simple.

Now, once Adam became aware of what he was creating, which is symbolic by eating of the apple and so forth, he didn't like it. He questioned his own purpose, and in questioning that he became aware of, "Perhaps I'm wrong. Maybe I'm not doing this right? Maybe I am not the Son of God? Maybe I've made a mistake?" And thus began the creation of what you term in this day in your time as sin; the first idea that maybe this isn't good.

Now once that happened, regaining this consciousness back in here was an impossibility because what did the Christ Consciousness know? No evil, no mistake, nothing wrong, no sin, everything is good. But Adam had created a *doubt* in the system. So, Adam represents a consciousness in form that tells you that maybe you're not acceptable to God—a loss of innocence.

Now, we come to the next one, the next state of consciousness. I don't know if these will all fit. You have your papers with these lists? Indeed. Alright! Getting pretty good at drawing eggs, don't you think?

Enoch

Now, we come to Enoch. Enoch is a state of consciousness that has a faint, vague, haunting memory of all of this back here—of the Christ, of the Spirit made manifest, of the good times, of the goodness—and Enoch represents that aspect of humankind that instinctively knew there was *more* than what was known by the five senses.

So Enoch represents that part of the human consciousness that never ceased to walk with God, whose ability to—I hesitate to use the word "remember" but I don't know another word of your language—whose ability to remember that somewhere back in the regions of the mind there was a time of love, a time of peace, a time when people loved and were safe *with* each other but not able to bring it forth into its full-blown realization. So Enoch represents then a passage of time in which the human mind longed for that total oneness with God and therefore sought, through various rituals and various ways of doing things, to find a connectedness to God. It represents that part of your awareness that never really left home but rather remained in its

17

connected mode, albeit overshadowed greatly by all the things that Adam, in that area, did.

Now this went on for a period of time. I would say by your earth years probably ten, fifteen thousand years, something of that sort.

Hermes

Now we come to a time when people have evolved mentally. They've grown considerably, not too much spiritually, but they have grown mentally. They are no longer cave people. The bodies have evolved. They are walking upright. They don't grunt at each other. Languages have been created and there has come into the consciousness of people an awareness of themselves as a part of, but not necessarily united with, other life forms.

Now, the place where this was the most prominent upon your earth was in Egypt, and it was in Egypt that the worship of a single God—as opposed to the God of thunder, the God of the wheat, the God of the rain, the God of this, the God of that—first made itself manifest in an entity, a mythical entity, a Pharaoh called Re.

Now, Re sought to know God, believed that he was God. However, he didn't have the full concept of the Son of God part. So his belief of being God was that *he* was God. But it bothered him that he was rather limited. For instance, he couldn't make the sun rise. He couldn't make it rain. There were certain things he couldn't do. So he sought help and lo and behold, there came a consciousness manifested in an individual called Hermes.

Now, Hermes was an alchemist. Hermes had developed the ability to take energy and manipulate it and change forms with it. Hermes came to Earth without benefit of mother or father. In as much as he hung around the earth in spirit form a very long time, and he remembered how, when back here—back in the First Spirit, back in the Spirit manifesting—you used to create bodies to run about in and have fun with and so forth and then get rid of when you didn't want it any more. So, Hermes took upon himself to create a human form and he occupied it. And he also brought with him into that brain—he worked on the brain a considerable length of time—and he opened the cells of the brain to the point where it could retain and use alchemist methods.

Know you what an alchemist is? It is one who has the ability to transform material things from one form into another, and this is done through the manipulation of the cells of the form. And that is accomplished by recognizing the source of the cells of the form, which is energy, and working first primarily with the energy, bringing it under one's control by bringing one's *mind* under its total control of the Spirit. It has nothing to do with religion; has to do with knowing.

Now Hermes quickly affiliated himself with Re because Re was powerful. People worshiped him and Hermes saw a road in which he could change things for the better and he did set about doing just that. But first he had to get it into Re's head, in what manner or form, he was God, and this was not successful. Re got so enthralled with himself and his ego became so thick and heavy and big that after a bit, Hermes decided, "This is a lost cause," and went off on his own to do his own thing.

Now, the thing is that this Hermes state of mind... Beloved woman, will thou write Hermes here please? Oh, by the way, I'm assuming that you know, but in case you don't, all of the lives that we've been talking about, all of the states of consciousness that you have on your paper, these are all of the lives of the Master Jesus *in that consciousness.*

Now, I want to digress a moment. In the Adam state of consciousness, the Son of God lost itself, so to speak, in its consciousness in form and because it represented the trend of the human being, it knew when it left the Adam consciousness that it had to do something to reinstate its own Christ awareness.

Now in the Hermes state of consciousness was the ability to manipulate form, and this was very good. However, the power that went with the manipulation of form was very great because he was the only one who could do it. He had a few disciples that he taught, but none of them reached the point that Hermes did.

Now, one of the reasons Hermes was so good at what he did was because he had a complete understanding of the Spirit manifestation of pulling in energy and using it *exactly* for the results that he wanted. Now, this was pretty good. He became quite popular. Kings would come to him and say, "I desire to become wealthy."

"Alright, bring me something," said Hermes, "and I shall turn it into gold," and he did. The only thing was he got lost again in his own popularity. He got lost again in the creative ability of himself and through it, although he was a great teacher, he didn't develop or reclaim the Christ love.

Now, we are going to take a little break because some of you need to get up and move around. The energy is getting droopy. Before we do, do you have any questions? Would you come up to the...

Questions

Participant: Beloved Gabriel, was there a time thousands of years ago when the Goddess creator, the sustainer, was really revered?

Gabriel: Oh, absolutely. Absolutely. There was a time when God was woman, as it is termed, in a sense that the female became the one worshipped. But you know men's egos. (Laughter) They're not going to let that one be and besides, women kind of took over...quite. And they were not above lopping off a head of a male who displeased them, however they displeased them. And so, the males realized after a bit this wasn't a good idea at all, so they began the systematic turning about and getting back into a male-dominant society, which of course as you know through your history is exactly what they did do.

Gabriel: What can I answer for you?

Participant: Thank you, Gabriel. I'm curious to know...recently, in my awareness, what's coming through is the seven deadly sins and I have actually seen them as seven stains of life or seven stains on spiritual evolution and progress. Is that right? Do you see them in that way or...in terms of being a receiving experiment?

Gabriel: I would say rather they are... I wouldn't say they were progress as much as I would say that in coming into the awareness of it, one could leave it behind.

Participant: Okay, so they're not impediments to spiritual growth or progress?

Gabriel: Oh, they are indeed if you believe in them and if you hold that they are the reason why you're not where you should be.

Participant: Okay. The other thing... I'm kind of seeing as we progress with this lesson, for instance, that the Adam state of consciousness represented doubt and I've taken it upon myself to see the Hermes state of consciousness as pride. So in these seven states that are presented before Jesus, can those seven—I hate to use the words "deadly sins,"—but are they applied to each one of these consciousness forms?

Gabriel: Well, I suppose you could, yes. I suppose you could. People believe in the downside of everything so if you want to put a downside to it, you can.

Participant: Okay, thank you.

Gabriel: Indeed.

Participant: Gabriel, because we humans are so tied to time, it's hard for us to imagine Divine Flame *always* being because we have a sense of there must have been a beginning somewhere. But what was it that impelled Divine Flame to go out into Christ consciousness and to Spirit manifested?

Gabriel: The desire to express, to be more.

Participant: But what first? I mean, here's Divine Flame always being...

Gabriel: Divine Flame has always expressed and become more. Your history that you are aware of is only a minute particle of it. You have no concept in your minds of the length of time that you have been. You date yourselves as probably four or five million years...drop in the bucket. Believe me, I know. (Laughter)

Participant: Thank you.

Gabriel: Any others, ere we take a little break away? Alright.

***

Lesson

Melchizedek

You are all gathered? We are running out of space here so I know you have the idea of each ring of consciousness, as it were, so we will not put any further up there since you have your list.

Melchizedek represents a state of consciousness that came into being through the result of the people seeking to explain life, to find a connectedness back to God. As is typical with any civilization that wafts its way off into the never-never land, there always comes a point at which home looks awfully good.

Melchizedek, when the Master incarnated as that state of consciousness, had brought with it from the Hermes part the realization of there being much more to life than the physical body and the earthly existence. He knew Abram before God renamed him or before Abram felt God renamed him Abraham.

Now Melchizedek was a *balance* of sorts in the sense that he could reach into a conscious state that Abram could not quite reach. Now Abram had...how might I tell? Abram knew there was something beyond what could be seen. Abram had a *faith* in the unseen while Melchizedek had a *knowledge* of the unseen. Abraham—Abram, when he became Abraham—knew in his heart that there was a spiritual existence. Now part of why he knew it was his association with Melchizedek.

Now Melchizedek—because of these other lives, especially the one of Hermes—had a very firm grasp of how to use the unseen, and he also realized that in the

23

last lifetime as Hermes, he really, in your terms of this day, messed up badly because he *mis*used the knowledge and this time he was determined not to. This time he was determined to use it in truth and so he saw in Abram an opportunity to bring into form some of the spiritual truths and so he taught Abram a lot.

One of the things in his teachings that he desired was for people to know that they could apprehend the spiritual energy—this truth, this power—and use it. But the minds of people back then were very dull. They still were in the mode of thinking of sacrifices. Even Abram believed in sacrifice; he was going to kill his son to sacrifice to God. Melchizedek had reached the point where he knew that sacrifice was no longer a workable thing, wasn't going to make any difference. You didn't obliterate your ignorance by slaying a lamb or a goat or any other thing. Melchizedek knew that it was the *internal* rather than the external that connected one with their communion with God.

And so he devised what is known in your world today as Holy Communion. And he used a physical thing because he was dealing with people who were very much grounded in physical existence and had little comprehension of anything as nebulous as a spiritual connectedness. So, bread was the staff of life, especially to the nomadic people. It was the one thing that they could travel with that didn't spoil too quickly. It was also something that could be made just about anywhere that they were. So Melchizedek reasoned that bread being the staff of life would be a good symbolism of the substance of God from which all things come forth.

Now, wine was used as equally with water. Even little children drank wine, a lesser wine than the adults drank, but it was a common thing, it was a common usage of the people. So he chose wine to represent the blood of life, the continuity of life, the ever ongoing-ness of life. And he felt that these two—the substance, which is God of all things, and the everlastingness, the eternalness of life—would be the two things that these people's minds could comprehend.

Now the thing is, beloveds, that this had to be brought forth in ritual form because these were people who were used to taking a little lamb, putting it on the altar, cutting its throat, and letting it bleed to death, all in the name of God. I am ever so grateful that God is not like that.

Now, Melchizedek was offering these people a *higher* way, a better way, a harmless way. And so he introduced to Abraham and Abraham introduced to the people the ritual of Holy Communion, of the breaking of the bread and the drinking of the wine as the outer act that represented an *internal connectedness to God*. In other words, they were taking *within* them all that they already had but needed to feel they were doing *something*.

Now remember, it was their belief system that whatever you ate you took on the power of. If you wanted to be courageous, then you ate a piece of a lion. If you wanted to be strong, then you ate a piece of a bull. If you wanted to epitomize the sacrifice of life unto God, then you slayed a little lamb.

So these people needed a physical act so they took bread. Now not just any bread, it had to be bread made specifically for that purpose; it could not be used for anything else. And the wine had to be the very finest wine, not just the everyday having-it-with-dinner wine, but the very finest wine.

Now the Master Jesus looked back upon this in the final hours before the Crucifixion as a method of getting it into the heads of the disciples the idea of the *internal process of the Spirit,* for they also were of dull minds. Peter...oof! (Laughter) Anyway...casting no aspersions upon them. The point is that this... In Melchizedek's thinking, he was lifting up the consciousness of humankind to the point where they did not think that what you did out here mattered half as much as what you did inside. Now he was more or less successful with that, especially within his *own* self. He was finally beginning to get the *ability* to bring his own consciousness back up to where it had begun. Now he worked at that and he got himself pretty much centered in that realization.

Joseph

Now comes the lifetime of Joseph. Now, the Joseph I am referring to is the son of Jacob and Rachel, whose brothers sold him into slavery and so forth. Now, here we have a situation representing a consciousness in humankind that was a *pivotal* point, it was a turning point. His actions on the earth as Joseph were perhaps the most important lifetime as far as turning—other than the one as Jesus—as far as turning the complete circle around of human thinking.

Now, let us go through the story briefly. Here is Joseph, favorite of his father, the youngest at that point, and certainly the most loved. Jacob made Joseph a coat of many colors, which is symbolic of the many states of consciousness that he recognized in Joseph.

Joseph was a gentle soul, a loving soul. He was beautiful to look at. His form was perfect. He was very fair to the eye. He was very bright. He was in touch with higher realms, for he had an understanding *beyond* what *appeared* to be of any given incident.

Now his brothers, who represent the old way of thinking, couldn't stand it. The brothers would represent the ego gone wild. Now, they had to get rid of this little troublemaker. First of all, he was getting all the goodies and they were getting what was left. So the first thing they had to do was to get rid of him. Well, their original plot was to kill him. Well, Reuben, who was a kinder soul than the others, said, "Oh, I can't bear the thought of...we can't kill him. That's...no, no, no...we mustn't kill him." So, as opportunity would present itself, along came some Egyptians on their way to Egypt and they were looking for slaves so they hauled Joseph out of the well where they had put him—which is also symbolic of a despaired state of thinking—and sold him for...are you ready for this one?...*thirty pieces of silver*. Where have you heard that before, eh?

Participant: Judas.

Gabriel: Indeed.

Now, off goes Joseph into the land of darkness; Egypt represents darkness or the uninformed. There he makes quite a name for himself. First of all, he's unbearably good looking, which found favor there because the Egyptians liked to look at good looking people. Secondly, he soon proved to be extremely bright and they thought, "We can learn from this little Jew boy."

So, he found himself in a position of power. First of all, they discovered he was extremely honest; he had no agenda hidden away and so it was not difficult to trust him implicitly. What does this remind you of? Back here...the Christ Consciousness *who embraces all*, does it not? That turns no one away? Joseph was extremely kind and gentle; he would help anyone.

Now, the Pharaoh quickly put him in charge of his household. Think on the symbolism of this. The Pharaoh—being the king, the final word, etc.—would represent the total consciousness of humankind, and who better to be in charge of it than the Christ awareness, eh?

Now this was an instinctive thing on the Pharaoh's part. Also, it freed him up to go lollygag with the ladies. Now, that Christ awareness working through Joseph was infiltrating, infiltrating, infiltrating throughout the consciousness of the people. Everything was going quite well. However, along came seven years of famine. Now, the king had a dream in which there were seven fat cows and seven lean cows and he called in all his advisors and said, "We've got seven fat cows and seven lean cows. What do you think it means?" They didn't know. They told him this, they told him that, they told him what they thought he wanted to hear, and when they all got through, they all lost their heads.

However, someone came to him and said, "Have you asked Joseph?" "No. Why do you ask?" "Because he knows." So in came Joseph and he told him, "The seven fat cows are seven years of great abundance. The seven lean cows are seven years of famine and you must prepare."

Now, what happens when one turns one's consciousness over to the Christ awareness? Is there not an infiltration of abundance? Do you not *feel* full of the Spirit? Do you not feel that everything in your life is really alright because you have in charge something, someone, who knows everything? So there came into the consciousness of humankind a great influx of sense of well-being as symbolized by the fat cows, the years of abundance.

Now, as often happens when one is settled in complacency, one gets a little lazy with the spiritual stuff. But the Christ awareness...that is never lazy, that is never unaware. So Joseph said to the king, "If you are smart, old boy, you're going to put away for the seven years of famine." And so he said to Joseph, "Do it. Just go do it." So Joseph set up a system by which one fifth of everyone's wages—or grain, cattle, whatever—had to be brought to the king, and it was put in storehouses. And when the seven years of famine came, the Egyptians were well prepared. And they could come and buy from the king food to feed their families.

Now, when the Christ Consciousness is allowed to work through human consciousness, it produces answers. Ever have I told you, when you have a question, the answer is beside it. Joseph proved that. "We've got seven years of abundance, seven years of famine, what do we do? Well, we prepare for the seven years of famine." So the Egyptians were quite well off. Not so the rest of the then-known world.

Now, chickens come home to roost. Jacob and his sons... Oh, by the way, the sons went back with Joseph's bloodied-up coat. They killed some poor little goat, dripped its blood all over the coat, and took it back to the father and said, "He's dead. Lion got him. Hyenas ate him up. All we found was his coat." And Jacob mourned.

Now comes the famine. And Jacob says to his sons, "You've got to go to Egypt. There's plenty there and buy food. Now the brothers, they are all assuming that Joseph is long since dead so they are not going to look for anybody. They're just going off to buy food and so all but Benjamin, who is now the youngest, all but Benjamin go. And off they go and *who do they run into?* Joseph. But Joseph is now a man, not a boy, and since they already think he's dead, they don't even recognize him, but Joseph recognizes them.

Now Joseph, by the very authority of his position, could have said, "You see those guys over there... [Gabriel draws his hand across his throat] But he didn't. Now we have the first powerful manifestation of Christ awareness. Beloved woman, would you write Joseph here? Ah indeed, thank you. Now we have the first manifestation of the Christ Consciousness coming *into the consciousness of a person who will live it.*

Now, there are his brothers—who tried to kill him, send him off to slavery, etc.—and Joseph looked at them and his heart was filled with love, so much so that he couldn't bear to look upon them. He had to leave the room and he wept. He wept with love, "Behold, the transgressor is returning."

This is told in a different form by the Master Jesus in the story of the Prodigal Son. When the Prodigal Son returned, his father didn't turn him away and say, "Go off, you beggar. You went and spent all your money. Get out of my sight." He welcomed him. He killed the fatted calf. He gave him a new coat, etc., etc. This is Jesus' story of himself as Joseph.

Now, he couldn't reveal himself immediately to them because he wanted to find out, was Jacob alive? What was going on? And so he made it appear that he distrusted them, that he thought they were spies and so on and so forth. Scared the bedoodles out of them. Anyway, he commanded them, if they valued their life, that they had to go and bring back Benjamin.

Now, Jacob had transferred his affection from the now supposedly dead Joseph to Benjamin, who was his youngest. Now everybody knows that the child of the...what do you call changing of the age? Change of life. Any of you here change-of-life babies? A few of you. Ah ha. Kind of a favorite? Get all the goodies, eh? We know another one back there.

Now the thing is, Jacob didn't want Benjamin to leave his side because the last time his favorite son went off, he never came back. Now the brothers returned with this story, "We have to bring Benjamin back or we can't get food." Well, now Jacob is really in a state. He's got two choices: send Benjamin and take a chance that he's never going to return, or let everybody starve to death.

Well, the end of the story is Benjamin went. Then they went back and they got Jacob and Joseph revealed himself to them. And they were fearful that he was going to destroy them because the brothers *knew* what they had done and they knew he had the power to wipe them out. But he didn't. He said, "Come, live in this land. Let me love you. Let me be with you." And he gave them the finest... He went to the Pharaoh and he said, "My father and brothers are here and they desire to live here. I desire them...," and the Pharaoh said, "Hey, whatever you want, kid. You've done good by me." (Laughter) So he sent them forth into the valley to give them the very best land and best place for their flocks and so on and so forth, and Jacob lived another fifteen or eighteen years after that, happy, happy, happy that his beloved Joseph had been restored to him.

Now what is the theme of all of this? That out of disaster comes goodness. Joseph's life in Egypt was wonderful. He couldn't have been treated better. He had absolute authority anywhere he wanted it. Even when the Pharaoh's wife tried to seduce him and he escaped and she went back and told her husband that Joseph tried to seduce her, what did he do? Nothing. He said, "Well, we'll put him in jail for a little bit but no big deal." Probably was thinking, "Too bad he didn't run off with you!" (Laughter) But anyway...nothing bad happened to Joseph and in turn, *this sacred consciousness, this state of knowing,* connected *absolutely* with the Christ.

Joseph used forgiveness. He forgave his brothers. He used love. He embraced them. He loved them. He restored their lives to them. He at no point entertained any thought of revenge, of "Boy, have I got my chance now." He never recalled to them, "Look what you did to me." Rather, when they were flabbergasted—is that your word?—that here was their brother next to the king, good heavens to Betsy, the heads will roll type of thinking, Joseph said, "No big deal. You intended evil but God intended good." That is the connectedness. Joseph knew that despite appearances, despite how things appeared, that once that connectedness to the Christ awareness was made, that *only* good could come forth because that was God's intent from the beginning, was only good. So here we have a kind of Christ made manifest in Joseph: forgiveness, love, nurturing, all of the things that constitute the highest consciousness in humankind.

Well, the Master made a great step forward with that one. He didn't quite get all of it but he got most of it. Now, it is my opinion that he should have left well enough alone but he didn't. (Laughter) Instead, he decided to come back as Joshua.

Joshua

Joshua was a very complex person. Joshua had power. Sometimes he knew where the source of his power was and sometimes he didn't, but Joshua came in in a time of conflict. Now, Moses had the Israelites roaming around the desert because he wouldn't stop and ask directions, (laughter) but along came Joshua.

Now Joshua was a real take-charge individual. Joshua's power was different than Moses. Moses kind of knew it up here [Gabriel points to his head] but didn't know how to get it into action. But Joshua was different. Joshua was a "let's do it now" type of person, so Moses said to him, "You know, I'm going to die soon and we're still out here wandering about. Can you do something?"

"Oh, I thought you'd never ask."

Now, Moses represents law, unbreakable law. Moses would symbolize that aspect of the human consciousness that is in strict obeyance to its ideals, even if those ideals be not true. Moses would represent law, unforgiving law, a kind of "If you do this, then you're going to get that." Through Moses, karma became a kind of law. They took the wonderful Law of Cause and Effect and they relegated it to one of "I'm going to get you back somewhere, sometime. A little voice is going to say, 'Smile, you're on karmic camera.'" (Laughter)

Now the thing is, that type of thinking was losing control of the mass consciousness of the people, thus symbolized by Moses dying. Now in came Joshua. Joshua was a warrior. Joshua had no problem going in and sacking a city and carrying off its goods. What happened to Joseph, you say? Thought he had the Christ Consciousness? Well, he did, but what happens when a person incarnates and they become enthralled with their surroundings and their circumstances?

Here came a man of great power into a situation where he was under the rule of a man who had great power but didn't know how to *use* it. Moses was so taken up with the idea that he didn't want to *dis*please God that he was afraid to take action. He also was extremely aware of a speech impediment that he had that he was very, very conscious of and didn't feel comfortable getting up and talking to the people, and so he had poor little Aaron get up and do the thing.

But anyway, the point is Joshua came in with this power. Now he's in a situation where he must be subservient to a person or a state of consciousness that is powerful but *non-acting*. Sound familiar? "I really ought to do that but..." "I really should have thought of that but..." "You know, I could have gone there but..." Recognize it? Sound familiar, little children? Oh yeah, well, that's your Moses consciousness.

Now, Moses was extremely intuitive. He had the ability to tune into the higher realms. What he didn't have was the ability to bring that wisdom that he obtained there into action. Thusly symbolized by the tablets of stone. Stone is unyielding. The unyielding "I shall follow the letter of the law no matter what, but I shall not rise to my highest potential."

Now Joshua comes. So Moses says to Joshua, "You've got to get these kids to the promised land."

Joshua says, "Hey! Hah ha! This is right up my ally. Yes, indeed it is!" So, Joshua rallies the forces about and starts them off and what happens? They come to the River Jordan. Now listen...Moses got them across the river so Joshua stood there and said, "If Moses can do it, I can do it; piece of cake."

Now Joshua was a very clever thinker, and Joshua knew how to read the signs of the earth. And Joshua knew from sleeping on the ground that there were some earth tremors going on. And Joshua knew that it was not without impossibility that they were due for a wee bit of an earthquake. So Joshua decided to use this, much to his advantage, so he got all the people to the river. Then he thought, "Now wait a minute. I've got to make this look good." A little angel whispered in his ear and said, "You've got the Ark of the Covenant, Joshua. You might as well use it."

"Good thought," says Joshua. So he gets the seven priests to take the Ark of the Covenant out into the water and stand there with it. Well, there they stood thinking, "What are we doing here? I don't know."

Now, up the river comes this earthquake and it was enough of a tremor and enough of a bother that the water of the Jordan got stopped about ten miles up. First thing you know, the waters going, they're standing on dry land, and Joshua's saying, "Thank you." (Laughter) "Now, everybody get across." So everybody got across and after everybody got across, Joshua said to the priests, "Okay guys, come on with the Covenant." So off they went across the river, greatly relieved, for they thought surely they would drown. Then he had them do...

Now Joshua also realized he was still dealing with the consciousness of the people where an action had to be made manifest, so he had them gather up twelve stones, representing the twelve tribes of Israel, and make a kind of a little makeshift altar there in the middle of the riverbed. Now after they all got across and the earthquake has subsided, the river began to flow again and Joshua looked awfully good. He looked really good. (Laughter)

Now, they went into the land of Canaan, which represents a state of consciousness in which one *knows* there's something better, *knows* that there is an ability to *be* more, to *have* more, to manifest abundance. But there were enemies in that land. The enemy of "I don't know if I deserve this. Maybe I better not take all this abundance that God's willing to give me because I might *misuse* it. Then I'd be in big trouble." "I'm not sure I deserve all this because I didn't treat my little brother very good when we were kids." "I better not do this because my friends won't like me because they are going to say, 'What is he or she doing with all of that?'" Familiar? "Can't win the lottery because it's going to ruin your life" type of thinking. Okay. Now, we're meeting this kind of consciousness. Now the people are afraid to go forward. Sound familiar? But not Joshua. Joshua says, "Let's do it guys!"

"Oh, I don't think so. No, no, no. We're not going to do this."

Now, the Christ awareness is saying, "Why not? Why not have abundance? Why not have all this stuff?"

And the little ego self is saying, *"Because I don't deserve it."*

Now Joshua, not to be put down...he's a warrior. He goes and he looks and there's a vast plain with cities and there is Jerusalem—well, well guarded—and he thinks, "They've got chariots with wheels with blades. I've got men on foot. They'll chop us to pieces. But you can't take a chariot up into the hills; horses can't get it over the rocks, the paths aren't wide enough, and so forth." So Joshua decided to bring the battle to his own territory. So Joshua went into the hills and he burned and sacked all the cities. He killed all the people—men, women, children—didn't make any difference. "Take no prisoners." And he went through the hill country and he slaughtered and he plundered and he took everything.

Now, what's going on in the plain? The plain's people are hearing of this mighty army, this invincible leader. And what happens when a well-protected fort learns that there is someone coming whose got an A-bomb? Fear. Fear rolled over the plains like a great flood. A frightened soldier is not a very brave one. He doesn't think clearly either.

Now Joshua knew well how to use the forces of nature for his benefit. Now we come to Jericho. Jericho was an extremely difficult city to penetrate. It had great thick walls. It had been defended successfully for generations and Joshua knew he had to take Jericho.

Now Jericho represents a state of mind that you refuse to leave, an old wound that you don't let heal, an old belief system that limits you, binds you in, holds you in, but it's safe because you're familiar with it. It's the kind of thinking that makes women stay with abusive husbands, makes people stay in unfulfilling jobs, makes people sacrifice their lives for something that doesn't really matter after all. Now, that has to be taken. That has to be destroyed.

So, Joshua flattens himself out onto the ground and he asks the God of his being to tell him when is the next earthquake. "In about a week."

"Alright, let's do it!"

Now he's got these people thinking, "We're invincible. Are we not?" So he says to them, "Guess what, guys? We're going down and take Jericho."

"Oh, Jericho? Oh, nobody's ever taken Jericho."

"Not yet," says Joshua.

"But they've got walls and they've got men and they've got...we can't do that."

Now Joshua can't do anything with that kind of thinking. "So," he says, "but we have a method, for the Lord God has told me how to do this." Oh, now he's got their attention. After all, they watched the river dry up while they marched across with the Covenant. So...now Joshua knew—don't forget he was Hermes—Joshua knew how to use the power of vibration and he knew that the walls of Jericho were very, very old. Albeit strong and sturdy, they were still very old and the mortar and stuff between the stones and bricks was a little dry and crusty.

If it had been modern times, he would have taken one of your fighter jets and he would have buzzed it and got the same results. Now, what he did was he got them to march around blowing horns. Now you all know that sound produces a reverberation and sound can knock a picture off your walls, can it not? Well, six days they marched around the walls of Jericho blowing horns, clanging symbols, shouting and yelling, and the walls are getting a little more tremulous and a little more tremulous. In the meantime, Joshua is listening for the earthquake on day seven. He knew it was going to hit so he said to his priests, "At the precise time that I tell you to blow your horns, I want all of you to give a mighty shout in the praising of God."

Now Joshua took off his shoes and he walked barefoot upon the ground because he could *feel* the tremors in the earth. And at precisely the moment when the tremor was at its peak, he gave the order to blow the trumpets and to shout and they did and the walls of Jericho went kaplunk.

Well, guess what that did for them? They went into Jericho and there was not any resistance because the people already had been terrified into submission by the rumors of this invincible leader. "Take no prisoners." That was always Joshua's rule. And so they slaughtered every man, woman, and child.

Now, can you write Joshua somewhere? That's fine. Now we go from Joseph to Joshua. Joseph, the forgiver. Joseph, the lover. Joseph, the sustainer of life. Joseph, the Christ awareness awakened. And we go to Joshua who...

Participant: Gabriel, I'm sorry to interrupt, but isn't that backwards? I thought we couldn't go backwards?

Gabriel: Oh, but let me finish. Now, your time in which you are born, your circumstances in your formative years, the things that you are taught all have as tremendous bearing on you. Now remember Joshua's background. It was one of survival of the fittest. The people who wandered around for forty years produced children. These children grew up wandering the desert. They had no sense of stability, no sense of anywhere to call home, always moving from one place to another. There was nothing to anchor into that made them feel safe.

Now Joshua was a survivor, but Joshua also had this aspect of him: he had the Hermes aspect of consciousness, which could manipulate energy. He had the Joseph, which used power lovingly, and he came into

39

a set of circumstances where lovingness, kindness, wasn't going to cut it.

He used his power with the intent of bringing the Israelites into the land of milk and honey, into the promised land. So, his intention was to bring the consciousness into a state of *abundance* and *acceptance* and in order to do that, he had to do what? He had to cut a path through error perception. He took down Jericho, the unyielding. He took the hill countries, the little hidden error perceptions that sneak up at you in the middle of the night just when you think you're doing really well.

He went through the human consciousness and he destroyed limitation. He got rid of anything in the human consciousness that would have prevented the return to the promised land, which is what? The Christ awareness. As Joseph, he used this gentleness, the sweetness that is the Christ. As Joshua, he used the *power* that *is* the only begotten Son of God. He combined these things in Joshua.

Now, this is all allegory. This is all symbolic of the human progress in consciousness. You cannot leave in your awareness the newborn of any error perception, and as ruthless as it sounds to say that Joshua went through and killed women and children and the elderly and all that, you've got to put it in the perspective of its symbolism. If, through the kindness of your heart, you allow a viper to remain alive and well in your awareness, how long do you think it will take before it turns and bites you? Know you what I say?

So Joshua's raiding and seeming conscious-less slaughter symbolizes... In your Scripture it says, "Every knee will bend to me," meaning every error perception, every *mis*conception, every form of illusion will bow before the power of the almighty God, which is in you.

So Joshua's acts, although they *appear* in written form to be quite without conscience, have nothing to do with the physical slaying of anyone. It has to do with the *absolute* power of the God Christ within—to go into the secret hill places, the hidden places of the consciousness of the human being and *get rid of* forever all misperceptions.

What time do you take your break away? I desire to use the whole afternoon for the Master's life.

Leader: Whenever you're ready.

Gabriel: Alright, we've got one more to go. We'll do Buddha, then we'll go for your food.

Now you will take note that all of these lifetimes up to now have been in the Hebrew trend of thought. Now the Hebrew trend of thought represents the "chosen" of God. Now, that is symbolic of...we're going right back up here...that is symbolic of the Christ Consciousness, the Spirit manifested, the First Spirit. Its right back into that connectedness to God.

Now this awareness has to reach out further. Remember, the Christ Consciousness is all inclusive. It is not for the Hebrew people only. It is for all forms of consciousness, all thinking, all...it must be all inclusive.

Buddha

Now we find this soul manifesting outside of the Hebrew teachings. India is a melting pot. It is a country of extremes. You can find there unbelievable wealth and you can find there unspeakable poverty. You can find there a great deal of compassion and you can find there

41

an absolute disregard for human life. So India would represent the extreme opposites in the human mind; the person who would lay down their life to save another and yet has no qualms about destroying the confidence of a child by belittling them and browbeating them...is your term, I believe. And yet, there are the people who go to the churches and the synagogues every single week faithfully, doing all manner of community service, and go home and beat their wife half to death. There are all manner of forms of extremes in opposition, one to the other, within the human psyche.

So, into this realm of extremes came Buddha. Now before he became the Buddha, he was the son of a raja, quite well respected, somewhat educated, highly thought of, had anything and everything he wanted, did what he pleased, when he pleased, and how he pleased, and so on and so forth. He lived a rather protected life. His ventures out into the world consisted mostly of going to beautiful places and doing beautiful things with beautiful people. And for the first twenty-nine years of his life, he lived in this little ivory tower of wealth and power and having everything he desired given to him.

Now, that little ivory tower consciousness is extremely limiting because it gives you only one perspective. It doesn't allow your thinking ability to stretch itself, to go out beyond that. So, the Buddha to be had to get out of that ivory tower so he decided to go on a little sojourn and in so doing, there he encountered for the very first time in his whole twenty-nine years something that wasn't lovely, pleasurable, pleasant, fun, comfortable. He encountered death, disease, living a life in such abject poverty that there was no flesh on the bones of a living person. He encountered the stench of decaying bodies, the sight of a person in the throes of breathing their last. All of a sudden his world wasn't lovely and beautiful and perfect anymore. All of a sudden there were things in it he could not comprehend. "Why was this old man dying? Why was that other body dead? Why was this monk sitting on a corner looking so awful and smelling so bad? Who *are* these people? Why are they like this?"

Now he could have scurried back to his ivory tower but his mind wouldn't let him. He went back home and he thought and he thought, "Why was that…why did I see that? What is that?" And he suddenly realized that there were two sides to life and that what is real is not always what you see. He went upon a quest. He decided that he had to know why there were such things in the world.

First of all, he left his wife and *was she angry.* Ooooh! Well, I tell you what… What is it you have a saying upon your… "There is no wrath like a woman scorned." (Laughter) Well, this lady was scorned! He was younger than her…pretty good looking fellow. They had children and who did he think he was, he was going to run off and leave all of this? Well anyway, she needn't have worried because her in-laws took very good care of her and the family and she was alright, but *he* was off and going.

Now the first thing he decided he would do is to reject all form of any kind of opulence, any kind of anything good and comfortable, so he put upon his body some old raggedy clothes and refused to eat, and he starved himself to the point where his intestines and stomach were nearly, almost completely, withered to the point where they were totally useless. And he went to a pool of water and he looked in and was absolutely

43

horrified at the reflection looking back at him and said, "This can't be me! I'm thinner, I'm wretched, but I'm not any smarter. I still don't know why there's death or anything so I guess I don't think I want to do this anymore."

So he went and he got food and he bathed himself and he cleaned himself up and he decided that wasn't the answer. Then he came to the conclusion that nothing in the outer world was going to explain to him what was going on out there, so the only way he was going to know this was to go where? Within. And so he found himself a comfortable spot, sat himself down, and he went into meditation. Well, he sat there so serenely that people passing by decided that he must be some sort of a guru, so they began to come and sit with him and bring him food and so on and so forth.

And as enlightenments came to him, he shared them and the more he shared them, the more people came until after a while he reached a point where he recognized one great truth: compassion, respect, love for all living things was the only way to leave behind forever the wheel of karma...was to not build any.

Now there are two religious trends of thought in India: one comes from the Vedas, which believed in sacrifice and so forth; the Upanishads, which did not believe in sacrifice but rather believed in the internalness of God, and Buddha *followed that trend*—that all life, the meaning of all life, is found within.

"Do no harm." Buddha said, "Do not do unto anyone that which you would not want them to do to you." Sound familiar? Jesus said, "Do unto others as you would have them do unto you." In this state the soul recognized that the power is from within. The power that comes from the within has one singular purpose and one only: the *transformation of the human back to its original state,* the only begotten Son of God. So the Buddha knew that the only truth that was worth anything had *nothing* to do with the world of form; it had to do with the world within—it had to do with the compassion, the love, the forgiveness, the willingness to *help* others.

Now everybody thinks that Buddha spent his time sitting under a tree contemplating and meditating and spewing out pearls of wisdom. No, he didn't. He walked about and where there was a need, he helped. He found a beggar, too weak to get up out of his own bodily dirt, and he carried him in his arms to the river and he bathed him and he gave him new clothes and he fed him. And he said to those who watched in wonderment, "Whatever you do, be *kind always,* for what you do to others, you do to yourself." The Master Jesus said, "Whatsoever ye do to the least of these, my brethren, you do unto me." "Me," being who? The Christ awareness, the Spirit manifested, the only begotten Son of God.

Now as Buddha, the soul learned how to *live* these truths, and so he did.

His teachings, if you care to study them, are almost identical with the teachings of the Master Jesus. There are some variations due to time and country and so forth, but there is an extreme unification in both of those teachings.

Now, you shall take your food break. Have you any questions before we break away for food because the whole afternoon will be given over to the Master Jesus?

Questions

45

Participant: I was just curious that through the different evolutionary stages, the various archangels assisted?

Gabriel: Oh, indeed.

Participant: Was there a particular... Here's what I'm thinking...I'm thinking if this is the path of human evolution, we're probably going through it...

Gabriel: Probably? Oh! Well...

Participant: Like we're spiraling through it, so that...like Archangel Metatron, if I recall, is the Archangel of spiritual transformation. So, supposing we were aware...

Gabriel: And who was he with, beloved woman?

Participant: Enoch.

Gabriel: And...

Participant: I guess that's what I am not getting. What I'm not getting is...

Gabriel: He was with Enoch and he was with another.

Participant: Yeah, he was with—here it is down here...I circled it—he was with Joshua.

Gabriel: Ah hah! Joshua! Metatron is probably as powerful as... I would say he was equal to Michael. Metatron is an angel of transformation from the standpoint of what isn't pliable will break.

Participant: Okay.

Gabriel: Think of the life of Joshua. What did Joshua do? He conquered. He wiped out. He went in, he took no prisoners.

Participant: Okay, so if we were to notice that we were in a particular aspect of this evolution... We've become familiar with calling on our angels for assistance, so I guess I'm looking at applying to ourselves...

Gabriel: Could you call on Metatron? Is that what you are asking?

Participant: Metatron or Michael or...which one would be appropriate? That's what I'm thinking.

Gabriel: Well, how do you want it done?

Participant: I don't know.

Gabriel: Well, let me tell you what the differences might be and then you can choose.

Participant: Okay.

Gabriel: Michael comes in swift. Michael is more swift than your words could ever imply. Michael comes with a tremendous amount of sense of justice. Michael takes no prisoners, as it were. He banishes without any thought. You call on Michael and you've got war, in a sense. Metatron comes in like rolling thunder and Metatron comes with the idea of transforming. Before Metatron comes, a feeling of, "You've got a choice, honey. Think quick."

Participant: Okay.

Gabriel: Michael gives no choices.

Participant: Okay.

Gabriel: Metatron will come in with this, "I'm going to let you think about this. You've got three seconds. Then, what will not be lifted up will be destroyed."

Participant: Oh, Okay. Okay, thank you.

Gabriel: Michael is the banisher. He banishes. He casts out. Metatron lifts up, if possible.

Participant: Beloved Gabriel.

Gabriel: Beloved woman.

Participant: You were talking about Melchizedek. If I heard you correctly, you said he got his own awareness from the external to the internal and that reminded me of something you said about "We teach what we need to learn." Was that in that same sense?

Gabriel: Indeed. Indeed. You will always teach what you need to learn, with exception of myself. (Laughter)

Gabriel: Beloved woman.

Participant: Now Adam was just...

Gabriel: Adam is symbolic of human consciousness at the time.

Participant: And it was not a person, but Enoch, Hermes, Joseph, and Joshua were actual people as well as symbols of states of consciousness?

Gabriel: Hermes was definitely. Enoch was a state of consciousness. Hermes, Joseph, Joshua, Buddha, Jesus. They were people.

Participant: Thank you.

Participant: What I wanted to know is, these lives that you've discussed, were they landmark lives or were there other lives...?

Gabriel: Oh, there were many other lives. He had many, many lives upon the earth as do you all. These were the ones where there was a decided shift, where there was an absolute upsurge.

Participant: What was, in effect, the purpose of those in-between lives?

Gabriel: Learning, the same as everyone...learning.

Participant: Thank you.

Gabriel: Indeed. Beloved woman.

Participant: Beloved Gabriel. You didn't mention Melchizedek in that list of things. I had always thought of

Melchizedek as being an energy rather than an individual. Was he an individual?

Gabriel: He was an individual, but he... First of all, please understand, these are states of *consciousness* that are within all people. Whether there was an actual person personifying it or not really doesn't matter. The soul of the Master Jesus entered into these states as a form, just as you and you and all of you. So yes. In that respect, yes, there was a person as that, but there were... First of all, there were millions of Adams, millions of Enochs, millions of Hermes, millions of Josephs, millions of Joshuas. It's the state of consciousness of that thinking mode.

Participant: Okay, thanks.

Gabriel: Any others? And you take your food break and this afternoon we shall do the Master Jesus.

***

Lesson

Master Jesus

You are refreshed? Indeed!

Now we will discuss the Master Jesus. After his incarnation as Buddha, he recognized that he had reached a point of mental understanding of the needs of humankind and a kind of a mental understanding of compassion, and through Joseph's incarnation, of forgiveness and so forth. And he contemplated long and hard how he had brought these aspects of himself to the point where he could bring in its fullness all of these things, which constituted the Christ awareness.

And so, for five hundred years of your time, he took himself into a state of absolute surrender unto the will of God. Now I know you have nothing upon your earth with which to compare this, but if you could think of a time in your life when you were so completely desirous of an attunement to something or someone, then perhaps you can begin to grasp his total, absolute, complete surrender.

Now, as he did this on the spiritual plane, it was without too much difficulty because he understood from that vantage point all of the lessons, as it were, involved in these various incarnations and the ones in between. Now he did incarnate many more times than this and as I said early on, I chose those or we chose those through which there could be seen the absolute turning, a changing made.

In the spirit world, after he had brought himself into that At-one-ment, he recognized that there was but one thing left to make this Christ awareness complete in form, and that was to come back yet one more time into the body of flesh to walk the path of humanity and to employ what he *was,* as opposed to what he knew.

Now you will recall that in these other lifetimes, especially from Hermes... In Hermes incarnation, he knew *intellectually* how to manipulate energy. As Melchizedek, he knew how to bring in certain ways the truth of Spirit into form and into ritual. As Joseph, there came forgiveness and love. As Joshua, there came the courage, if you will, to go into the hidden places of the consciousness and to completely annihilate anything that would keep him from his awareness. As Buddha, he learned how to discern what *appears* to be a need from the true real need within of the human Spirit to join once more in consciousness with its Creator.

Now, these were all things that he learned in his mind; some things in his heart. Now he had to pull it altogether into a singular form whereby these things could be manifested on all levels. The manipulation of energy, the bringing into form of Spirit truth, uncomplicated, unreserved love and forgiveness, *extreme* courage, wisdom, and now all of this, all of these aspects had to be collected up and brought into the fold, as it were, of the human consciousness and established there forever. Forever.

Know you the parable of the lost sheep that the Master gave in which the shepherd had ninety and nine sheep and there was one lost upon the hill? And he left the ninety and nine and he went forth to save, as it were, the last sheep and he rejoiced more in the finding thereof of that one sheep than in the safety of all of the other flock.

That, beloveds, is a very concise truth of your evolution, for indeed, he left this state of Christ awareness and he foraged forth upon the hills of illusion and deception and disappointment and pain and death to bring at last into *your* fold of awareness one truth: your At-one-ment, your God Self, your Christ, as well as his own. And when he told that parable, he told it not in the terms of lost souls, but rather in the terms of lost awareness.

Now, what he was about to embark upon was not an easy task. He needed cohorts in crime, as it were, to make this a possibility. And so his other self—his other half, if you will—Mary, agreed to be the vehicle through which this Christ awareness could be made into form. Now, you must understand, not everyone accepts the Immaculate Conception. They see it as a physical impossibility, but let me tell you what; it is real and I shall explain to you how it came to be.

Back before you were Adam, when you wanted a form, you simply thought it. You created it in your mind. You went through the process of manipulating energy and bringing it forth into form. And so, back to the knowledge of Spirit manifested as individual, Mary went through the process of these states of consciousness and prepared herself: in mind—the ability to conceive of this ideal person; in feeling nature—the ability to love enough to bring forth something holy; in physical body—to have the molecular structure, to live in the pureness of her diet, of her way of life, to prepare the cells of her body to be able to bring from a *thought* an energy unit so loved and so *believed in,* so *known* within her, that it could take from the cells of her body everything it needed to create itself.

This meant lifetimes of preparation for her, and even as he was going through these, she was going through her own—and I won't get into that because it would be a whole day's lesson—but she prepared herself on every single level to be able to bring forth within her physical form a spiritual truth.

Now, he worked with her ardently from the spirit realm and together their combined energies of desire to bring forth into form that which was *truly,* absolutely, in every sense of the word, the Son of God. And so Mary went into a cloistered life where she did not have to be infringed upon by the world, and she lived in a very sheltered, very protected atmosphere.

Now, the only thing she did not know, could not feel within her, when the time was right, when she had reached that state where this could become real, and that was my part. That was when I came to her and I told her, "It is now," and she rejoiced greatly, for at last it had come to be.

Now, from that point on, the Spirit of Jesus worked to assist and aide the development, within the womb of Mary, of this form he was to take. She ate special foods. She lived in an atmosphere of pureness. In her mind, her thoughts were ever pure. Her feeling nature, ever directed to the love and the praise of God, and her whole attunement into the service of humanity, for she knew the power of that which was about to be. She also recognized that this would be a completion of the turning of the consciousness of humankind, for this time the Christ would be grounded in form. Before, it was known, especially in Joseph, as an ideal, as a feeling, but in Jesus it would be *in form*.

Now, the molecular structure of his body had to be capable of being in two places at the same time—two states of consciousness, two states of awareness at once. He had to be enough grounded in the physical to occupy a body to eat, to sleep, to commune with people, to be a *real* person. He also had to be enough centered in *who he is* to *never* lose the Christ awareness, to *never* be *without* it.

Now, he had a practice run as a child. As a little child, he would do little things. He restored a bird that a friend had stoned and killed, and Jesus went over and picked it up and saw therein an opportunity to bring Lazarus from the tomb, and so he restored the bird to life.

He saw opportunities to prophesy with his little playmates. He would say, "Behold, your mother is preparing such and such a dinner for you this eve, and she shall call you at such and such a time," and it would be exactly as he said.

He practiced reading minds and used to greatly disturb the teachers in the temple because he would go in there and say, "This day, you are going to teach such and such and so and so, are you not?"

And they would look at him and say, "How did you know that?" And he would just smile. (Laughter)

Now remember, he was raised in the community of the Essenes and they knew who he was. Right from the very beginning they knew who he was because they knew who Mary was and Mary lived among them. So there never was any doubt in their mind as to what he would become, what he would manifest.

Their problem was that they were people—albeit good people, but they were people—and they frequently forgot that this little red-haired child running amongst them was practicing what he would later do when he would run up and say to them, "You are thinking thus and so," and they would become a little annoyed. "My thoughts are my own, you little bugger!" (Laughter) But nonetheless, on a higher level, they revered him, for they knew that he was indeed sent forth to save the consciousness of humankind, to bring people back in a *conscious knowing* of who they were. And this was it, folks. This was the time, and they all participated in that.

When he was six years of age, he was taken from the Essenes and he was sent abroad to the then-known world. He was sent first to India and there he studied with the great Masters there, which was very familiar to him because his last incarnation had been in India, so he felt right at home there. He loved India. He loved the people and he loved the teachings that he gleaned there. And by the same way, he taught them things that he had since learned.

He went from there to Egypt and the same thing; it was familiar territory to him. He also, because he had been there before, knew how they thought and he was able to communicate with them on their thought level process, as well as learn and teach. He was ever the teacher. From a little fellow up, he was ever a teacher.

Now as he grew into manhood, the realization of all that he had chosen began to weigh heavy upon his mind and he began to wonder, "What was I thinking?" Sound familiar? And yet within him was this flame, this fire, that told him he could be nothing less. This was it. He could be nothing less than this.

Now there was certain symbolic outer expressions that represented his inner trend of thought. It tells you in your Scriptures that when he was twelve years old, he got lost, as it were. Well, one of the things about being a Christ is you're rather headstrong, and since you already know the outcome of things, you don't always listen to Mommy and Daddy.

And one of the things that Mary used to trouble herself greatly—oh, and poor Joseph, who felt totally responsible for this little fellow—was the fact that he would go off and not tell them where he was going or that he was going and they were frequently scurrying about hunting for him. Since they lived in a safe community, they never worried about his well-being...simply where he was and had he eaten. But now at the age of twelve when they were traveling, he saw an opportunity to go to the temple and there to bestir the minds of the priests.

Now, let us follow this symbolically. Here is the young Christ, the as yet undeveloped, fully developed Christ, entering into the temple—the awareness of the individual *as* an individual—and challenging, if you will, the concepts held in that temple. He walked up to the priests and he listened to what they had to say and then he said, "Well, that sounds pretty good, but let me tell you how it really is." And he amazed them with his wisdom— wisdom from Buddha. Now, they were enthralled. Here was this child boy teaching them, revealing to them truths hidden in their own religion.

Now, symbolically, this young Christ comes into the temple of your concepts, of your belief system, of the things that you have always held to be true from Abraham, Moses, from all of the old concepts, the old prophets, the old Masters of your belief system. In comes this upstart and challenges your belief system and at first you think, "Who are you?" And then you realize that this Christ within you is presenting a truth that you cannot deny. They didn't throw him out. They listened. They questioned him. They were amazed. And so, as this young Christ comes into *your* awareness, you listen and you begin to recognize that this new thing in you is very real and has something of value to give you.

Mary, representing the balance of Jesus... When they found him, she said, "How could you do this to us?" In other words, the support system questions the— (snaps fingers) what did I teach you this morn?—the male energy that comes, does, goes, comes, does, goes. Now, Mary was bringing him back in consciousness to the fact that he had to allow a nurturing of the seeds he was sowing. He couldn't just drop some seeds and run away. He said to her, "I am about my Father's business." Audacious little upstart, eh? (Laughter)

And she reminded him, "You are under our care." As the nurturing aspect of you desires for you to allow your spiritual truths to develop and unfold, to grow rather than to grasp an idea and think, "Oh, I know that," and run to the next one before the seed has a chance to take root and establish itself as your reality.

Now, Jesus comes into...and he traveled about the world. He came to your continent here and he traveled for many, many years, returning when he was approximately twenty-eight to thirty years old, depending on whose books you are looking at. And he realized that now he had to come to the point where he had to choose, forever...even at that point, did he have free will.

Now John the Baptist, as he is come to be known, came before Jesus to prepare the consciousness of the people. Now, the John the Baptist consciousness is one of "Better watch out. You're in big trouble. He's watching. He's going to get you." Sound familiar? Now, that type of consciousness does what? It awakens the mind (snaps fingers) to be alert. "Something more is coming. I'd better make straight the crooked ways of my thinking here."

Now Jesus knew that he had to decide. This was it. He had come to the point where he could say "yes" or "no" at this point. Interestingly, he returned yet again...remember Joshua at the River Jordan? So he came to the River Jordan. Now the last time he was at the River Jordan, he used a little mental wit to get across. The only ones who got wet were the poor priests holding

57

the Covenant. A little humor there. (Laughter) Now, the thing is that once again, he came to the crossing over.

Jesus knew from that point on, once he had been what you term "baptized" or taken in his awareness to that state where he is the Son of God, that there was no turning back. At that point, that was it. And when he approached John, John hesitated, for John knew the full impact of what, from that moment on, would be taking place. And he went to Jesus and he said, "This is it, my brother. Are you ready? Do you really want to go through with this?" And Jesus said, "Yes, I must do this now." And so John, that aspect of consciousness which *makes way,* made way and he baptized him.

Now it tells you in your Scriptures that a dove appeared and a voice from Heaven saying, "This is my beloved Son in whom I am well pleased." The actuality of it was that the energy, that Christ energy, came at that moment from a realm beyond the consciousness of the man, Jesus, and it entered into, fully entered into the soul properties of this entity. Up to this point, it had all of these things in a scattered way, even as *you* do in your souls—your scattered wisdom, your scattered love, your scattered everything.

Now came that sacred moment in which the sheep were called into the fold. As John put his hand upon him and submersed him into the water and brought him up, it symbolized the washing away of Joshua, Buddha, Joseph, Hermes, all of them. All of the error perceptions of any limitation whatsoever was *gone!* And the energy that came in from above connected and there was, from this point to this point [diagram], a *Oneness* that would *never,* ever be gone. It was forever, this divine connection.

When Jesus emerged, he was transformed, every little residue of any error perception in him had literally been washed away. Now, he needed time to allow the cells of his body to acclimate to this change. He needed time to get used to it. He needed time to let it become an integral part of him in such a way that he was familiar with it, that it was not strange or different to him.

And so he went off into the desert by himself—by himself, in terms of any physical company—but there he communed, first with angels, then beyond angels into High Masters, beyond High Masters, until he could open this man totally in consciousness to the Christ and there would be *nothing* in between. He could do the things of Hermes. He could love as Joseph loved. He could have the wisdom of a Buddha. He was that which was the truly, only begotten Son of God.

Now during that time, he was shown in great detail the unfoldment of the next few years of his life, and he was given time to assimilate that, to weep over it, to rejoice in it, to walk through the fears and to come at last to a sense of peace.

When he emerged from the desert...and by the way, this is the symbolism of all the temptations of the so-called Satan. It wasn't Satan at all; it was his own ego self that challenged the right of the Christ to be there. Remember, he was taken upon the temple and told to cast himself off? You all know the stories of that.

When he came forth, now he had to call forth the twelve faculties within man, as represented by the twelve disciples. And so he chose them. He handpicked them. Now the interesting thing was, of course, before they all came to Earth, they all knew what their job was. They had been handpicked before they even reached the earth plane to do this and asked if they would participate and they said, "Yes."

As with all of the people in Jesus' life—the same, Mary Magdalene—all of them chose to be with him at this time. As he went forth to teach, he realized that there was a difficulty in putting into words what he knew. I can relate to that. But he also recognized how needy were the souls of the people to whom he taught, and he also recognized the familiar faces of the people in the cities, in the hills, in Jericho, the women, the children, the old people. "Take no prisoners," Joshua said, and before him were the multitudes, and guess who the multitudes were? The people in the cities, the people in Jericho, the people that Joshua had slain. Here was the redemptive life force restoring what had once been slain. Not the error perception, not that, but redeeming in truth what had been slain in error. Know you what I say?

Now, the teachings of Jesus were given on two levels: one on the level of the average individual who was raised as Jew or gentile who had old stuff to get through, and on the level of the higher ones who had evolved and could take in and know what he was speaking of. He also recognized within them a sense of hopelessness—a hope that there was something and yet not a faith to acknowledge that "Yes indeed, there is something." And so much of the healing that he did was not of the physical form but was of the soul.

Now you must remember that no healing of the physical form ever takes place until that aspect of the soul is healed, for the healing that comes from the Spirit is first activated in the soul and the activation in the soul then proceeds to work through the body chemistry to produce healing. So when Jesus would restore sight, he wasn't just restoring physical eyesight, he was restoring the sight of the Spirit into the soul, and sight represents understanding. He was restoring a truth through understanding to these people.

Now, each of the disciples presented a different kind of a challenge to Jesus. I'll mention only a few because it would take up the rest of the day to go through them all. But he recognized that he had redeemed these aspects within himself in these various and sundry lifetimes that he had lived before.

Peter, for example, was *absolutely, one hundred percent with the Master* as long as the road was pretty smooth and things were going along good and he was more or less comfortable. But Peter didn't have a lot of courage. He was very loud and very boisterous, quick to make an opinion, quick to judge, but he didn't have conviction behind it in terms of himself. He relied on the Master Jesus and that is why, when it came down to the final hours, Peter denied him because Peter didn't have the courage to stand behind his convictions.

Thomas knew in theory what Jesus was doing and he thought, "Oh, this is very good. Yes, yes, yes. This is very good," but when it came to the phenomenal part of it, Thomas couldn't grasp the idea...the things that Hermes knew kind of escaped Thomas. Therefore, Thomas had to see to believe.

The one who knew with his feeling nature the truths that Jesus taught was John. John was very young when he came to Jesus. He was—what is your term?—hardly more than a teenager and he came to him with an innocence of youth. And he came in a manner that "I just want to know what you know. I want to know how you know what you know." And there was never in John's mind any doubt as to the truth of Jesus' teachings or of the miracles that he did. He believed what he saw. He believed what he heard. He instinctively connected with that love energy there. But John was a sweet and gentle soul and it didn't occur to him that at any point there would ever be any reason for there to be danger or any kind of thing like that because after all, we've got Jesus here and he can do anything.

And then there was Mary Magdalene, whom Jesus loved. Now Mary was a person of great wealth. She was born to it—her parents were wealthy and their parents before them and so forth—so Mary had what would be termed "old money." Because of the position of her family in the community through the years, Mary had a position of authority. Now, it was not a common thing for women back then to be in positions of high authority openly. They were usually—what is it you say?—the power behind the throne, as it were.

And Mary started out the power behind the throne. She wasn't one to go forth openly and assert herself. She followed the mores of the day in which women were listened to occasionally, heard sometimes, but more or less expected to be sort of out of the way. And she followed along with that until the day that she met Jesus.

And she encountered him... She had been to the market and the day was lovely. It was early in the morn and she decided she would take...she gave her purchases to her servant and said, "Take these home. I'm going for a walk." The air was fresh with the bloom of flowers and she just wanted to be out of doors. She's walking along and she encounters this man sitting under a tree, his head back against a tree, his eyes closed. And she came up the path, he opened his eyes and he looked at her and he said, "Hello." She, being a proper woman... Mary was never a harlot, never. That is a misconception brought about later by a later generation of priests who had to discredit the female. Mary was never a harlot.

So when this stranger spoke to her, she was not of a mind to answer him. After all, she was a lady of means. And she kind of gathered her skirts about her and politely started to walk past and he said, "Mary," and she turned and looked at him, at first thinking, "How did he know my name?"

And in the meantime, he stood up and she looked at him and she said, "Sir, I do not believe I know you."

And he walked over to her and he did a very unprecedented thing; he reached out and he touched her face and he said, "You know me well."

And something in her knew the truth of his words and she said, "Who are you?"

And he said, "I am Jesus."

And it was as though an old memory, an old calling, something from the soul of her, knew this was the love of her life. And he said to her, "Will you help me?"

And she said, "Yes. What would you have me do?"

And he said, "I need someone to make way for me and my students when we travel. Would you do that?"

She said, "I will do it if you will take me as a student."

And he said, "Of course. Why would I not?"

And there began a friendship, a love, a bonding between them that is unto this day, for Jesus loved her deeply and she, him. And from that moment on, she saw to his every need and to the needs of the men—their food, their lodging, any monies they might require—anything to make their journey and their teaching and their learning all the more better.

Jesus would often walk with Mary in the evening and he would explain to her why he was where he was and what he was doing, and she took it in but not with the recognition of it being an actual event in the terms of his leaving the earth. It didn't occur to her that she would ever, ever be without him. Ever. And when the time came for him to leave, when the Crucifixion came, Mary could not bear it. She was the last one to leave the cross. The others... John took the mother away and the others... Mary would not leave and she pleaded with him, even as he hung there, "Don't do this to me. Don't leave me. I will have no breath in my body when you're gone. Do not ever require me to go from you."

And she pleaded and he said, "Mary, it is finished."

And she was desolate, absolutely desolate. She hid herself away. She wouldn't even go where the others were. They looked for her but they couldn't find her. And finally, at last, she said, "I have to go where he is," and she went into the garden.

Now Mary, the mother of Jesus, and Joanna went early in the morning and it was they who were there first and it was Mary, his mother, to whom Jesus presented himself first, not to Mary Magdalene.

They came and he showed himself to them and Joanna, being so full of enthusiasm, she went running back to the disciples and then came back to get Mary, and they had just left when Mary Magdalene came. And Mary Magdalene was so filled with grief that she didn't...she walked more on instinct than anything and when she got there, there was this gaping hole and she stood there and the first thought was, "They have robbed him. They have taken his body and I shall *never* see him again," and her devastation became even deeper and she was sobbing so

64

that when he stood before her, she couldn't see through her tears who he was. And he said, "Mary, it is me."

And it was as though the breath came back into her body. It was as though life was restored to her and she said, "My Lord and my God."

Through this, there came into Mary a kind of a mightiness in her understanding. There came a courage and a determination that had not been there before. Her first desire was to run and throw her arms around him as she had done so many times—they embraced, they kissed, they loved...he loved her...she loved him—and he said, "No, not now, for I have not yet changed the molecular structure of the form you see to be such that it can be touched. Just suffice it to know that I live and because I live..."

And she finished the sentence for him, "Because you live, I live." And that bond is as present today as it was then.

When he had come to the point where he knew the Crucifixion was within days, a great battle went on within him. On the one hand, he knew, "Yes, I have chosen this and this is the culmination of all that I have been through all this time. This is the totality of it coming to its fullness." And on the other hand, the flesh and body man said, "I don't think I can do this." There is this battle within.

Now when he went into the garden, he went there to establish his Christ awareness completely within him because he knew that was the *only* way that he was going to go forth and do what he had to do, that was the only way it would carry off. He could not let any aspect of the man, Jesus, be in consciousness; he had to be totally in the Christ.

Now, here was a situation. He had people he loved, he was attached to, people he enjoyed the company of—people he laughed with, walked with, ate with, people who were beloved to him—and he felt the sorrow that they would feel. How could they understand that this mighty God-man could be rendered dead? How could they grasp that all that died was every error perception of humanity that had ever been and that the truth lived on forever?

The man took over and he said, "I'm out of here," and he went out of the garden and there were the disciples snoozing away on full bellies. And he looked at them and he said, "There is humanity asleep to the God-ness. If I leave, they will sleep on forever. I cannot let them sleep. I cannot come this far and not complete it." He went back into the garden and he prayed again, and again the man took over and said, "Go! Go! Nobody's going to blame you. Just go!" And he went out and there they were, snoring away, oblivious to the night flies and mosquitoes, oblivious to all the little natty things that beleaguer humanity. And he looked at them and he wept and he said, "I cannot leave them like this."

And so he went yet again into the garden. Now in the meantime, we were told to stay away from him, to let him come into his own without intervening, and that was one of the most difficult things for us to do, was to remain apart from him and to observe. In his mind, he went through his life, and in the going through, he brought himself back to the River Jordan and to John, who said, "Are you sure you want to do this because you know once you have been immersed, the die is cast. You cannot go back."

And Jesus remembered the power and the dignity that he said, "I am ready," and that flooded in and he remembered going under the water and having the water cut off his hearing—no sound from the earth to interfere, no breath of air to sustain, only the Spirit of almighty God within to give life. To come up out of the murky waters— you cannot see through the waters of the River Jordan— into the clarity of the light and the warmth of the day.

And he remembered the *power* that came *into* him and the absolute *knowingness,* "I *am* the *begotten Son of God* and *all of this* is under my dominion." And as he remembered, he called on that power and it manifested in him again, and he stood up and he said, allowed, "I *am* the begotten Son of God! The Father *within* me doeth the works." And he went forth and he woke up the sleeping disciples and he said, "The hour is come." But it was this manifestation of the Christ brought to Earth in form and *grounded for you forever in form*—in your physical bodies, in your mind bodies, in your feeling nature, in every aspect of your being is this God-ness established and brought to your memory as your reality, because of this. And then he went forth.

Now Pilate was an Essene, and so was his wife. They were ardent followers of the Master Jesus, although be it secretly so, for if Rome found out, Pilate would have lost his head.

Now Pilate's wife was a very astute person, and being a woman, she gossiped with the other women, so when Jesus was taken captive, Pilate's wife was one of the first ones in the authority to know of it and also to recognize the sleazy way in which it was done, for it was done extremely underhanded. Oh, before I get into that, I want to speak of Judas.

The night before the Passover, Jesus called Judas aside and he said to him, "Judas, the time is at hand when you must do what you came to do."

And Judas looked at him blankly and said, "My Lord, what have I come to do?"

And he said, "You have come to dip your hand into the bowl of deception and you are to betray me."

And Judas stared at him in disbelief and he said, "My Lord, I could not betray you."

Jesus put his hand on Judas's head and he caused him to remember, back before they came to Earth, the vow that Judas had taken to do this terrible thing.

Now, of all of the things that the disciples had chosen to do, Judas' task was the most difficult. Think about it, beloveds. He traveled with this man. He lived with him. He learned from him. He observed him doing miracles. He loved him! How could he betray him? He could not. Yet Judas knew that if he did not, there would be no symbolism to the betrayal of the five senses. There would be no symbolism in the realization of humankind recognizing how *betraying* belief in the external world, as opposed to the knowing of the internal world, can be. There is nothing more beguiling than the outer world.

And so when Jesus put his hand on Judas and caused him to remember, Judas wept. He said, "My Lord, I do not have the strength."

And Jesus said, "Go into your ego. Go into the part of you that *questions* everything I do and stay there."

Didn't work. Judas tried it, came to Jesus in the middle of the night, he said, "My Lord, I said I cannot. I cannot."

Jesus said, "Judas Iscariot, upon you rests the salvation of the consciousness of humankind, for if you do not, then how will they know what I have taught? You must. You must and the angels will give you strength."

Now, something that is hardly known: Judas called upon Metatron and Metatron came, but Metatron is the transformer and he kept giving Judas time to think. (Laughter) Not so good. Metatron withdrew and he went and he found Lucifer and he said, "Lucifer, our Lord has need of thee."

And Lucifer—Son of Light, obedient servant of the Most High—said, "I come."

And he went to Judas and he said to him, "You will do as you're told, you know."

And Judas said, "But I am so weak."

And he said, "Then rest upon my strength."

Now you must know something about Lucifer. Lucifer can present himself in any way that he chooses. That's what makes him so beguiling at times. And so he presented himself to Judas as the great warrior-king—the great courage-maker, the lion-hearted, if you will—and he placed in Judas' mind all of the old, misleading, disillusioning concepts that would have you believe in death.

And for about two hours, it worked, and then all of the teachings of the Master Jesus flooded in upon Judas and Judas collapsed on the road in tears and said, "I cannot! What have I done?" and he raced back to the men and he threw the money at them and he said, "Take it and put it where you will. I am out of here. I am not going to do this."

And as he went forth, there upon the path stood the Master Jesus and he said, "Judas Iscariot, you cannot betray me in this way. You *must* follow with your

69

promise, for if you betray me by *not* betraying me, then all of this will have been for naught."

And Judas said to him, "Lucifer has come to me and visited me."

And Jesus said, "Lucifer's power is not greater than mine, and the power of the Christ in you has risen above the power of Lucifer. Do not call upon Lucifer."

And he went and he helped Judas to his feet and he looked at him and he said, "Because you love me, do this."

And Judas said, "I love you enough, if this is your bidding."

And Jesus said, "It is."

And so Judas went forth and he betrayed the man he loved.

Now in the meantime, back at the ranch—is that your term?—Pilate's wife come rushing into him and she said, "You've got to saddle up your horses. You've got to get out of here right now!" She said, "They have taken the man, Jesus, and they are bringing him before you to be condemned."

And Pilate looked at her and said, "Woman, what are you talking about?"

And she said, "They have taken him and they will bring him before you. The women have told me. They are on their way ere as I speak."

And sure enough, in came the soldiers and they acknowledged Pilate and they said, "We have a Jew that the others wish to have crucified. He is come before you to be condemned," and in came Jesus and Pilate froze. Here was a man he loved. He was his teacher.

Anyway, they brought him in and Pilate said, "Well, what have you got against him?"

"Well, he healed on Sunday. (Laughter) He is against Rome. He is this. He is that. He is all manner of lies," and Pilate knew they were lying.

And he said to Jesus. "What have you to say?"

Now the story says that Jesus stood silent before Pilate, but rather Jesus looked up at Pilate and he winked. Pilate looked at him. Pilate said, "Clear the room! Get out, all of you. Leave me with this man!"

So, they all left and he walked down to Jesus and he said to him, "What are you doing with the winking?"

He said, "The time has come."

He said, "What do you want me to do?"

He said, "What you promised in the beginning."

Pilate said, "No, no, not I. I will *never* condemn you."

And Jesus said, "Then pass it on to someone else, but I must be condemned," and Pilate could not.

Now, of course, in the background, he's got his wife sobbing, sitting there on the chair saying, "You can't do this to him! You can't, you can't, you can't!" And Pilate is between a rock and a very hard place here.

He said to Jesus, "I cannot do this. I will not have your blood upon my hands."

And Jesus said, "So be it. Give it over to another."

Pilate called them back in and he ordered a basin of water and he said, "I find *no* wrong in this man and I wash my hands of him. His blood does not rest upon my soul. Do with him what you will."

Now he's got his wife wrapped around his knees sobbing and saying, "Stop them! *Do* something!"

And Pilate said, "I cannot. I cannot."

Now the thing was that Pilate knew, for Jesus came to him approximately a week ahead of time and he said to him, "They are going to capture me and they're going to bring me before you and you must condemn me."

And the very thought of it, the very idea of it, affected Pilate so that he excused himself and he went forth and he vomited, and he came back and he said, "Don't ask this of me."

And Jesus said, "Someone has got to condemn me."

And Pilate said, "Never me." He said, "You will not come before me and be condemned," and he wasn't.

When they come to do the crucifixion, the only disciple that didn't run away and hide was innocent John, who didn't think this thing was ever going to come off. Something would stop it. Someone would make it go away. Somebody would do something. Mary Magdalene did not believe it could be happening. "This cannot be. Surely, he will raise a legion of angels and this thing will all be over!"

Peter said, "Maybe not, and I'm not going to be a part of this," and the rest of them fled for their lives.

But John remained. John remained in his childlike innocence of firmly believing that Jesus was going to do some great miracle and none of this would happen and Mary Magdalene believed it too. "This cannot be."

And it wasn't until they brought him out and placed the cross upon him to carry that John realized this was happening. And John knelt beside Jesus to wipe his face and he said, "Master, what can we do?"

And Jesus said, "Let it be. Just let it be."

Well, Mary Magdalene decided she was going to do something about it so she stated pulling in favors and all of the way up the road, there were officials who were going, "I don't know...tell her I'm not here!" because they could not... They feared the Jewish people. They feared

Rome! And there was Mary Magdalene running along saying, "You owe me."

"Ho ho...well, I'll give you three camels, but I am not getting involved in *this* one!"

Until finally, she looked up and there was the cross and there was John and Mother Mary and there were the Roman soldiers and the people, and there was darkness within her and without. And within John there was a great sorrow, a wound that seemed never to heal. And Mother Mary was the only one who closed her eyes and remembered that first born cry, "When this is the issue of my womb, the Christ in form." And that's all she let herself see was that.

After it was all over and they took him down, they were all in such a state of shock that none of them could conceive of the idea that in a little while, he was going to say, "Hi guys! I'm back and *I* am and it's all over." They were lost in their grief, blinded to truth by their sorrow. Sound familiar? How many times have you been so blinded by your sorrow or your grief that you do not see the truth of a situation, that you do not see that even in the midst of death, there is life? In the midst of illusion, there is truth? How many times, beloveds, have you been there at that cross?

John took Mother Mary back to her home and he went out into the street and he leaned against the wall and he wept bitter hard tears. And Jesus came to him and he called his name and John looked up and he stared at him and he said, "How can you be here? You're there."

And Jesus said, "No." He said, "What you see is the body of the man, Jesus, and I, as the Son of God, am the truth. What you behold is the illusion. What you see, I am. I AM."

And it was then that John took within himself the truth of Jesus' words and it was like all the lessons through the years suddenly flooded in upon him with a new and righteous understanding. And he said, "Then you live?"

And he said, "Indeed, I live."

And John's sorrow was eased, for he knew what he had seen.

Now in the meantime, Joanna had come running back to the disciples and she said, "We just saw Jesus in the garden! He's alive!"

And Peter slapped her and he said, "How dare you come in here, woman, and lie?" Now, Joanna was a timid soul, so she just quietly left.

Now, a little while later, in come Mary Magdalene, her face alight with joy and she said, "I have seen him in the garden. He spoke my name."

And Peter stood up and he raised his hand to her and she looked him in the face and she said, "Give it your best shot!" (Laughter) Well, not those words but... (Laughter)

And he looked at her and the power of what she had just experienced radiated from her in a light so bright that Peter backed away in fear, and they listened. "He lives," she said. "I saw him. He lives."

And a rumble of hope began to go through them. "Can it be? Can it be?" And there were those who said, "Well, we saw him dead upon the cross! We know all of the city is in desperation because of this. How could it be?" And yet, inside of them was this hope, this eternal spring of "Can it be?" And "Yes, it is," and they began to know. They began to know with an internal-ness that was not of the external world at all. It was of the *inside*—the Christ in them recognizing the victorious Christ in Jesus and what that all had meant to them in every way. In every way.

And the whole of his life took on a new meaning and they said, "Now we understand so many of the things that he said that we couldn't seem to grasp before." And that prepared them for the coming of the Holy Spirit, which Jesus promised.

Of course you know, he appeared to all of them, each in turn, each at the appropriate time. By the time he got to Thomas, he had solidified his body, his astral body, enough and had transformed the molecular structure of his physical body enough that he could be touched.

Now Thomas was a very analytical person. I suspect if he lived upon your Earth this day in your time, he would be a nuclear physicist or something of that sort. Because when Jesus appeared before him, Thomas's first reaction was, "This is no big deal. You're nothing but a spirit. I've seen spirits before!"

And Jesus held out his hand and he said, "Look and touch."

Now it was in the *touching* of the hand, the touching of the side, that there infused into Thomas a new knowingness and all of the things that he had *reasoned* in his mind fell away and truth became real to him—very real, indeed—and he became a very ardent disciple and went forth and did much good.

The power of the Christ is upon your Earth this day in your time. Your New Age has brought to the point where what was grounded 2,000 years ago, sown the seeds of 2,000 years ago, is now producing a harvest, for now there comes into the consciousness of humankind the ability to take in and to understand and to *become* that which he did all those years ago.

Now you are going to see, and are already seeing, the results of what took place back then because all of these avenues of consciousness you are going through—sometimes you're in one state, sometimes you're in another—but you all recognize these, I'm sure, within yourself. And you have this to come to—this Jesus state of mind, this Christ awareness—and you're well on the road, all of you, well on the road to it. And each day of your time you come a little closer.

Each time a truth becomes your reality, you've made another step forward. Each time you love someone who is not particularly lovable, each time you forgive and forget and let it be, each time you honor yourself by saying, "I'm worth that blessing," each time you can see truth through illusion, you've come that much closer.

Have you learned this day? Have you anything to ask of me?

Questions

Participant: Gabriel, that was beautiful, wonderful to hear. I really couldn't help it but feel that with the stories that you've told, why has this not been embraced by the Jewish people?

Gabriel: They look for a Messiah to come with great power, a warlike Messiah to come and sweep away the past. They do not recognize that the only way the past will be erased is within themselves. Each individual must be willing to walk away from an old, out-worn, though time-honored belief system and embrace the new reality that God is indeed within.

Participant: And so the state of Israel is in a ways mired in that, but the old orthodox way is not willing to move forward to a new light?

Gabriel: Indeed. They believe in persecution and so they are persecuted. They believe in war and so they are made war upon. They believe in loss and so they lose. When they stop pouring their energy into those negative things, their lives will change greatly, and they must learn to remember that Jesus was a very fine Jew indeed.

Participant: Thanks.

Participant: One of the things that is attributed to Jesus saying when he was on the cross is "sabachthani" and this has been translated as "Eli, eli, lama sabachthani,"..."My God, my God, why have you forsaken me?" That doesn't sound in character.

Gabriel: No, he did not say that. He did not say that. The sky had grown extremely dark and he was very cold, for there was no circulation going through his body, and his words were, "Even the sun seems to have forsaken me."

Participant: Which would be... Can you tell me how that would be different from "sabachthani"?

Gabriel: No, because her voice, her speaking mechanism, would not embrace that. I can only say through her what I can manipulate her tongue, mouth, voice, etc., into...unfortunately. I could tell you if I were using someone who spoke the language, but because she does not, I cannot through her.

Participant: Okay, thank you.

Participant: Hi Gabriel. I don't have a question but wanted to share something briefly with the group. The last time I was here, my grandmother had just undergone heart surgery and actually made a transition into spirit while we were leaving and while you were taking your leave, which is very beautiful, but the doctor, the heart surgeon that worked on her, allowed me to come in and do healing work as she was recovering. And I just had a meeting with this fellow two days ago to discuss an alliance with his practice. He is interested in having this healing work for his patients as they're receiving the surgery and recovering, and as I was sitting with him, he said to me, "I realize that there is a spiritual deficit in Western medicine." And I never really felt grief when my grandmother died because I realized that her spirit was so involved in this transition and its beautiful manifestation of truth. It's very similar to this, to look upon that aspect of death on a cross but to see it as a life-affirming and life-sustaining experience.

Gabriel: Indeed.

Participant: And I just wanted to thank you and all of you and all that is here for offering me that awareness into truth and love.

Gabriel: You are very welcome.

Participant: Thank you.

Gabriel: Any others?

Participant: On the list that we have, there are certain archangels mentioned. Can we assume that you were present with the soul through all these incarnations?

Gabriel: Through a lot of them, depending on whether I could be of use or not. Certainly with the Jesus.

Participant: And when someone asked who to call upon, could we assume that we have actually called upon you to be our...

Gabriel: My phone never stops ringing. (Laughter) I'm thinking of getting one of your answering things. (Laughter) Indeed, of course you call upon me.

Participant: I also wanted to know, did...I'm assuming that Jesus consciously knew that he was going to arise, to come back in three days?

Gabriel: Oh, indeed.

Participant: Was it three days?

Gabriel: Indeed.

Participant: Did he not tell the disciples that?

Gabriel: He did but they didn't understand it. Nobody had ever done it as far as they were concerned, so they didn't grasp the meaning of his words.

Participant: And were there other souls going through this evolutionary process at the same time as the soul who is Jesus...?

Gabriel: Yes, but none of them had reached a point where they could collect up the sheep, as it were, of these incarnations of their own and bring it to this point.

Participant: So he was the very first one

Gabriel: Yes, he was the only one at this point, at *this* point. Now there have been some since who have done it quietly, not in this universal way, but at this point, he was the one to do it.

Participant: And he did it in this manner so that it would be known and remembered?

Gabriel: Oh, indeed. If he passed quietly away of pneumonia or something, who'd know?

Participant: Is that also why the disciples died such...?

Gabriel: No. You must understand that after he left them, after the Ascension and they were no longer in direct communication with him, they fell back into a lot of their old belief systems, and one of the belief systems was sacrifice, the sacrificial lamb, the making burnt offering and so forth. That was very much practiced back in those days, much to Jesus' dismay. That was one of the reasons he went in and cleaned out the temple when he did because they were sacrificing little turtle doves—little doves and little birds and so forth, and he found this absolutely terrible—so he went in and he threw them all out, turned the animals loose, and so forth.

A lot of the disciples took on the idea of the old ways of sacrifice and believed that the only way they could become holy would be to be sacrificed. It was totally unnecessary, and they all found it out after they got over there. "You mean I didn't have to do that?" (Laughter) What is your term? "Oy vey"?

Participant: Have the disciples learned and have they ascended as Jesus did?

Gabriel: Yes and no. Yes, they have learned. Not all of them have ascended, no. A lot of them want to; a lot of them are in the process of rectifying a lot of wrongs, Peter and Paul especially. They taught a lot of misperceptions to the people and made it the word of the Lord, so to speak...especially Paul.

Participant: Thank you.

Participant: Since Jesus chose to go through with what he had come to do, had he chose to let it pass, had he chose not to go through with it, would he have come again at a later time?

Gabriel: He would have to have come and do it at some point in order for him to... You know, he did this as much for himself, too, because he also desired to get back up here, back up to the Christ awareness and to be able to be it totally, as he once was, as you *all* once were. But he knew he had to go through these states of consciousness, even as you went through them to come *away* from your awareness of God, so you go through them to come *to* your awareness of God. And so, after the first Adam incident, he systematically was making his way back again.

Participant: Could you give us some sort of idea what our world would be like now had he not made that choice at that time?

Gabriel: Just briefly, I would say Atlantis probably.

Participant: Thank you. And could you describe for just a little bit what the actual Ascension was like, what that event was like?

Gabriel: Well, first of all, it was easier for him because at that point, his body had already gone through what you perceive to be death. So to reestablish life in it simply meant to reverse the process, so to say. Now when it come time for him to ascend, he merely had to let go of that energy that held the body in a physical sense and allow it to go through the changes that had brought it up into a finer, non-physical form.

It tells you in your Scriptures that he ascended up through the clouds. Now the actuality was that he simply dematerialized and then went up in that manner. There was no actual rising up of the physical body, disappearing into the clouds. That is all symbolic. He simply dematerialized it and rose away from the pull of the earth.

Participant: Thank you.

Participant: I feel awful about this, you know, act and all...

Gabriel: Beloved woman, why should you feel awful? You weren't even there.

Participant: But you know that I could never...when they had the stations of the cross...all of a sudden, I could never do it because I would cry like as if it was happening, you know, and really, right then and there and I would feel this pain and I would suffer. People would look at me and say, "What's going on with her?" Maybe I had problems at home, but it wasn't so. It was really...I couldn't re-enact this whole thing. And now, again, this picture of it...he had to have some suffering because they gave him a crown of thorns, blood, they always say, is leaking out of his head, the nails had to go through his body at one point before he would know how to go out of it, maybe even before. Did he suffer a lot?

Gabriel: No.

Participant: Thank goodness.

Gabriel: Beloved woman, you must understand that to be completely in the Christ is to leave behind all illusion and suffering and pain is one of the grandest illusions, so there was no way his consciousness entered into that aspect of it. What they saw, this man dragging this cross, all bloodied and everything, was what they *needed* to see, what they *knew* they would see.

Participant: But he then...?

Gabriel: He was far removed from that.

Participant: Oh, great. Great.

Gabriel: He could not have appeared to John and said, "Here I am. I'm alright."

Participant: I understand that, but at that point...there was a point where I felt that the nails had to go wherever...you see the way they did this thing. His body, the bones had to be broken.

Gabriel: There is an aspect in the physical body, in the brain...I do not know your term for it. Where is our doctor person? There you are. What is that little thing in the brain, when a person goes into shock, causes them to feel no pain? Endorphins...that's the word. So, when you are the Christ, you can kick in anything you want, and that's all he did was get himself in that state of consciousness where whatever happened to the body didn't bother him at all.

Participant: Great.

Gabriel: Now he had to *hold* himself in that quite completely, which was one of the reasons he didn't answer his tormentors when they questioned him. He didn't allow his consciousness to come into the earth enough to answer them because if he had, then he would have been into the pain and once he got into the pain, it would have been extremely difficult for him to get back out of it, so he just never went into it in the first place.

Participant: I understand, great. Thank you so much. It helped me a lot.

Gabriel: Don't suffer, little soul. There is no need.

Participant: Hi Gabriel. Obviously, Jesus was into this big production because he wanted to get the attention. However, everybody's interpreted it incorrectly, so for 2,000 years, you have a lot of people interpreting things and they didn't really get it.

Gabriel: I do not care for your term, "into this big production because he wanted the attention." No, he didn't.

Participant: No, not he wanting the attention. He wanted to show...

Gabriel: He wanted to serve as an example.

Participant: Right, but everybody's twisted it.

Gabriel: Of course it has been twisted. The whole thing has been brought all out of proportion.

Participant: Did he know that they would be twisted?

Gabriel: Well, he was hoping that they wouldn't but the point is, it's the consciousness of the people. Always there has to be control, control, control, and there's nothing more controlling then politics—and I mean this sincerely, and for all politicians and priests or what have you, forgive me—but there's nothing more controlling then a person in power in politics or the church.

Participant: Oh, I know.

Gabriel: Now, here comes this little Jewish man who's going to come in here and do all this stuff, so what have they got to do? They've got to discredit him. Now, along comes these well-meaning disciples, who only half understand this stuff, and there the balance between *total,* absolute, complete misinterpretation and truth.

Participant: It seems that maybe the few of us here are getting it and it took 2,000 years and...

Gabriel: Oh, it took longer than that but I haven't the heart to tell you! (Laughter)

Participant: Okay, I know its longer. However, it seems like...how do we get it? How do you get people to get it?

Gabriel: Unfortunately, the method we have determined to be the most effective is repetition. If you tell it long enough, somebody somewhere gets it. Now, out of the thousands of people that Jesus talked to and instructed, thousands of people, probably out of all of them, maybe a hundred people truly got the message.

Participant: It's not really encouraging.

Gabriel: No, it isn't.

Participant: But even as you speak, you're in a classroom where how many of us are getting it?

Gabriel: Well, I would say more of you are getting it than *you* would probably think. I would say not quite half of them really have a good handle on it and the rest are going to... You know, one thing about truth; truth will present itself again and again and again. If you don't get it the first time around... Truth is never discouraged; it circles around, comes in with a new presentation. If you don't get that, okay, you'll go back and...I *know*...

Participant: I understand that. However, I see myself as saying, "Gee, did I get it?" So it's like we want to ascend and we want to get it and that is not enough to want it.

Gabriel: No, it isn't enough. It's enough to *be* it; that is enough. To *be* the truth that you are learning, to live it, to make it a reality so much so that there is no way that you would *not* live it.

Participant: However, it seems to me that we can delude ourselves so easily and it's like...

Gabriel: When you can do...when you can love—how can I put this?—when you can do miracles, then you will know you've got it.

Participant: I guess I don't have it. (Laughter)

Gabriel: Well, you're not alone.

Participant: I know.

Gabriel: Beloved woman.

Participant: I have two questions. Why did Jesus choose to come to the Jewish community and not somewhere else?

Gabriel: Because at that point in the evolution of humankind was the fertile soil. The Jewish mindset was to worship God, however they thought Him to be at the moment, and it was in this sense that it was the consciousness that could be *most* influenced.

Now the other thing is, he had to come to what is termed the "cradle of civilization," which is that whole area of your earth, of the then-known earth. Now he did come to other...he came here to this very continent, presented himself to the native people here. He traveled worldwide. He has been in every country in every culture and presented his truth, and it has been embraced and embroidered and worked into the system of religions in every country—called different things, but nonetheless the same truth.

Participant: Now, I belong to...I grew up in India within the community that believes...they became Christians because of Thomas, the doubting disciple, came on a trade ship to Syria. You know, that's legend. They claim he was buried there. Is that true?

Gabriel: That is true, he did. Thomas was infused with a lot more understanding and a lot more courage after he touched the wounds of Jesus. Partly from a purely psychological point of where he saw, touched, knew, and partly from the fact that it awakened within his Spiritual Self a new understanding. All of a sudden, he realized that death was not the end; there was life and that the body could be resurrected, and this put a whole new avenue of thought into his mind, and he also gleaned a great deal of courage.

Participant: The question I wanted to ask is, as I've been sitting here listening to what you had to say today, it seems like there's been an awful lot of violence and suffering going along with each step or each incarnation, and I just wondered why we have to learn that we can only...it seems we are only getting the messages through extreme violence.

Gabriel: That's humankind's perception that violence is a part of life. It isn't. But if you will notice throughout these lives that always good came out of it, even with Joseph now. Poor little Joseph being cast into a well and sold into slavery and all that sort of thing, yet he got a bunch of lemons and he made lemonade.

Now the point is that each one of these lives, they went to the opposite extreme before they came back around to the truth. And people always do that. Can't understand why you do, but you always do that. Have you not noticed in your own life, beloved woman, that you went through a lot of suffering before you came into truth?

Participant: Absolutely.

Gabriel: Well, anyone here think they haven't done that?

Participant: It just seems so extreme to have him, you know, his body...to pound nails through his body and all that sort of thing.

Gabriel: That was a very common way of executing criminals back then, you know. It wasn't particular to him only. And usually, they did it upside down because they died faster.

Participant: Hello Gabriel. Thanks again. This is great. I have a couple of questions. One, you mentioned that Jesus had many, many incarnations in addition to his pivotal ones. Was he ever a woman?

Gabriel: Yes. Yes, he was.

Participant: So, was Mary ever a man?

Gabriel: Yes.

Participant: At the same time that Jesus was a woman, then?

Gabriel: No, they didn't incarnate together. Sometimes he remained in the spirit to assist her. Sometimes the other way around. Sometimes they came back as brother and sister. Sometimes as good friends. You know... depended.

Participant: Now, you said not all the apostles have ascended. Are some on the earth plane today?

Gabriel: Mmm hmm.

Participant: Are some of them in this room today?

Gabriel: Mmm hmm.

Participant: More than one? (Laughter)

Gabriel: No.

Participant: Okay. Do they sometimes take the same name as they had before? (Laughter)

Gabriel: On occasion. I answered you incorrectly, beloved woman. There are two here.

Participant: Is one a female?

Gabriel: Yes.

Participant: Thank you. So, the other question: You mentioned each of these consciousness things. In order for us to get to the point where we ascend—you know, to be back to our Christ Consciousness—do we have to go through those same...?

Gabriel: Oh, you are.

Participant: Every one of us has to go through...?

Gabriel: Oh, you are already progressing through these stages.

Participant: Okay. I forgot my next question. Thank you. This was amazing. What are we getting next? (Laughter)

Gabriel: I have to take it into counsel...

Participant: Okay.

Gabriel: ...because we gave you these past two times, we gave you a lot and we want you to have time to digest all of this before we go into something as heavy as this.

Participant: That's why we got it on tape, right?

Gabriel: Oh, yeah.

Participant: Because you said everything is happening faster and faster, and you know, as usual, you're right. (Laughter) Not like I questioned it! But it's because, you know, I was scared about you being right before. Now, I gave up on it.

Gabriel: I'd be very scared if I wasn't right. (Laughter)

Participant: When I personally first heard you talk, it seemed a mote difficult to believe, and I am grateful that I've been blessed to keep coming and be in your presence because I think we all, speaking for myself, I think I feel the benefit of this and I really, really appreciate it. Now, are we learning from you when we're not in the same room with you, too?

Gabriel: Yes.

Participant: Thank you.

Gabriel: Not only from *me* personally but from those who work with me and other angel groups as well.

Gabriel: Beloved woman.

Participant: Beloved Gabriel. Thank you for this lesson. The life of Jesus really...I was very moved by that, especially the part with Mary Magdalene, and thank you for that. My question pertains to Joshua and the Moses energy in terms of states of consciousness going back and going through that bearer. As you stated that we swing, you know, to the extreme...

Gabriel: It is true.

Participant: The question I pose to you is that in terms of "taking no prisoners" and translating it in my own mind in terms of the ego and the error perceptions, it seems to me that that could be perceived as an attack on the ego and when one attacks that form, that energy, doesn't that also feed that energy so that the walls become thicker?

Gabriel: Well, he was not attacking the ego. He was attacking the concepts and perceptions *of* the ego, the illusion.

Participant: Oh, okay. Okay.

Gabriel: It was a case of truly cleansing every aspect of the consciousness.

Participant: Okay, so it would be the product that was created by the ego?

Gabriel: Indeed.

Participant: Okay, so we can move through that and not the ego?

Gabriel: Indeed.

Participant: And moving through that, the ego's creation, in terms of illusion, moving past illusion, the thought comes up to me in terms of the Moses energy, there's almost an un-forgiveness to that.

Gabriel: Oh, there is. Indeed.

Participant: So that's part of our learning in terms of moving past that?

Gabriel: Indeed.

Participant: I know that you've given us many lessons in terms of moving past that, so we are, right now, in a healthy state of beingness, we are in alignment with the God of us, and we are actually in our aim going towards our Source?

Gabriel: You are moving along very nicely, all of you are. All of you are. If you didn't, you wouldn't be here.

Participant: I guess what I wanted was an affirmation in terms of…that we are indeed, and when we go through a lot of deep barriers, we are actually making way.

Gabriel: You are, indeed. A lot of you are in your Joshua state of consciousness and that's alright to be there, as long as you don't physically slay your neighbor. (Laughter) But to go forth with that determination to cleanse and purify every aspect of your consciousness and to not be put off by the fact that some of the negative aspects in your consciousness are infant in form…

Participant: Explain that. I don't understand.

Gabriel: When Joshua went through the hills and through Jericho and everything, he told his warriors, "Take no prisoners. Slay everyone, children and all." In other words, he granted no amnesty to any error perception whatsoever, even if it was cute and cuddly and pink-cheeked and what have you not…didn't matter. If it was an error perception, it was slain.

Participant: Okay. Take no prisoners.

Gabriel: Take no prisoners.

Participant: The other question that comes to mind is the Joseph energy, and I liked your presentation in terms of that there's lemonade out of lemons. And so that energy is always with us.

Gabriel: Oh, indeed.

Participant: Always with us. We just have to call that forth and allow that to guide us.

Gabriel: Indeed.

Participant: Okay, thank you.

Gabriel: You're very welcome.

Participant: Some of us have to come a long way to be here.

Gabriel: I heard horror stories. (Laughter)

Participant: My question is: I'm sure that all of us consciously would like to be here every time you are here, but it's almost impossible for some of us to do that. And my question is, if we choose everything, why in the world did we choose not to be here all the time?

Gabriel: First of all, remember, on a higher level, you all know what the lesson is going to be before it's presented. Some of you are willing to accept that lesson to learn from it, to hear it, to *hear* it, and to work with it, and sometimes there comes a lesson that you are not willing to work with yet and those are the times when you find it impossible to get here because that defense mechanism of the ego comes up and says, "Oh, you don't really want to hear that, do you? Do you know if you hear that, you're going to have to do this, this, this, and this," and you think, "Oh, I'm not ready for that. Alright, let's get a blooming blizzard going here or let's get a mode of transportation that suddenly expires in the drive. Let us do *something*. We'll get a neighbor way up the road to come down with the heebie jeebies and I have to go care for her or whatever, but we will not come forth and meet this lesson because we aren't ready to deal with it right now. We'll catch it another time around."

Participant: And why is it that we would like so much to just go out and bring hundreds of people and...?

Gabriel: Be my guest.

Participant: But they don't respond.

Gabriel: Beloved woman, as I have told this Beloved Woman [Rev. Penny] many a time, whoever is ready to hear will come, and those who are not ready to hear, even if they came, would hear nothing of value to them. Your desire to share your truth is because it resonates from within you a sense of truth. You know it is true, so therefore you want to spread the word, but not everyone is ready to hear the truth. And those are the ones who don't listen, who don't believe, who think it's a bunch of—what is it?...your huggywuggy?—hogwash, whatever that be. It is the desire of the Spirit in you to *retrieve* your brethren that makes you want to go forth and spread the word. But not all of the brethren are ready to come back to the fold. A lot of them are really having a grand time out there.

Participant: Thank you.

Gabriel: You're welcome.

Participant: On today's lesson of Jesus, it brought back...not that it hadn't brought back many, many other times, but when I was a child just about six years old, I saw the story of the life of Jesus as they portrayed it on video—not video at that time, just on screen. I was so overwhelmed at that time that I can remember, "Don't they know he's innocent?" And I was so devastated, I have never forgotten how I felt at that time and this kind of brought it back, but it was so long ago.

Gabriel: Those of you who wept this day—and there were many of you who wept—were among those...some of you among those who persecuted and realized later you made a mistake. Some of you were among followers who, as you, "Why don't they know he is innocent?" Some of you were among the observers who were greatly moved by the courage and quiet dignity of this man.

Remember, beloveds, crucifixion was a common way of killing criminals, and it was not an uncommon sight to see one or two dragging their crosses through the streets, being flogged as they went and so forth, and crying and pleading and falling down and begging for mercy and so forth. And here came a man who asked nothing, nothing of anyone.

Interestingly enough, on an occasion while Jesus was teaching, he encountered a slave who had been flogged greatly for some perceived wrong by the master, the owner, and left to die of thirst. And the Master came by and he looked at this poor wretch and he fetched water and he gave him to drink and he bathed his wounds and he brought him back to a place where he could live.

When Jesus was going up the street carrying this cross, one of the times he fell, this slave...he fell in front of this slave and he looked up at the slave and the slave recognized his face, and he immediately took a goatskin flask from his side with water in it and he poured it on his head and he gave him to drink before the soldiers pulled him away and told him he couldn't do that.

And as Jesus looked at him, a great heaviness that had been within this man's heart—he had been wrenched from his family, sold into slavery for debts that he owed, and never had any hope of ever seeing his wife and children again—and as he did this kindness to the Master and Jesus looked at him, Jesus said to him, "Look behind you," and the man was pulled away by the soldiers and flung into the crowd and as he turned, he looked and there stood his wife and children, whom he had not seen in many a year.

These little miracles happened all along the way— little things, but very profound things. This was part of the healing that went on. One of the soldiers whose task it was to nail him to the cross had twin sons and both of them suffered from epilepsy, which was, in those days, considered to be possessed of demons. And as he knelt to nail the hands of Jesus, Jesus looked at him and he said, "In this hour, thy sons shall be healed." And the man looked at him, not understanding the words, but at the end of the day when he went home, his wife greeted him with great enthusiasm and she said, "Behold, our sons are healed. Look!" And they were healed, and then he remembered the words of the man whose hands he was nailing and he was filled with a great sorrow over what he had done. Have I answered you?

Participant: Yes, thank you.

Participant: Gabriel, did Jesus have brothers and sisters?

Gabriel: Yes, he did. After his birth, yes.

Participant: And was there a family life that he was part of?

Gabriel: Yes, his mother and Joseph had children after him and... It is interesting that Mary never let Joseph forget that he wasn't Jesus' father. (Laughter) She still was a Jewish mother. (Laughter) And Joseph never took offense. Yes, there was a family life within the community of the Essenes. Yes, indeed. Very much so.

Participant: Thank you very much.

Participant: For those of us who wept as we heard this story, is there any value or benefit in finding out why? Knowing our role or...?

Gabriel: No, because you would latch on to it and you wouldn't let it go. It was 2,000 years of your time ago and whatever the reason for your tears, let it be.

Participant: In healing—I don't know if healing is the word—in understanding the evolution, one of the things about the Joshua part, about "take no prisoners," I understand on the one hand it's symbolic, but on the other hand it's sounding like it actually happened historically.

Gabriel: It happened historically, yes, but it was all... Anything that happens has an inner meaning. All of your history has an inner meaning. Remember, your history, your outer expression, is only the outer expression of a higher, deeper manifestation. So, Joshua did indeed ride through the hills and slay, but as Jesus, every single one that was slain by Joshua was touched by Jesus either by word or physical touch.

Participant: So can we look at it as the people who were slain by Joshua... I mean, we know that based upon what you have taught us in the past that each and every person has agreed to participate in some way...

Gabriel: Oh, indeed.

Participant: ...on our journey home.

Gabriel: Oh, they all agreed to participate. All of you agreed to participate in all manner of things, so no one was slain unaware.

Participant: So as they participated in this, they didn't know it was symbolic of anything...

Gabriel: At the moment, no, but they had agreed to it because they knew it before they came, just as you all do.

Participant: Okay, thank you.

Participant: Could you tell us a little bit about Joseph's role in Jesus' life as Mary's husband because he kind of disappears out of Scripture after about the age of twelve?

Gabriel: No, actually he had a very profound effect upon Jesus. Jesus as a child loved Joseph greatly and followed him about and tagged him all over the place and frequently slipped away from Mary and went with Joseph to do "man stuff," you know. And Joseph taught Jesus the value of wood, how to use wood with respect for the life therein. Jesus grew in many, many ways because of Joseph. Joseph was a very wise man—a very gentle man but a very quietly *strong* man, and a lot of the strength, the quiet strength, that Jesus had he learned from Joseph. And Joseph loved Jesus deeply as his very own and never minded the remarks that Mary made from occasion to occasion, "Well, he's not *your* son." Joseph felt in his heart that indeed he was, and he treated him with the same love and the same fatherly caring that he did all the other children.

Participant: How many children were there?

Gabriel: Four altogether.

Participant: Did Joseph live past the Crucifixion?

Gabriel: No, Joseph died when Jesus was in his early twenties. Jesus was actually out of the country when word came to him of Joseph's death—Joseph was a lot older than Mary—and Jesus sent word to his grieving mother because Mary loved Joseph deeply. She...they were very contented with each other. And when Jesus heard of Joseph's passing, he communicated with his mother and asked of her to realize his great light and his great freedom now, as opposed to her loss, which she needed to be reminded of.

Participant: And after the Crucifixion, what was Mary's life like? Were any of the other children still living?

Gabriel: The other children took care of her. John took a great deal of care of her until his calling took him away, in which case he left her in the care of her own children, who looked after her till her end.

Participant: Thank you.

Gabriel: One more and then Beloved Woman's body is going to be sat down. I am told she's getting weary.

Participant: Okay, you had mentioned Essenes a lot. Would it help us at all to know more about the Essenes and maybe follow their lifestyle? And if so, where would I get that information?

Gabriel: You couldn't follow their life style, beloved woman, because it was another country and another time.

Participant: Okay.

Gabriel: You could follow their spiritual mindset. Where would you learn of them?

Participant: Right.

Gabriel: Well, where would she learn of them? Are there library books?

Participant: I have some books, only I find reading them intolerable.

Gabriel: Well, then I don't know how to answer you because the spiritual aspect of the Essenes is very prevalent upon the earth now.

Participant: Okay, fine. Thank you. I'll find it.

Gabriel: I am going to have a prayer and close because Beloved Woman's body is getting a little weary I am told.

Prayer

The Divine Light, the Eternalness that is,
unto Thee, I offer this day,
unto Thee, I offer all that I have done,
unto Thee, I bring these, Thy children,
on their homeward journey,
that they might come close to that flame
and feel the warmth of Your love
and the light of Your truth.

Divine Master Jesus, Who has shared so much
on levels yet unknown
with these, Thy brethren,
Unto Thee, I offer my service ever,
Unto Thou, Who art all life,
I give You thanks that I have been
in the presence of Thy beloveds.

And so it is.

And I shall see you all next time.

The Life of Jesus
May 17, 1997

Lesson

Archangel Gabriel: This day we will discuss the further explanation of the Master Jesus.

As you all know, he was a member of the Essenes, and they were one of many religious groups among the Jewish people. They were known as the Healers, for their purpose was to bring healing to the masses. They used spiritual truths, they used herbs, they used flowers and remedies of the land in which they lived.

They were a very select group and very exclusive. They kept much to themselves and formed little communities wherein those who wished to dwell had to pass certain tests. They did not live as the average person lived. Rather, their whole attention was devoted mostly to the spiritual path. However, they had their segregations because they separated even within their own group into ideals and practices that were not used universally.

The various groups of the Essenes—in various parts of the country and parts of the world—all had their own way of living. Jesus was a member of that, as was his mother, Mary, and Joseph, as was most of the disciples who followed him with the exceptions of Peter and Andrew; they were not members of the Essenes.

Now some of the apostles, some of the disciples, were rather high-ranking in the Essenes. They held positions of power there. They were not of the group that Jesus was. Jesus was of the Hellenist group and he was raised in this strict code.

Now, one of the rules and regulations of the Essenes was that married couples did not live together. They came together and made physical contact for the idea of bringing forth children only in the month of December so that all of the children would be born in the month of September.

Now this was done for a purpose, and the male, the father, did not father a child until he was thirty-six years old, and then he fathered a child four years after that, and four years after that, and four years after that, and so on.

Now they were divided into groups that followed certain teachers of the old—what you would term the Old Testament, the old prophets. There was the Abram group—Abraham group. There was the Davidic group, which Jesus was a part, descendant of David.

Now the descendants of David were the only ones considered to be *true rulers*. The rest of the Essene groups who belonged to the various other followers— such as Moses and Jacob and so forth—they were not considered to be kingly or of royal blood. Only those of the David line or the Davidic line was considered to be any way a proper heir to rule.

Jesus was the first born. His brother, James, followed thereafter, four years after. Now, the situation that arose that caused such controversy, and one of the reasons why Jesus did the things he did, was the fact...two elements entered in there.

One, Jesus was not born in September. Now, it was in this wise. There would be a wedding feast. A host would be selected and that host had no connection whatsoever with the bride or the groom. It was simply someone who served as host to make sure that everything went well, that the wine was served and the food and the fruit and the fish and so on and so forth, and that everyone at the wedding dinner was very happy.

After that, the couple had what was termed to be their first marriage. Now, this usually took place in the fall of the year. However, they did not come together as man and wife until the month of December. During the month of December, they lived together and they engaged in intercourse for the purpose of producing a child. Now this was *extremely* important, especially in the Davidic line, because the Davidic line had to produce an heir, so it was imperative that the males of the Davidic line produce an heir...at least two sons were required.

Now, before the woman would be considered truly married, there had to be a second ceremony, a second wedding. This was usually done when she was three months pregnant, and then she was considered to be a true wife or spouse to her husband. Before that, she was considered to be the equivalent of a single woman.

Now the thing is that the children were all born in September. Now along came Mary, Jesus' mother, who was with child that would be born in the spring. Now this was not allowed. This was considered breaking the rules. This was considered dishonorable, and that is the meaning of the words in your Scripture where it says, "Joseph was of a mind to put her away privately." Now what that meant was there was a group in the Essenes who took care of what was considered illegitimate children. Jesus was considered illegitimate because he was not born in September. So anyone who produced a child—be it male or female and especially male—that was not born in September, these children were usually not raised in the family circle but rather raised in a commune who did nothing but raise children. Now it was debated whether or not Jesus should end up there.

Now Mary and Joseph knew the truth about Jesus. Some of the Essenes accepted their story, some of them did not, and especially those who wanted to be in a position of ruler. So therefore, there was some question as to what would become of Jesus when he was born.

Now the story goes that they had to leave and go to be registered in Bethlehem. Think, beloveds. Why would one have to be registered in a census in a town in which you did not live? Wouldn't make any sense. Doesn't make any sense now; didn't make any sense then. But because Jesus was considered illegitimate and because he would be taken from them, Joseph and Mary decided to leave the compound. A few devoted people went with them, and they journeyed to Bethlehem thinking to find a place.

There is so much symbolism in the Bible that you have to consider. Where in the Scriptures it says, "Let he who has ears to hear, hear," usually meant what you were reading didn't mean what you thought it did. There was a code that the Essenes used to get political and religious information to those who were members who were not in the compound, and so a lot of your Scripture was written in that code. The compound, the Qumran, which is where Jesus was from, was referred to as "the way," and where you read in Scripture, "the way," when Jesus, says "I am the way," he was telling those who could understand what sect he was from. When he said, "I am the way," he was saying, "I am a Hellenistic Jew and I am from Qumran."

Now, when Mary and Joseph got to Bethlehem, they sought other Essenes to assist them. They went to an inn whose owner was a member of a different group of Essenes and they presented their case: "Here we are, Mary obviously very pregnant." And this was in March. Now, the owner of the inn was not a Hellenist Jew. He was not of the House of David and here he had two refugees seeking his help.

Despite the myth concerning the Essenes, they did not all get along. This was not a utopia of peace and love. There was political undercurrents there, the same as there is everywhere. Now here we have a man who doesn't like Hellenist Jews—certainly isn't happy with Qumran—and here he's got two...well actually, there were five people asking for a place to stay. Now one thing that did run common through all of this, all of the Essene beliefs, was the fact that they had to be kind to strangers. They had to extend common courtesy. It is written, "Entertain strangers, for there by you meet the angels unaware." So this man *could not* turn them away completely because that would be going opposite of the code of ethics of the belief system of the Essenes, so he *had* to provide somewhere for them to be, but he didn't have to take them into the inn. So he offered them a cave where animals were kept because that allowed him to *not* give them kindness and yet not break the code. So, Jesus was born in a cave.

Now, because the Hellenist Jews did not want a king of their group to be born out of the code, they decided

105

that Jesus did not warrant inheriting the Davidic line of reign. If they had returned to the compound, he would have been taken from Mary and placed in the sect that raised the children. So they had to go somewhere else, and so they fled to Egypt. Now it tells you in the Scriptures that Herod was after them. Well, I'll tell you a little secret: Herod wasn't after them at all. Herod didn't even know about them. It was within their own group that they fled.

One of the things that you will find holds true in politics throughout your world—has ever been so, probably will be so for a considerably long time—that when someone becomes a radical or when someone is a threat, that someone is gotten rid of.

They remained in Egypt until there was a transition in the power in the Qumran and it was safe for them to return. Now, office was held only for a certain period of time and only by certain Jews. Not everyone held office.

A lot of the symbolism that they wrote in and left their mark with represents rank and order, for even in that, not everyone was considered equal. The Davidic line was considered the kingly line. The line of Moses was considered the line of the law. The Jews belonging to the Moses sect were the ones who made the laws and saw to it that they were carried out. The Abram line was the one who took care of the temples and saw to it that there were proper rituals carried out from time to time according to the code.

Now when they returned, Jesus was nearly twelve years old. Now in that belief system, when a boy was twelve years old, he went through an initiation; he was taken to a temple and the priests questioned him. Sound familiar?

Now Mary, Jesus' mother, was very *protective* of Jesus and when he came up missing one day and they told her he had gone to the temple, Mary panicked because children that were not accepted by the priests in the temple were banned from the commune.

Now in the meantime, when Jesus was four, Mary bore another son, James. Now James was properly born in the month of September. Therefore, James was considered by the Qumran sect to be the legal heir to the throne, as it were, or to leadership. All the priest had to do to take Jesus out of there was to say that he couldn't answer anything satisfactorily and Jesus would have been put in with the other children or taken completely out.

This is why Mary went running. Mary and Joseph both went running, looking for Jesus, because he was in the temple and he was being questioned. Now the thing was, Jesus was smart as a fox and he could answer them even before they asked him. So they had no way of disinheriting him on the basis of that. The only problem he had was that he was still considered illegitimate.

Now when James was four years old, Mary bore another son, Joseph. Now Joseph, being the youngest, was not considered a threat to James at all, for it was the eldest son. And up to this point, James was considered the only one to be a legal heir to the rulership of the Qumran sect of the Essenes. But James did not have the knowledge, the spirituality, or the background that Jesus had. Jesus could out-talk James like that, and they all knew it. They knew in Jesus, they had a leader, and in James, they had an heir.

Now, they didn't throw him out because they feared there were too many who listened to Jesus and knew that he was someone to be reckoned with, and he, even as a youngster, had a certain amount of people who favored him.

Now, they lived there for quite a while. When Jesus was about fourteen, he began to travel. He went...well, a little younger than that. Not younger than twelve but younger than fourteen. [To Tinkerbell] Yes, I know that makes it thirteen. He began to travel. Now they sent him off traveling for two reasons: one, Mary and Joseph were concerned for his life; the other thing was he wanted out of there. He wasn't happy with the situation; it was too restricting. Too many rules and regulations, and if there's one thing Jesus knew how to do was to break a regulation. So Jesus went off traveling.

Now, the three wise men who came to see Jesus— actually Jesus was almost three years old before they found him—these were also of the Essenes but they were of a different group. They were not Hellenist Jews; they were of the Judah group.

Now, they believed in astrology. They believed in what the other Jews termed "magic," so the Qumran kind of stayed away from them a little bit. But to Jesus, magic was fun. So he went off traveling with the three wise men and they taught him all manner of things. That, plus the fact he had the Hermes remembrance, which knew how to do alchemy and so forth like that, so as he traveled, he learned.

He traveled most of his young years. He went all over. I told you that before. When he returned to Qumran, he was a young man. Now he knew things they didn't know, and this was very disturbing to them. Up to this point, his brother James was the uncontested heir to the throne, as it were, and back came Jesus. Know you the story of the Prodigal Son? Well, Jesus was talking about himself. Now he didn't go off squandering his father's riches, but he did go off and he did come back and he was a threat to the heir of authority.

Now, Jesus was not above doing a little mischief, you know. Nothing to harm anyone, but he certainly knew how to hold his position and to make his presence known. When he came back to Qumran, he was not welcomed there. There were only a few, a handful, who welcomed him and the rest of them didn't want him there and made no bones about it, so his stay there was brief.

Now in the meantime, his cousin, John, who came to be known as John the Baptist—who was also of the Judah line, not of the Davidic line—he had developed a kind of following. So Jesus went and he talked with John. Now John knew that Jesus was no threat to him because he was of the Davidic line and John was not, so...we didn't cross lines back then. So John welcomed Jesus and they became good friends.

In the meantime, there was a lot of political unrest, a lot going on.

Now the apostle, Thomas, was the brother-in-law to Herod. Herod married his brother's widow, Herodias, and Herodias was the sister-in-law, *had been* the sister-in-law of Thomas, so Herod knew of John and he didn't like him because John denounced him.

Now John's belief system was very narrow. The Judah's sect was extremely strict, very unyielding, very narrow minded, and closed off to any other type of teaching. So John getting up and denouncing Herod for marrying his sister-in-law didn't go over well, so Thomas stayed pretty much away from Herod. But Thomas was also privy to all the information of what was going on in

Herod's home. Now this was of a great benefit to Jesus because it gave Jesus all the information he needed on the political scene. Jesus knew he somehow had to establish himself as a teacher. He had to be recognized. He could not gain recognition from his own sect because he was considered illegitimate.

So he decided—since he had all this palace information, so to speak, from John—that he was going to use it to his advantage, and he did. And Jesus began his own campaign, not to rule, but to teach. And one of the things that Jesus wanted to change was this sectarianism, this division. He knew the only way that they were going to overpower Rome was to unite, and if it's anything at all that Jews have never been, it's united. They have never united outside of their own little groups.

So Jesus set about trying to establish himself as a teacher and a healer. Now don't forget, when he was a child, he was of the group who did healing. He knew how to heal. That was one of the things that they were taught right from the git-go, was how to heal. So Jesus had this power. He also had the Hermes ancestry and he also had learned from the magi and he had learned from other teachers as well, so Jesus had a lot of power.

He also was learning more and more about his own divinity. He was discovering more and more the power that he had came not from what he knew of the earth but rather from what he knew bringing in through the Spirit. So he began to teach.

Now he had to get some support. He couldn't just go walking about barefoot teaching, so he started out to find some followers. And he wasn't stupid. He knew he had to have people in high places, and so he went to Matthew.

Now Matthew was a tax collector on the outside—that's how he earned his living—but Matthew was also a member of the Essenes and he held a high position there, so Jesus went to visit him. Now Matthew remembered Jesus from when he was little, and Jesus made friends with Matthew. He did the same thing with the rest of them. The only two were Peter and Andrew; they were not members.

Within the sect, there were priests who were called "fishers," and when a gentile desired to join in their sect, the gentile went through a considerable amount of instruction, testing, and so forth. They were never fully accepted as far as any authority was concerned...that never came to them. However, they were allowed to join, and one of the initiations to which they were subjected before they could become a member was to walk out through water to a boat, out in the sea aways, and to be submersed under the water and then hauled in nets into the boat. The priest who did the ceremony were called "fishers." The men who pulled them in the boats were called "fishers of men."

When Jesus went to Peter and Andrew and asked them if they would care to follow him...they were very practical, uneducated men and their first question of Jesus was, "What's in it for us?"

And Jesus said, "I will make you fishers of men." Now this gave them a little power. This gave them the ability to belong to a very restricted sect.

Now, Jesus had a certain amount of clout because he was of the Davidic line, even though he was considered to be illegitimate. He still could walk in Qumran and command a little bit of respect; resented as it was, they had to give it to him. So Jesus went to Qumran with Peter and Andrew and said, "I desire for these two men to be taken in." Well, that added to the furor. They were not welcome. They did not belong. They were of the low caste. They were laborers. They worked with their hands. They were uneducated. They didn't know how to read or write. They were simply village people.

But...Jesus went to James, who was fearful of Jesus. James feared Jesus. Not feared for his life or anything of that sort, but he feared the power that Jesus had. So Jesus went to James, who was quite highly regarded, and said to him, "These two friends of mine wish to become members. What are you going to do about that?" Now here was James between a rock and a hard place. James had authority, James was high up there, but James also knew that was one of the most unpopular things that he could do, was to ask that Peter and Andrew be brought in as members of that group. But here stood Jesus, truly the legal heir, the first born of the Davidic line from his mother.

Back in those days—I'm not sure if this holds true today upon your earth—but back in those days, you were not considered a Jew unless your mother was a Jew. If your mother was Jewish, then you were a Jew. If your father was Jewish and your mother a gentile, you were not a Jew. Now Mary was of the Davidic line and they could trace Mary back to David, and here was her first born son, illegitimate though he be, there he was and James recognized the power Jesus had if Jesus cared to exercise it.

So James went and pulled in some favors and Peter and Andrew were accepted in. I guess the equivalent of that in your day and time would be to put a street person in the White House. It would be comparable to that. Well, the Qumran people were extremely unhappy. They didn't like Jesus. They didn't like what he was doing. He was flaunting their code of ethics. He was flaunting their everything. So, they had to figure a way of getting rid of him.

Now at that time, Herod had decided he was going to clean up the countryside because he didn't like what was going on. There were too many groups of Jews getting together. There was too much rebellion rumbling underneath the surface, and Herod decided that he had to do some things to get things straightened out, so he indiscriminately sent—well, he got authority from Rome—and he sent the soldiers out and they grabbed up three thousand Jews and crucified them. Now you don't find that in your Scriptures.

Now, while this was going on, the Essenes began to fear for their lives because all of a sudden this was not a friendly place to be, and they decided that they needed to defend themselves and so they hired themselves a "hit man," by your terms, and that "hit man" was Judas. Judas was a paid assassin.

Now, they didn't have anyone in particular in mind when they hired him. They just simply wanted protection from whomever. And they knew that Judas would do whatever they bid him to do. For one thing, Judas was very happy, indeed, to be taken in the Qumran sect and he was immediately given a certain amount of authority. Now while he was there, who do you suppose he met? He met Jesus.

Now Judas wasn't used to rules and regulations; these things were rather new to him. And here was Jesus who didn't *like* rules and regulations, and he and Judas would sit and talk and Jesus would say to Judas, "You know, this would be a better place if..." So Judas decided to take up with Jesus, which you know what that did to James. Whoa. Talk about a viper being invited to dinner.

Well anyway, Jesus left Qumran and he went out to teach and Judas went with him, Peter and Andrew went with him, Matthew went with him, and the rest of the apostles that he had chosen who had been sitting and listening to Jesus. He went out. Now he had friends in high places. He also had an assassin with him.

He had Peter, who was loud and boisterous and bullyish. And Peter, who had ears to hear; Peter could get all the gossip. Judas was accepted in low places, so he could get all the news of the day as well.

Now Jesus meets Mary Magdalene, and that put another aspect into his life because Jesus fell passionately in love with Mary Magdalene. Now Mary Magdalene was also a member of the Essenes but she was a member of the Judah aspect, and while she loved Jesus greatly, she was divided, greatly divided. Her belief system didn't match his belief system; his belief system didn't match anybody's. He came to teach unity. He came to teach the oneness of humanity, the oneness of life. He came to teach love and compassion and respect, and this was much wanting in any of the Essene sects, some more than in others, but nonetheless, they all had their own code of ethics and none of it matched Jesus' teachings.

Jesus would not dishonor Mary Magdalene. He loved her too much and he knew the only way that he could be with her would be to marry her. Now he hadn't planned exactly on getting married, but he wanted her to be with him and the only way that that could happen in a way that would not dishonor her or discredit her would be for him to marry her.

Now we come to the wedding in Cana. Now you have to understand how things were back then. The mother of the groom was the top authority at any wedding. It was she who said, "Do this, do that," and this and that was done.

Now the wedding feast at Canna was not a marriage. It was the dinner that *preceded* the actual marriage, and it was at this dinner that Jesus' mother, Mary, ordered the water to be turned into wine, and the only way she had the authority to do that was because Jesus was the bridegroom. And she, as his mother, had top authority. When she said, "Jump," they said, "How high?" So, even Jesus was under her authority at that event. And when she came to him, she said, "We're running out of good wine. We need good wine."

And he said to her, "What do you want me to do?"

"Make some wine."

He said to her, "I can't do that. I'm not...we're not ready to go public just yet."

"Make the wine!" She called the servants, they brought the vessels of water, and she stood there. (Laughter) Now, he may have broken the codes and ethics of the Essenes, but he never crossed his mother. (Laughter) So Jesus made the wine at his own wedding feast.

Now politically, the scene was getting very rough at this time, a lot of turmoil. Roman soldiers were everywhere. Rome was on the march. The Jews were fearing for their lives whether they belonged to the Essenes or not. They really needed to unify. Now, from the high priests in the temples we're hearing murmurings...this is the time of the Messiah.

Now you have to understand, life for the Jewish people under the rule of Rome was horrible. The Roman soldiers had no qualms about taking what they wanted, who they wanted; rape and murder were a common thing every day. So they seriously were looking for someone to save them from this. They were looking for a Savior, truly a Savior. This was the opportunity that Jesus needed. They were looking for a Savior.

Now, however, they were looking for a Savior who would come in with a sword and an army and rout out Rome. They weren't looking for a teacher; they had teachers in Abraham and in Moses. They weren't looking for someone to come and give them words; they were looking for someone to come in with power.

Now, the thing was that Jesus knew that he *had* the greatest power. He had power from on high—he had spiritual power—and he knew that if he could get them to change their thinking and get rid of some rules and regulations, that they could unite and they would be rid of their Roman oppressors. So he and the disciples went about talking to the people.

The things that Jesus taught were spiritual truths, but hidden in among them were words of instruction from a political sense. Now Jesus had no dream of being king or ruler of the earth, but he did have this ideal of people living in love and peace and harmony, and he knew that as long as the dividing lines of can and cannot's, who's accepted and who isn't, and all of that was in force, that there would be no unification of the Jewish people. He never started a new religion. Jesus was a good Jew. It was Peter and more, Paul, the fanatic, who got the new religion going.

Now, Jesus had to work with what he had and what he had were men who held high positions in the Essenes who were not exactly comfortable with breaking all the codes and rules and regulations. There was a lot of resistance among the disciples. The only two who said, "Let's do it!" was Peter and Andrew. They were willing to take up swords and fight.

Judas, by this time, had decided, "Hey, this is pretty good. I think I'm going to sit back and watch." Judas quickly had assessed the situation and he knew that Jesus had no army.

Judas lived by a different code of ethics. If someone was going to harm you or threaten you, you got rid of them. That was not an uncommon thing. There were many paid assassins in that day and time, just as you have them in your day and time. So for Judas to understand that the takeover that Jesus was doing was of a spiritual, loving nature and not of a violent one...this was very difficult for Judas and he confronted Jesus on many an occasion—"What do you think you're doing? You're going to get us all killed. Nobody's going to do this this way. You've got to get an army. I know guys. I can get you an army." And Judas could have gotten him all manner of men who would have been willing to go forth and have a field day killing Romans.

But Jesus said to Judas, "My kingdom is not of this earth. We are going to bring the spirit of the people together in the unity of love and compassion."

"Well," Judas said, "you're out of your mind."

So Judas decided he was going to go out and about and see how many people he could rally up if he needed to and he did. But something was bothering Judas. As Judas went back into the world from which he came, he didn't fit now because his spirituality had been awakened. He had been in a place of love, where love was shown, where harmony and peace were part of the inner circle.

Judas, for the first time in his *whole life,* felt loved. The radical, Jesus, was not the radical that Judas had hoped he would be. And so, when Judas tried to go out and rally up an army, he found he didn't have it in him. He couldn't bring himself to do these hard things anymore. Rather, instead, he found himself talking about the teachings of Jesus and telling people about the love and the healing and the things that were going on that were good and whole and holy.

And the things that Judas started to do began to not come out the way he intended, and he realized that through the love that had come to him, he had lost his edge, as it were, in the world of violence.

So he came back to Jesus and he said, "I have gone to seek an army."

And Jesus said, "Did you find one?"

He said, "I did, but I cannot call them forth."

And Jesus said, "Blessed art thou, Judas, for thou has learned greatly this day."

Now that began a different kind of relationship between Judas and Jesus. Now Judas protected him. Now Judas didn't always understand what Jesus was doing or saying, but love him, yes, indeed he did.

Now in the meantime, Jesus has Mary Magdalene. Now Jesus is in a quandary. By the Davidic law, Jesus has to marry her and in four years produce a son. Jesus knows that in four years he isn't going to be there, and what will happen to Mary Magdalene and any child they had? If the Romans didn't get them, the Qumran would, and so he decided that children could not be an option for them.

This put him in a difficult place. He wanted Mary very much to be his wife but he also knew that it would be a great threat to her life. Now they also already had their wedding dinner. If Jesus didn't marry her now, that would be a dishonor to *her*. She would be thought to be a harlot. She would be thought to be an unclean woman and this would not only sever their relationship, it would end her life as a woman of respect.

Jesus turned to his brother, James, and he said, "I desire greatly for you to take Mary Magdalene into the Qumran."

"Well, I tell you what. We've already done two. Now you've got a third? What is this?"

Now James was really frightened and very much opposed to this, but Mary, Jesus' mother, loved Mary Magdalene. She saw in her the love that her son had for her and she also saw how devoted Mary was to Jesus. So Mary, having quite a bit of clout in the Qumran Essenes, decided to advocate the inclusion of Mary Magdalene in that group. Mary, the mother of Jesus, got Mary Magdalene into the Qumran, and just in time because a great revolt was going on.

Now Thomas took it upon himself to confront Pilate. Now Pilate was also a member of the Essenes but he was not a member of the Davidic group, he was a member of the Judah group, and their rules and regulations were a little different. And Thomas knew, of course, as everyone did, that Pilate worked for Rome, and Thomas felt that Pilate was showing more favoritism to Rome than he was to the Essenes and decided that something needed to be brought to Pilate's attention.

So Thomas went to Pilate and he said, "What are you doing?" He said, "The Romans are coming in here, they're doing this, this, this, and this, and you're sitting back on your laurels and you're letting it happen. You are either with us or you are against us. You choose."

Well at that point, Pilate had not met Jesus and Pilate's affiliation with the Essenes had grown rather weak and watery, but his affiliation with Rome had grown rather powerful, rather strong. He could see a great future for himself with Rome, not so much so with the Essenes.

So Pilate, at that point, sided with the Romans. This infuriated Thomas and some of the other hierarchy of the Qumran group, and so they got a hold of Judas and they said to him, "We need to be rid of Pilate."

Judas said, "Why are you telling me?"

"Well, that's what we hired you for."

Judas said, "I can't do it."

He said, "Why not?"

He said, "Because I can't. I can't kill."

Well, this didn't make them very happy at all. But Judas, in order to stay in their favor, said, "I'll tell you what I will do." He said, "I will go and do the necessary background work to find out how this might be accomplished and I shall find you an assassin."

"Alright, we'll do that."

So Judas went out and he found out the schedule of Pilate—where he would be, certain times, certain places, and so on and so forth—and he brought back...are you ready for this? He brought back an assassin named Barabbas. And Barabbas, who had been in prison many times by Pilate and had a gut level hatred for Pilate, said, "Piece of cake. Consider it done."

However, Pilate still had friends among the Essenes, friends who benefitted by knowing Pilate. Their families were not harangued by the Roman soldiers. Their monies were not taken from them and so forth, so it was good to be a friend of Pilate.

So, someone came to Pilate and said, "Your life is in jeopardy. Barabbas is after you. His intent is to slay you and get rid of you." Well, Pilate was used to these kind of things. However, this came from a reliable source. This came from Matthew.

Pilate listened. Pilate knew who Matthew was. Pilate knew what his position was with Jesus, although he had not met Jesus. He considered Jesus an inconsequential rabble...rebel that wouldn't amount to anything. So Pilate said, "Alright." He said, "I desire to go into hiding for a little bit. In the meantime, I think we need to teach these Jews a lesson." So he sent his soldiers forth, they killed some, they captured some—Barabbas among them—and threw them into prison.

In the ensuing conflict, Jesus walked into the palace where Pilate was and stood before him and said, "What are you doing with my people?"

Now this unsettled Pilate considerably because number one, he didn't know how Jesus got there. Where were the guards? Number two, he didn't know Jesus. Maybe he had a dagger. Instead, Jesus walked up the steps to where Pilate was, sat himself down opposite him, and he said, "We're going to talk," and they did. They talked all the day and in through the night. And by the time Jesus got through, Pilate understood that Jesus was not the threat to Rome at all, not in the sense of being a militant. Jesus was teaching love and unity and harmony and peace. The ideal that Jesus presented to Pilate was one of compassion, of everyone living equally.

Pilate sat and listened, and he saw in this man not a rebel with an army hidden in the hills but a profound spiritual teacher who harkened back to the old "love thy neighbor." This was the part that Pilate began to remember from his early years as a member of the Essenes. There were no rules and regulations with Jesus; it was just open love and unity and peace. And Pilate saw that beyond all of the rules and regulations the Essenes had created, this was the foundation of their belief in the *beginning,* and his yearning to return to that, to believe as he once believed and had long since ceased to believe, this was the man who was the truth of "the way," and Pilate knew it.

And Pilate became a supporter...quietly, without Roman knowledge. It would have been worth his head if he had been open about it. But Pilate supported Jesus greatly. Pilate afforded Jesus safe places to be when the soldiers were around about.

Now Pilate's position was very unsteady, for Herod had relatives that looked upon Pilate's position with a great deal of greed, and Pilate knew if he crossed Herod that his position was over with just like that, and perhaps even his life. Quietly listening, without being seen, was Pilate's wife, and Pilate's wife sought out members of the Qumran women and talked to them, and she asked to be taken in.

Now she was taking her life in her hands to do this. The wife of Pilate, a member of the Essenes...ooh! They decided not to take her in as a full-fledged member because it would threaten her life and theirs as well, but they did allow her to come and learn. She was allowed certain lessons, certain things that she was permitted, and she formed a great bond with both Mary's and with Martha.

Now Jesus was separated from Mary Magdalene because Mary Magdalene had been taken into the Qumran and even if Jesus had gone in there, he wouldn't have been allowed to see her. He wanted to see her very much. After all, he was very much in love with her and was still in the quandary whether or not they should wed. Now the good thing was there were no time limits on when there was the wedding dinner and when the wedding happened. It could happen within a few months or within a few years, as long as the betrothal wasn't broken.

Jesus concluded that if he were to marry Mary Magdalene, it would have to be very quietly and with no one the wiser. He couldn't let it be known that she was his wife because *he knew* what was coming and he knew that even as they would kill him, they would hunt her down and kill her too, that there would not be enough protection among the Essenes to keep her alive. He wanted very much to meet with her but he wasn't sure how he could do this. He didn't want to dishonor her.

Now, Peter didn't like Mary Magdalene. I don't think that's any secret. Peter took issue with the fact that Jesus wanted to wed. "Why would you want to take a wife? I have one. They're terrible!" (Laughter) That was Peter's philosophy. Peter also resented the time and the teachings that were given to Mary Magdalene. After all, she was merely a woman. Now, you remember, by Peter's code of ethics, women were subservient to men. They were in the same classification as camels and donkeys. They served a purpose; beyond that, no value.

He also resented the fact that Mary Magdalene wasn't afraid of him. She took all five foot three inches of her stature and stood up to him, and Peter didn't like that. Peter felt that if Mary Magdalene were out of the way, that Jesus would go forth in battle. He knew about Judas. He knew that they could rally an army. He knew they could go forth with and they could overthrow Rome. But here was Jesus, mooning over Mary Magdalene instead of rallying an army.

So Peter, not knowing all the rules and regulations by heart of the Essenes, decided that since such a length of time had passed between the dinner, the bridal dinner, and there was still no wedding, that it wouldn't be hard to start the rumor that Jesus had found out some unpleasant things about Mary Magdalene and was probably not going to marry her. Well, that wasn't too smart of Peter.

Jesus had a great love for Peter but a greater love for Mary Magdalene. He wanted to confront Peter but not in an antagonistic way. He wanted Peter to recognize the power of the *Spirit* rather than the power of the earth. So, he waited until Peter was out in a boat, he and the others, and Jesus walked across the water just a little ways and he called to Peter and he said, "Come to me."

Now Peter thought, "Oh well, this is great!" He said, "But if I do, shall I not fall in?"

And Jesus said, "Well, I haven't fallen in. Come on, Peter." (Laughter)

So, Peter scrambled over the side of the boat into the water and, with a little help from Jesus, began to walk toward him. And then—this is not in your Scripture— Jesus said to Peter, "Peter, I don't think it's very smart of you to carry out what you think you're going to do concerning the woman I love." And where do you think Peter went? (Laughter)

Now he had Peter's attention grandly. He raised Peter up, gasping for breath, and he said, "Peter, have I not taught you love?"

"Oh, indeed."

"And do you not think that *all* of God's people are worthy of love?"

"Well, I do now." (Laughter)

Peter realized the power of Jesus, but *more* than this, Peter learned something in that incident and that was that when your thoughts are concentrated on love, there is power, but when your thoughts are concentrated on harming another by word or by deed, you sink beneath the waves of your own ill-doing and only the power of love can save you.

There was a lot of lesson in that for Peter, and while he really didn't like Mary any better, he certainly respected her position in Jesus' life and he certainly respected the code of love and compassion.

Jesus desired greatly to have Mary Magdalene become his wife, but he also needed to be able to guarantee her *safety,* for he knew their time together would be very brief and he did not want to jeopardize her life in any way.

So Jesus went to Pilate and he said to him, "I desire to take to me a wife and I desire that you give me your word that she will come to no harm."

And Pilate said, "As it is within my power and while I am magistrate here, I give you my word, she will not be persecuted."

And so Jesus went to his mother and he told her. A good son always tells his mother first when he intends to wed. And Mary was greatly pleased, for in Mary's mind, she saw coming forth an issue from Jesus that would carry on the Davidic line of that which would be king—not king of the earth, but king of the Spirit—and so she gave her approval and she immediately set about making the arrangements. Now the thing was, it had to be a very quiet wedding. It couldn't be the usual thing because Jesus didn't want to have everyone know and therefore put Mary's life in danger. And so they had a quiet gathering within the confines of the Qumran and Jesus and Mary Magdalene were married.

Now usually the procedure was in this wise: They would be married in September and not until December would they come together as husband and wife. Then they would be separate again until the following year. Jesus knew he didn't have that kind of time, and so after a few weeks of living in the confines of the Qumran, he took Mary and they left.

Now, Jesus' mother was not happy with this. This wasn't good. She felt there would be another illegitimate child, as it would be termed, one not born in September, and so she worried greatly.

Joseph was not well. He was considerably older than Mary and his health was failing, had been failing for some time. And Jesus went to him and he offered him healing and Joseph said, "No, let me be, for my time upon the earth is drawing to a close and I desire that it be so."

So Jesus took Mary Magdalene and they left and went out into the hill country and they spent time there teaching, and the disciples followed afterward...came with them.

Now Peter wasn't aware that Jesus had married Mary Magdalene. He wasn't at the ceremony, as it were, and when they reached the place where they were staying, Peter was shocked to find Mary there. Quite indignant, and he said to Jesus, "Why do you love her more than us?"

And Jesus replied, "It is one of the mysteries of marriage," and that's the first time that Peter heard of it and Peter fled from the room, wrath at the idea that this audacious woman should occupy a place so close to the Master.

Now everyone thinks that Jesus and the disciples had this wonderful communication and that everybody loved everybody and everyone got along. Didn't happen. There was a lot of jealousy among them. There was a lot of resentment, especially with Matthew and those who were of an important part of the Essene community. They resented Peter and Andrew, and of course there was resentment going the other way. They even disagreed among themselves on a lot of things.

One of the things that troubled them was the fact that they did not see Jesus rising up armies and going forth to overcome Rome. And this disturbed them greatly, and it especially disturbed Judas. Judas didn't see why they couldn't overthrow Rome. That seemed to be a rather simple thing if they would just get together. And so Jesus tried to teach them about this and one of the things he used was what you have come to call the "Sermon on the Mount."

"Blessed are the meek, for they shall inherit the earth. Blessed are those who mourn, for they shall be comforted," and so forth. And for the most part, it went right over their heads. They still were looking for the Messiah to be the *Savior*. They were not looking for a spiritual teacher.

Jesus preached all through the countryside, for the most part avoiding Jerusalem, more because of Mary than anything else. He found sanctuary in people's homes, and Mary had a lot of influence—don't forget, she came from a wealthy family and wealth is power, even back then. And so between who she knew and who believed in him, they always had a place to stay where they were safe.

One of the "codes" that was used... In your Scriptures you will read, "And the way was made safe," or "The way was made straight," meaning, to those who had ears to hear, that Jesus was in a safe place and not to worry.

But things were getting worse and worse in Jerusalem. The Jews were acting up, Roman soldiers were everywhere, and there was a great deal of turmoil and unsettledness there. One never knew whether their neighbor was a spy under the Roman payroll or not.

Among the Essenes, there was a lot of unrest. They felt betrayed by Jesus. He had come into the sanctuary and he had married and he had not honored the code of not coming together until December. He had taken his bride and he had left. This was unheard of. What's more, they had heard that he had had a feast and he had invited publicans and he had invited gentiles.

Now Jesus was of the conviction that God was for everyone, not just for the Jews, but God was for *every living person* and the love and the teachings of God was to be *shared,* not to be secreted away. And secrecy was one of the things the Essenes practiced most ardently, was secrecy, even among themselves. One sect did not share with the other. They were very political. This was not what it was about and Jesus knew it, and he tried very hard to bring that truth home to them but they saw in his words a rebellion. They saw in his words usurping the old Masters, the old teachings of Moses, and so forth.

Do you recall in your Scriptures where an expensive ointment was used to rub on Jesus' head and feet, and Judas said, "Why are you doing that? You could take that ointment and you could sell it and we could give the money to the poor."

And Jesus said, "You will always have the poor with you, but the bridegroom is soon to leave." Now what he was saying in code, what Judas was saying in code, was, "We could use that money to rise an army."

And what Jesus was replying was...the poor representing those of the underlings, the lower class, as it were, in those days and those were the ones who constituted most of the mercenaries and the soldiers for hire and the assassins for hire and so forth. So Jesus was in fact saying, "You will always have those kind of people with you, but what is being done this day is an honor to me as the Messiah."

Well, Judas had little use for a Messiah; the thought was an army. Now Judas was even in more of a quandary because while the human part of him wanted to rise an army, the spiritual part of him was being taken over, so as it were, by the Christ awareness, the love, and so forth. So Judas's punch or power was lessening considerably.

In the meantime, Rome was having a hard time. More and more crucifixions were going on. It was a daily thing for the Jews to be dragged through the streets and crucified. Six or eight or ten or twenty at a time. The survivors were getting more terrified and in their terror, plotting more and more against Rome. Rome was getting word that Pilate was not in control anymore and Pilate had better do something to show Rome his allegiance or he was out of there.

So Pilate sent forth more soldiers and more soldiers. Now came the time when every radical, every rebel, was being rounded up. Even if they were just suspect, they were still rounded up.

Now, Jesus knew his time was near. He knew he had to go into Jerusalem. Now all the apostles said, "Are you crazy? That's where they're killing people in there? What do you want to go there for?" But Jesus knew this was bringing into the culmination of his purpose upon Earth, but he also knew that he had to bring the message even more profoundly.

Now it tells you in the Scriptures—in the Old Testament as you have come to call it—that the Messiah shall ride into Jerusalem on a donkey. Now this is an old, old myth, an old belief system that goes way back long before Jesus' time. It was always considered an act of humility and service to the people for the king to arrive at his throne on the back of a donkey. That was the outward display of what was supposed to be an internal service to the people.

That was the way it was. It had been that way for centuries. Jesus also needed to let the authorities know that he was coming into Jerusalem. He also needed to let Qumran know that he was coming into Jerusalem. So, he said to his disciples, "I'm going into Jerusalem riding on a donkey."

Well, this did not meet with any kind of support or approval whatsoever. They saw it as an outward act of suicide. "You *know* they will capture you. You *know* they will slay you. What is going to happen to the rest of us and so forth? How are we going to overthrow Rome if this is what is going on?"

But Jesus was adamant. He said, "Leave it be. It has to be thus," and he set them forth.

Now in the meantime, of course, you know, the word of these activities of Jesus was also reaching Qumran. There were people there who still supported Jesus, and when the word came that Jesus was going to present himself in Jerusalem riding on a donkey, they all knew the significance of that. They all knew that he was making an *open threat* to Rome and to his brother James.

Now James, in the meantime, had acquired quite a bit of status in Qumran and he saw himself—with Jesus' radical activities and total disregard for the code and all that—James saw himself as the Davidic heir to the throne. Now, Jesus was doing an act that would have been James' way of claiming his inheritance. It would have been *his* way of triumphful entry into the Qumran and claiming to be king.

Now Jesus never aspired to be king. Jesus was trying to draw the people together in unification. When the word came that he was going to do this, James went to his mother and he said, "Do you know what Jesus is doing?"

And Mary said, "I've heard."

And he said, "Well, you're not going to let him, are you?" ...because Mary had a lot of clout there.

And Mary closed her eyes and she said, "The purpose for which he came is unknown to you—indeed, is unknown to the world—but this day in your time you will come to see the word of God in action." And Mary went straight way out, made the connections where the donkey was to be left for Jesus to find, and James went away with his head hanging down.

Now you all know the triumph ride into Jerusalem. He went to the temple. Now, he had *flaunted the code* of the Essenes. He had flaunted in their faces, "I don't abide by your code. I'm going into Jerusalem on a donkey." Now, Qumran was certainly not behind that. James was the one they had planned to put in the Davidic line. *He* was to be the king. Now, Jesus had no help from the Qumran. Even those who believed in him feared to show it.

Now, the disciples are wondering what form of insanity has overtaken Jesus that he is doing this kind of a thing. Nonetheless, they believed. They believed and they did his bidding. They got the donkey. They got the crowds gathered. It wasn't hard to get a crowd rallied in Jerusalem in those days, not at all, because anyone who thought that there was anything that was going to get...overthrow Rome, they are for that. And so it wasn't hard for the masses to get behind Jesus to make this great greeting because they felt he was coming to take over the temple, to take over Jerusalem, and throw out the Romans.

Jesus came into Jerusalem, and having flaunted the rules and regulations of the Qumran, now he went to the temple—the holy of holies where all the Jews met to worship—and he went in there and he threw everybody out. There were money changers in there, there were people selling little creatures for sacrifice and so forth, and he went in there and he threw them all out.

Well now, where do you think that put him in the eyes of the Jews? Not in a very good spot. They got together and they saw in him a rebel that was dangerous indeed. Now, the Romans had their hands full with all these revolting Jewish people and they were weary and tired of the revolt and now, just when they think they're getting things settled down, along comes this upstart who's starting things up all over again.

So he had Rome against him. He had the Jews against him. He even had Qumran against him.

After he went to the temple, Jesus went to see Pilate. Now, Pilate had his own problems. Rome was not happy with Pilate. Pilate feared for his life. Jesus went to Pilate and he said, "They're going to take me captive soon and they're going to crucify me."

Well, Pilate hit the roof. "Just what I need on top of everything else. Now, we're not going to let this happen. I'm going to do this and I'm going to…"

And Jesus said to Pilate, "No, you can't. You have to let it be."

Pilate was not happy. Pilate was on the verge of insanity from all of the problems he had. He was getting messages from Rome that if he didn't clean up Jerusalem, he was out of there. He had great problems and now, a man he dearly loved and respected, was coming and telling him that he was deliberately coming in to cause trouble, and of course this meant more trouble for Pilate.

By the way, after the Crucifixion, Pilate was assassinated. Rome was unhappy with him. There were so many people unhappy with him and most certainly, the Essenes were not happy with him, and so he was assassinated.

You all know the story of the Crucifixion. I told you that the last time so I won't go into that. And after you take your food break, I shall bring you up to date on what happened to everybody afterward, including Mary Magdalene.

Questions

Participant: I'm curious. You said that he belonged to a Hellenic Group?
Gabriel: Hellenist.
Participant: Were they Hellenist because they were from Greece?
Gabriel: A lot of Greece, yes. A lot of Greek people were part of it...the Greek Jews. Now the thing is, you must remember that Jerusalem was kind of a melting pot and a lot of influence came in here—a lot of Jesus' teachings, a lot of the way he believed, the Qumran he was a part of, had a lot of Greek influence in it.
Participant: Okay. The Qumran...where does that word come from?
Gabriel: That was a name that they chose, just a name they chose.
Participant: It sounds like it might be oriental of some sort.
Gabriel: No, it was quite...in fact that's where some of the Dead Sea Scrolls were found, was in Qumran.
Participant: Oh, okay. It was a place, too.
Gabriel: It is a place, indeed.
Participant: Thank you.

Participant: Gabriel, you said earlier that Jesus began to campaign to teach because he wanted to change the sectarianism among his people...
Gabriel: Indeed, he did.

Participant: ...and unite them against Rome. Is there not a parallel in modern Israel today where there's a lot of sectarianism dividing up the people more so than ever? And if so, does this preclude that eventually there will be another teacher coming to help the people?

Gabriel: How can I answer you? Yes, there is another teacher, and whether or not the Jewish people unite is still up for opinion.

Participant: It hasn't happened in thousands of years.

Gabriel: It hasn't, and the sad thing is if the Jewish people were to unite and come together in agreement and leave behind the old mosaic thinking, they would rule the world. The Jewish mind is extremely bright, extremely clear, but their belief system gets in their way.

Participant: Thank you.

Gabriel: Beloved woman.

Participant: Greetings Gabriel. While I'm listening to the story here, I know that I came looking for, "I wonder how Jesus practiced the spiritual truths that Gabriel's been teaching us for all these years," and I know that the...I suspect that Jesus came in the spring verses September because it was a designed obstacle to produce the desired result at the end. Things like...I mean they lived in an awful, awful time—the power struggles, the suffrages, the assassinations, all of that sort of stuff—and in the meantime, I'm hearing statements of, "Jesus feared for the life of Mary Magdalene," and I'm saying to myself, "Gee, I'm sure Jesus and Mary Magdalene had designed this beforehand and I wonder what Jesus was thinking because he must have known...so I have this confusion in my mind and this question in my mind that says...

Gabriel: Why didn't he know she would be alright?

Participant: Something like that. And you know, it's like the illusion of death, the power of the Higher Self, releasing our desire of outcome and all of that stuff that we've been taught to practice.

Gabriel: Beloved woman, do not forget that Jesus was a man, a human being, who *became* the Christ. You are on the path, all of you, and do you not have times of thinking, "Is this going to be alright?"

Participant: Boy, do I have times.

Gabriel: You have an offspring that you concern yourself about several times in a year?

Participant: Hmm...okay.

Gabriel: Do you not know in your heart of hearts that ultimately he will be alright, but in the meantime, what if?

Participant: True.

Gabriel: I rest my case.

Participant: Okay. Okay.

Gabriel: Beloved woman.

Participant: Hello. I think that I have the same sort of question as she had. I was thinking of Mary and how she must have felt, knowing what was going to happen.

Gabriel: Oh, but she didn't.

Participant: Oh, she didn't know?

Gabriel: He never told her.

Participant: How did she have the strength to get through that? I would assume she was, at that time, looking at things from a larger perspective that she must have felt or known there was a purpose for all this?

Gabriel: He told her many times in such a way that she did not... When he said to her, "Soon, I must go to my

Father and prepare the way," she assumed that he meant go some*where* and make ready for them to come, for he said to her, "Where I go, you shall be also." And she believed that, but she didn't know in her mind, she wouldn't let herself take in the *real* meaning of his words. Rather, she chose to believe he's going to some geographical place and we shall follow after, for he often did that and then he would send for them.

Participant: So she went through the Crucifixion on a very human level?

Gabriel: Oh, indeed. Indeed.

Participant: But did she see the bigger picture?

Gabriel: She is beginning to see the bigger picture.

Participant: Thank you.

Gabriel: Beloved entity.

Participant: [Young boy] Pardon?

Gabriel: I greeted you. I called you beloved entity.

Participant: Oh, thank you. After Judas told the Romans where Jesus was staying and he got paid for it, did he hang himself?

Gabriel: No, he didn't. Judas actually was murdered.

Participant: Oh okay, thanks.

Gabriel: Actually, Judas was murdered by those who had an old debt against him. You know, Judas had been the assassin, and they found him in a very distraught state of mind afterward, for Judas did not want to do what he did. It was totally against everything within him. And after the deed was done, he was most distraught, terribly distraught, and he was not hard to find, nor was he hard to get rid of, because there was no defense left in him. And he didn't even put up a fight. They simply slew him and threw him over a wall, and he never even said, "Don't touch me."

Gabriel: Beloved entity.

Participant: Would you discuss the Kaloo and the men of Ur and their relationship to the Essenes?

Gabriel: They were a part of a...they were rather a distant part of the Essene group. Their belief system differed quite a bit. They didn't follow so closely the teachings of Moses. They were more liberal in some ways than the Essenes, the core Essene group. They also were extremely...very much not allowing women into their group. They were very masculine-minded and the women that were allowed in were more like mothers or sisters. Marriage was not encouraged; although it was not prohibited, it was not encouraged. They relied more on conversion rather than birthing and bringing up the children in that way.

Participant: Was there any relationship between them and the Atlanteans?

Gabriel: In consciousness somewhat, yes. Yes. They were...their belief system was very stringent. They were quite a mental group rather than a loving group. Their rules were hard to bear and if one could not bear them, then one was not included.

Participant: Thank you.

Gabriel: Indeed.

Participant: Gabriel, you said that Judas was murdered. Why did they put it in the Scriptures that he hanged himself?

Gabriel: Oh well, they're not going to confess to anything like that, are they? People didn't go around saying, "Oh, guess what I did this morning? I went out and killed somebody!" They kept it to themselves, beloved.

Participant: So he was killed by his own?

Gabriel: He was killed by his own, indeed.

Participant: Were they members of the Essenes?

Gabriel: No, no. He was slain by those...he used to be a paid assassin and there were people who had cause to hate him greatly. A father is slain, a brother is slain, a husband is slain...and when they saw this opportunity to slay him, they took it.

Participant: But, how did they it get handed down to those who wrote the Scriptures that he had hanged himself?

Gabriel: We'll discuss that after your food break. You're going to learn things today about your Scripture that may not make me popular at all. (Laughter)

Participant: Oh, okay.

Participant: Beloved Gabriel.

Gabriel: Beloved woman.

Participant: Was there ever an issue of the marriage of Mary and Jesus?

Gabriel: Oh indeed, because the Essenes did not recognize it as being a legal marriage because he took her off before the appointed time of separation. He broke the rules, as it were, so they were considered to be living in sin. Sound familiar to you, does it? Living in sin? (Laughter)

Participant: Did they have children though? Did they have any children?

Gabriel: No. Jesus knew his time with Mary was very short and he knew that her time upon the earth would be difficult enough without having to have children to look after.

Participant: Gabriel.
Gabriel: Beloved woman.
Participant: I'm concerned about the response that you gave to a previous question in terms of time. If... We think linearly so we think of a past, present, and a future, and in truth we live in eternity.
Gabriel: Indeed.
Participant: So my confusion comes from the fact that from a perspective, from the eternal perspective, that there can be a doubt about the choice that the Jews will make.
Gabriel: Only from this perspective, beloved woman: For more time than your mind could comprehend, teachers, prophets, healers, rulers, kings—whatever you care to call them—have been sent to the Jewish people to raise their consciousness. As true with all people, and yet you all are so slow, so slow to come up, to come up. I did not say there would *never* be a time when they would know, but to know it soon, that is a question.
Participant: So...because "when" doesn't really matter because there is no time.
Gabriel: That's true. If there were, I would have been worn out long ago. (Laughter)
Participant: Okay, thank you.

Participant: Gabriel, I actually have two questions and possibly you've already responded to them and I noticed there was a tape called "Master Jesus" so you can stop me. First question is: You mentioned that Jesus had two brothers; did he have any sisters?

Gabriel: Yes, he had one...Tamar.

Participant: And she was the youngest child?

Gabriel: She was the youngest child.

Participant: And you'll tell us about her afterwards or she doesn't figure in...

Gabriel: She remained with the Essenes. Don't forget, the rest of the children of Mary and Joseph were legitimate by the ideals of the Essenes. Jesus was the only one that was born what they term to be "out of wedlock," as it were. And they suspected...what *they* thought was that Joseph and Mary had not honored the code of remaining celibate until December. They took it to mean that after the first part of the marriage agreement, betrothal part, that they came together and created Jesus. A lot of the Essenes never believed that Jesus originated without Joseph as a father.

Participant: But some did.

Gabriel: Some did, a few did, but most of them considered him illegitimate. But the rest of their children were considered legitimate and honored as such.

Participant: Many years ago, I had read something by an American psychic called Edgar Cayce called *The Story of Jesus* where he—this was very interesting—that he came out with this idea that, for me at that time, which was very unique, that Joseph and Mary had other children besides Jesus. But two things he said: Number one was that originally, in the beginning, that Mary or the soul that was to be Mary and the soul that was to be Jesus were originally from the same...

Gabriel: They were...they are soulmates.

Participant: Yes, that was one thing. And have you discussed this before in other classes?

Gabriel: Yes.

Participant: Okay. Which tapes? (Laughter)

Gabriel: Which tapes? Does anybody know?

Participant: Does anybody know? Okay, in keeping with that...what was the other question? This same psychic had indicated that when Mary was a young girl, that she was chosen to be the mother of the Messiah, and that is also discussed in the...?

Gabriel: Yes.

Participant: Okay, thank you so much.

Gabriel: You are very welcome.

Participant: Hello Gabriel.

Gabriel: Beloved entity.

Participant: My head is really spinning on this one. Anyway, a lot of Christian fundamentalists see the apostles as being these great saviors of the world and I'm seeing that they're really kind of these really undesirable characters. (Laughter) I mean, God, one was an assassin, one did this, and you know.

Gabriel: They were people, beloved entity, simple people who were living in *extreme* times, searching for the answers, as is everyone always, looking for something outside of themselves to be their comfort. Jesus' purpose was to teach, "God lives within," and it is...they are no different than anyone else.

Participant: That's a very beautiful thing because it shows us that we have these similar tendencies and it is so easy to negate them within ourselves and...everybody knows what I'm talking about, yes? (Laughter)

Gabriel: Oh, wait till this afternoon and we get into Paul. (Laughter)

Participant: Okay, thanks.

Participant: Beloved Gabriel.

Gabriel: Beloved woman.

Participant: At another time, you have told us that when Mary Magdalene and Jesus first met, she said, "Do I know you? I don't believe I know you," and he looked at her and he said, "You know me well."

Gabriel: Indeed.

Participant: Can you tell us where it is that...in what context?

Gabriel: Oh, in many other lifetimes they were together. They were very much in love. Jesus was a very loving man. He was a very *romantic* man. He was the kind who brought flowers and sweet cakes, and he was the kind who would hold her hand. One of his greatest pleasures was to walk with her in the evening holding hands and to come upon flowers that he would break off and give to her. He kissed her publicly—which was not done back then, not at all—but he loved her so and if they were walking together, he had no qualms about leaning down and kissing her on the mouth, which was *totally*...well, you just didn't do that.

And he was the kind of man who loved openly, not just Mary Magdalene, but he loved his disciples. He had no qualms of walking up and clasping an arm around a shoulder, giving a hug, patting on the back. He was a *touching* person and indeed, they were together many times before. That's a whole other story.

Participant: Okay, thank you.

Gabriel: Indeed.

***

Lesson

I talked to you before about the Crucifixion, so I will not go into that again because you have already heard that. After the Crucifixion, Mary Magdalene hid herself away. She could not bear the pain of it. She didn't know who to trust. She wasn't sure what had happened, who had caused this betrayal. She didn't know about Judas. What had become of him? Judas had been murdered, as I told you.

She didn't communicate with anyone because she wasn't sure who her enemies were and if they would be so bold as to slay Jesus, then she knew that her own life was not truly protected; that was her fear. She also grieved, for while she did know he had returned to life, he had resurrected, it was not the same as the physical presence and he always protected her. He was the power that kept her safe and made her feel that she was loved and safe. And now, suddenly, he was gone.

She knew better than to talk to Peter. She didn't know exactly who to talk to. Matthew was high in the hierarchy of the Qumran and she wasn't quite sure just who her friends might be. So for several days she was...they could not find her. They didn't know where she went. Finally, Joanna, who was a follower of Jesus, found her and Joanna said, "I have friends...I have family in Greece and we can go there and you will be safe."

Now in the meantime, the crucifixion of Jesus was considered by most all of Jerusalem to be just another crucifixion. That was a common thing back then. Every day, as I said before, somebody died upon the cross. So, he wasn't any different to most of the people in

Jerusalem. It was only to his ardent followers that this was an unusual and tragic thing.

Pilate, in the meantime, knew that his life and his job were on the line. And Mary didn't feel—although Jesus had told her you can go to Pilate and he will make you safe—Mary didn't feel that that would be true now. There were already murmurings that Herod's nephew would inherit Pilate's place and that meant Pilate would leave Jerusalem and then, ultimately, Pilate would be slain, because that is how they did things back then; they transferred you into oblivion.

So, Joanna knew the one person she could trust would be Jesus' mother, so Joanna, who was welcomed into the Essene group, she went to see Mary, who was in proper grief and proper grieving, and she told her they needed very much to afford Mary Magdalene some kind of protection.

Now Mary, the mother of Jesus, was wise enough to know *not* to turn to James—although he was Jesus' brother, he also was his competitor—and she knew that any kind...she did not know whether Mary Magdalene would be with child, which, if she had been, would have usurped James' place if the child born had been a male.

Mary, the mother of Jesus, had friends in among the Essenes—women friends, especially, that she knew she could trust—and so she gathered a group about her and she told them of Mary's plight, and they agreed that they would make a way safe for the passage of Mary to go where she needed to be. Funds were collected, food for the journey, and so forth. And they found a friendly caravan driver who, while he didn't know Jesus, had heard stories and so forth, and he was not for Rome by any means. He did not belong to the Essenes so he had no political ax to grind, as it were, and he was willing to take a small group of women, which consisted of Joanna and Mary Magdalene and a few others, and take them to Greece, and that's what he did.

Now, from Greece, they went to other countries and Mary Magdalene ultimately ended up in France, and that is where she died at the age of sixty. She was nine years younger than Jesus. She lived there quietly, teaching quietly small groups of people, those who would come to listen and learn, but she never made public who she was or what her connection to the Essenes had been for fear of her life.

She also knew that Paul was out and about and she didn't trust Paul and she most assuredly did not trust Peter. Now Peter... In the meantime, Peter had political aspirations and he found favor with Rome, oddly enough, for the Romans decided that Peter would be a good ally because they thought he could bring them information quietly concerning the activities of the Essenes, but what they didn't know was that none of the Essenes trusted Peter either and they weren't going to tell him diddly squat. (Laughter) But Rome didn't know that. So Rome, more or less, took Peter under their wing.

Now, Paul... Even though Paul was a very learned Jew and certainly had money behind him and power and position and so forth, he also recognized there was a great deal of power to be had in the Essenes, and he had heard of Jesus and he had heard of all the revolt that was going on and so on and so forth. So, he decided he was going to side with... Well, he went to the Essenes, first of all, and asked to be a member. Well, he picked the worst possible time because the Essenes weren't taking in any strangers for fear of their very own survival, so he was turned away. He went to another group, from the Judah group, and they did the same thing. They knew he was a person of money, he held a high position and so forth, and they were not about to jeopardize their lives any more than they were already in jeopardy for this stranger. So, Paul was turned away from the Essenes. None of them wanted any part of him.

In the meantime, Pilate was assassinated and the new governor took over, and *he* had *no* qualms about slaughtering anybody that he perceived to be a threat to him in any way. If they thought Pilate was bad, they had not seen anything until this new one came in, Herod's nephew.

Now the thing is, Paul recognized that he was going to have to choose sides and choose them quickly because if he didn't, he was dead because he was a Jew. So he went to the governor and he said, "I can go among the people. They won't think anything about it because I am a member of them." He said, "I can go among them," and he said, "I can find out where these followers of this rebel, Jesus, are hiding and I can dispatch them readily."

"Wondrous! We shall hire you. We shall pay you thirty pieces of silver because thirty pieces of silver were returned to us by Judas Iscariot, and we have it in the treasury, not marked for anything, so consider yourself hired." So Paul was hired by Rome to hunt down the followers of Jesus—they were not known yet as Christians—and slay them.

Now in the meantime, of course, the disciples had gathered together and decided there was strength in numbers and decided that perhaps the best way to go was to stick together as much as possible. However, one thing they weren't counting on and that was Peter's idea that he was top dog now and he was going to run things. Well, Peter was not well thought of among the Essenes—and there was Matthew and all the rest of them who were part of the hierarchy of the Essenes—so they did not take much favor with Peter being considered their leader. So again, dissension reigned. There was not an agreement among any of them as to who was going to be what.

Now, in the meantime, there had been several people who saw Jesus. Oh, in the meantime too, Peter was hunting for Mary Magdalene, for he saw this as a great opportunity to at least get her out of his hair because, he thought, if she were with child, that was going to change everything.

Now, what happened was...Peter went looking for Mary Magdalene, and even though Peter had walked into the empty tomb and knew that Jesus had gone somewhere, Peter, up to that point, had not encountered the risen Jesus. So Peter's out hunting down Mary Magdalene and all of a sudden, there stood Jesus.

Well, Peter couldn't speak. Number one, he was shocked that there he was, appearing to be as he had seen him in the flesh. And number two, *he knew* Jesus knew what he was thinking and that put him in big doggy doo. (Laughter) So, they walked along the beach together and Jesus said to Peter, "I want you to go forth and feed my sheep."

Now, here we go back to allegories again. Sheep, among the Essenes, represented those people who desired to become a member but had not been accepted yet, those who were still in a state of transition where they were still learning but had not yet become really brought into the group. Now, this was an unusual thing of Jesus to ask of Peter because Peter had no clout in the Essenes at all.

[Gap in recording] ...Jesus of that. He said, "They're not going to listen to me."

And Jesus said to him, "You must go out and teach what I have taught you."

Well, that really left Peter in a quandary because Peter hadn't really gotten the whole idea of what Jesus was teaching. He followed him, loved him, would have laid his life down for him as long as it didn't require it of him exactly, but Peter was a lot of bluff. He was a big blocky man with a loud voice and a very egotistical manner about him, and for Jesus to ask of Peter to go teach was a very strange thing. It didn't fit in with Peter's character at all, nor did it fit into any of the things that Peter had thought he would be doing.

But Jesus had a method to his madness. He knew: one, it would make Peter...it would *force* Peter, actually, to learn more of the truths; and it would also put him in a position where he wouldn't be quite so free to roam around hunting down poor Mary Magdalene.

Now Peter, being a jealous man, he wanted to know, "What are you going to do with everybody else?"

Jesus said, "They will all meet me. They will all encounter me and I will speak to each one of them privately," and that's exactly what he did.

Now he did tell them to gather together in preparation for the coming of the Holy Spirit. Now here is something you must understand. In the Essenes, the highest priest of the wisdom part... Now you have to remember, some of the Essenes raised children, some of the Essenes did rituals, some of the Essenes did instruction, and the highest regarded one was frequently referred to as the "Father." He had two assistants: one, to see to it that everything run right and the other one to teach, and the one who saw that everything run right was often referred to as the "Son."

Beloved woman, how do you spell "son" when you need an heir? S-O-N, that kind of son.

The other one was referred to as the "Holy Spirit of the Word." So when Jesus said to Peter, "Gather up and the Holy Spirit will come to you," Peter assumed it would be Caiaphas, who was that aspect of the code. So, he gathered all the other disciples and they all met in this room and they were expecting Caiaphas to come and instead, that's not what happened. Not at all. Instead, the power of the Christ came. The true Holy Spirit came and it blew through there and blew away...

Now when I say it blew, I don't... They likened it to a wind because suddenly their understanding was open. Suddenly they recognized the lessons that Jesus had been teaching all this time. It wasn't a bunch of poppycock. He wasn't a coward running from the political things. He was a man of courage and he was teaching a law higher than the Essene law. He was teaching them a universal truth that the Essenes had only just nibbled at. Little by little... Now they tell you that it happened all at once. Well, let me tell you how it really happened.

There came to them... Know you how when you are in a state of meditation, you aren't sleeping but you're not awake? You know how you're in that little in-between, that kind of a quiet, lovely place to be? They were taken into that space where their conscious mind could not argue, and especially so Peter because Peter was the biggest arguer of all. Well, he argued with Jesus...what can I say? Now, in that state, the voice of the Master Jesus was heard and he talked to them and he opened their understanding and they began to *finally get it*.

Know the feeling? (Laughter) Indeed. It took three days for this to happen, not just a few moments. It took three days. Now when they went forth from there, because their understanding was opened, all of the plans that they had made—they had made plans—began to shift because now they knew a truth. Know you how when you come to a seminar or you go somewhere where someone has greatly inspired you and you leave there, for the first few days you're really gung ho? You've got it and life is going to be different, and then as you go along each day, life gets a little more like it used to be until after a bit, you kind of fall back into the old traps? Well, they're no different than anybody else.

Now, the thing was that they had had a *contact* with Jesus. They had lived with this man, ate with this man, traveled with this man, loved him, knew his power, so this was a little different. This was more brought home a little more solidly. Now, in the meantime, Paul decided he was going to make one more trek to the Essene group and see...because Paul didn't trust Rome. Paul was a Jew and he had seen what Romans did to Jews, so even though he was on the payroll, as it were, he still did not feel comfortable with the idea, so he decided he needed to make some contact, some safe place to be, so he decided to visit the Essenes.

Qumran was up in the hills. It was not easily accessible. It took a bit to get up there. And Paul was a man of wealth so Paul had himself a fine Arabian horse, and he's riding along and onto the path stepped Jesus.

Now Paul had never met Jesus, but he knew by looking at him this was no ordinary person; this was *someone* and he couldn't *quite* get a feel of who it was. But not wanting to offend, just in case it should be someone of high order from the Essenes, he greeted him. And Jesus said, "What do you think you're doing here?"

And Saul, as he was called at the time, looked at him and he said, "I have come for sanctuary."

And Jesus said, "Murderous viper, how dare you come here to this place of holiness when you have slain Stephen," which Paul did. Paul had Stephen stoned.

Paul became frightened. Contrary to what your Scriptures tell you, he was by himself. He was in a mountain path. He was with a person of great power. He didn't have anybody around, and because he wanted to come in peace, he brought no sword; he had nothing to defend himself with.

Now, horses represent emotion. They represent that aspect of you that needs to be kept under control because a horse not in control can be a dangerous creature, and especially so on a narrow mountain path.

Jesus began to approach Paul. Now Paul had not room enough to turn the horse around. He had one choice—go forward or go backward. Paul became very rattled. Now, if there's one thing a horse knows, it's when you're scared, and it will react accordingly. As Jesus walked toward Paul, he said, "I demand to know of you, what you are doing here!?" and his whole manner was one of authority. Now Paul wasn't used to that. *Paul* was a man of authority and here was someone who exercised authority greater than his, and Paul began to get frightened.

He couldn't turn around. He started to try to back the horse up. Well, that's not an easy task, especially on a narrow mountain path. Horses don't always back up the exact way you want them to. The horse became very upset, started to bolt. Paul lost his seat and fell flat on his bottom and away went the horse.

Now, Paul was terrified, absolutely *terrified*. Jesus stood over him and he said, "Why won't you see the truth of my words?"

And Paul realized how blind he had been to the truth, how completely self-satisfied and self-absorbed he was, and Paul—thinking he was pleading for his life, not realizing Jesus didn't mean to slay him or something—he said, "Please, let me live. Let me live. Please, let me live."

And Jesus said, "Why are you persecuting my followers?"

And Paul said, "Oh, I'm not." Well, you don't lie to somebody like that now, do you?

Jesus said, "I know your thoughts, Saul of Tarsus, and I know full well that you have slain Stephen and I know full well there are others who have met their end at your hand. Why do you think you can say to me that you have not?" And Paul's terror threw him into a trauma, which left him physically blind.

Now, here he was on this narrow mountain path and he couldn't see, couldn't see anything. And he pleaded with Jesus. He said, "Don't leave me here or I shall fall to my death!"

And Jesus said, "No, we have other plans for you. You're not going to die." So Jesus went and he appeared to Anaus and he said to him, "On the path, you will find Saul of Tarsus." *Well,* you don't bring the viper into the camp. And he said, "You must go and assist him. Get him to where he needs to be. It's alright."

Now when Paul was taken in, before his sight was restored... And remember, you're talking about a community whose whole purpose was healing. They knew how to heal all manner of things. But before they healed him, here they had the enemy, sitting there blind and frightened, and they walked around him and they looked at him and..."Here is Saul of Tarsus! Well, well, well, well! Now, isn't this interesting?" You know, they weren't above a little psychological terror either.

They said, "Before we restore your sight, you're going to hear some truth." And so, they talked to him and they told him of the life of Jesus, they told him of his teachings, they told him all of the things about Jesus that they knew, and Paul began to realize that this man had not been a threat to Rome, nor had he been a threat to the Sanhedrin or to any of the other Jewish sects at all, that he was trying to bring a revolution of understanding and truth, not a military revolution.

When they felt secure enough, they gave Paul back his sight. It took several days but they finally, with their little compresses and what not, they restored it...and talking and prayers and so forth.

Now, would you not think that here would be a convert who would go out and do a lot of good? As is so typical, when Paul left there, the truth that he had been told began to get strangely mixed with old Sanhedrin beliefs, old beliefs in the mosaic laws, old beliefs in *so* many things that had limited and held him.

Now, he also had the pressure of Rome because he was under Roman authority. They had *paid* him. Thirty pieces of silver is a large amount back then. Now Paul was really in a quandary. What was he to do? Here he knew the truth, or at least a part of it, and here he was bound by consignment to Rome. Now Paul recognized the feeling of fear for his life as the Jews had known. He recognized the unjustness of the Roman rule and of his part *in* it.

Paul decided to seek help. He went and he met with some of the disciples and they taught him things, as much as what he would take in, but you have to remember, Paul was a man who was not at peace with himself. Not at all. The strain of Rome, the strain of the Essenes, the mess he made of his life as he perceived it to be, all of this flooded in upon him in one fell swoop and Paul tinkered a little bit on the brink of insanity.

When he was with the...what was to be known as the Christians, he spoke ardently of Jesus. When he was in the company of the Romans, he spoke ardently of Caesar, of Herod, of whoever—Alexander the Great, you name it, anyone that he could bolster up. Now, he was trying to ride two horses across the stream and that doesn't work. One will win out over the other. You cannot serve two masters.

Plus, Paul was dealing with an internal demon as well. Paul was a homosexual and back in those days that meant you were killed. There was no ifs, ands, buts, or too bad, I know him well...he's a nice guy really. You just...that was the end of you. He was trapped by his perception, totally trapped.

Partly because of his homosexuality, partly because it was the nature of the man, and partly because of the way he had been trained when he was in the Sanhedrin and all of that, Paul had absolutely no regard for women at all. Women were, in his estimation, as they were in

Peter's, something that you had for a purpose and other than that, they served no good worth. So Paul's letters, Paul's teaching, and Paul's preaching were all based upon *where* he was and *who* he was with and what effect it would have on his life.

Many times it tells you that Paul was imprisoned and that is a grand truth. However, the prison was in his mind and not external. Paul was imprisoned only on a few occasions, actually physically in prison. The rest of the time the prison he dwelt in was of his own doing, of his own making.

Paul manufactured a Jesus that did not exist. He took his old ideas, what was required of him at the moment, and he fused them all together into this strange, twisted, unrealistic idea of what the man Jesus really was.

Paul literally and figuratively never knew Jesus. Now, does that make everything Paul ever said wrong or should it all be discounted? Indeed, not. From the depth of his own being and from the truth that he had learned as a good Jew, Paul brought forth a lot of truth, but Paul never brought forth love. "Let not the women be known in the churches." "Do not give a woman authority." "Slay a witch." These are all Peter and Paul's teachings.

Now after the physical presence of Jesus had left them, the disciples, each one by one, fell into patterns of old ways of living. They all found themselves in situations that they couldn't cope with and so they made do with what they could. The only one who stayed true as best he could and nearly so with a pure heart was John.

Now John was not of a fiery nature; John was a gentle soul, a true believer, a seeker of truth, one who did not put a whole lot of stock in the physical. John knew of life beyond the physical. That was the one thing that he and Jesus used to discuss in great depth. Jesus could teach John because John had an open heart and an open mind and he listened and he learned. And he learned not only the words, but he learned the truth and he internalized it. While the others were seeking to save their lives and to preach where and when they could, John was communing with God, John was learning his own internal power, John was keeping that spark of spirituality alive and growing. The others let theirs flicker. There were times when they were powerful speakers and there were times when they were little wimps...depended. And that was alright—that's human-kind. But John steadfastly stuck with the truth, and John was the only one who sought out Mary Magdalene to comfort her. John would send messengers to Mary Magdalene with words of encouragement and hope. John always wanted to know where she was and if she were well and he visited her twice.

He was the only one of all of them who really, truly got the message. The rest of them got little bits of pieces, turned it into their own, whatever they could make of it, and some of them lost it completely.

Paul was not a loving man; he was hard-hearted and hard-minded. Peter believed in sacrifice. Peter believed in all of the wrong things at the wrong time but Peter *meant* well. Paul was a survivor. Peter really *meant* to do good. Didn't quite make it, but he meant to do good.

Now one of the things that Peter had learned while he was with the Essenes was their system of hierarchy, and he set up certain rules and regulations that *he* felt would bring in the true Spirit, and it is from that that you have your rules and regulations of the papacy, because *they* built upon Peter's belief system, totally. Peter had it all written out. He didn't write it but he had it written out. And he made the rules and regulations that have followed down for many, many, many centuries since then—the rules and regulations that govern your churches.

Peter was crucified upside down. When Peter was asked, "How do you wish to die?" and Peter said, "Crucify me, for then I shall be like unto my Lord." It was Peter's choosing to be crucified. He chose upside down because you die quicker, you suffocate much faster.

All of this—the turmoil, the beauty, the joy and the sorrow, the truth and the error—all strangely mixed in, and from Paul and Peter came a very *mis*guided, although well-intended, concept of God, of Christianity, that was handed down and passed down through the ages to the priests and to the authorities who changed it and molded it and made it into what *they* felt would be acceptable, into what would give them absolute power and would make the people subservient. And that is the exact opposite of the message of Christ.

What you have learned in your doctrines through the years, if you will take it apart and dissect it with love, you will find little seeds of golden truth throughout it. But you will also find a great deal of malice, a great deal of greed and power.

Jesus never came to be king. He never came to start a new religion. He never came to set one against the other. When he said, "You think I have come to bring peace; I come to bring a sword," he was referring to the breaking down of the confines that separated the people, the rules and regulations that, instead of unifying them and bringing them together, separated and dispersed them.

He spoke of "loving your neighbor." Why? Because just about everyone back them distrusted their neighbor. You never knew who you were talking to.

He spoke of "honoring and respecting the life that was," and that was never thought of. When he went into the temple to throw out the money changers, he went in there trying to make them realize that this is not the purpose of the temple. God does not require blood sacrifice. For what? That's an old hanger-on of the pagan belief system.

All of the things that he came to teach and to bring to humankind were greatly distorted, a lot of them lost, and some of them downright changed. For instance, the marriage of him and Mary Magdalene. Go anywhere in your Church chronicles and you will find no trace of it. But if you were to look in the archives of where the Pope lives, down in the places where no eyes are allowed to see, you would find that Mary Magdalene and Jesus indeed had been married.

If you were to study the Dead Sea Scrolls, especially those from Qumran, you would discover that everything I have said to you this day is a grand truth, for it is written there. Someday, these truths will be made known, but only after those who are in religious power cease to be afraid of truth and are willing to listen and learn. Only when those who are politically minded do not perceive someone of spiritual intent as a *threat* to their well-being... [gap in recording] ...forth. But I tell you this: Now is the time when it has begun and this truth *will* be known upon your earth, and those who would seek to be first will be last and those who *think* they know will come to learn.

Because of the changes upon your earth, because of the spirituality that is coming forth with its own power, old things have to fall away. There has to be made ready a *space* for the *new*. The new? The new that is so old, older than time, and that's what this is all about.

When you love someone, you love them completely. You do not judge them by what you perceive to be those things in them that you do not agree with. You allow them their own beingness, even if that beingness contains things that are opposite of your belief system. You love them because they are, not because of what they do for you, not because of their position held in this earth, but simply because they are.

You recognize that in all of the differences, there is one single silver, binding truth and that is life. And that all living things have a right to *be just as they are*...just as they are. Do I have the right to say to this beauteous flower, "You are not a rose; therefore, I have the right to slay you"? Do *you* have the right to look at another and say, "You're different from me; therefore, I am not required to love and accept you"?

When Jesus went out to teach, unlike the priests of the Essenes, everyone was welcomed—Jew and Gentile, rich or poor, men or women. He would gather the women to the front of the crowd. By the Essene and Jewish tradition, they weren't even supposed to be there, let alone be up front. People of authority sat up front.

When he would teach the multitudes and they would gather, usually the women would sit to the side and in the back, and he would go over and he would say, "Sister, come...here," and they would look about like, "Me? Oh, no. Indeed." Then he would say to the most authoritative person in the front row, "Excuse me, would you step back and sit back there please? Thank you. Come sister... here." *Well, hoho,* you know how that went over.

When he would break bread, he frequently chose a piece of bread and offered it to a woman. Or he would pick the least among them by social status and he would come and say, "Here, sit beside me." And, if he *really* wanted to get their attention, he would pick a woman of low esteem and have her sit at his right hand.

He broke the rules. He did as best as he could in his time to desegregate, to bring unity. He honored everyone, everyone. What audacity did he have when he was on the cross to say to a *thief,* "This day thou shall be with me in paradise"?

These are the truths that he *lived.* This was what he was about. He was the rebel, not in a militant way. He was a rebel to bring spiritual truth, to break away the old codes, to break away from the old, rigid way.

A man and a woman who marry are meant to *live together.* What? One month out of a year? And the rest of the time, not speak, not touch? To what end? Did it make you more spiritual? If you think so, look at the Essenes, who hired assassins. People who love each other, if the love be true, what is the difference if they both are male or both female? Who cares? Is there a love? Is there a gentleness? Is there a compassion between them? Then let it be blessed.

Who has such wisdom that they can look into the heart of another and know what lies there? Who? Who can look at creatures and not see that God looked upon them and found them good? And what code of ethics is it that says that because a creature is not human, therefore it is subservient and should not have the right to its life as its own nature dictates?

Jesus never commanded anyone to do anything that was not in their nature, even when it came to raising Lazarus. He asked Lazarus, "Do you want to come back to the earth or not?"

And Lazarus said, "Indeed, I do."

And he said, "Come forth."

He *allowed* people to be who they were and *he loved* who they were. He never said, "Well, I will accept this one to come and hear me but that one can't come because he wears a turban upon his head. Whether they were Jew or Gentile, Greek, or Roman... Oh, the Roman soldiers used to sneak in to hear him. They would sit around upon their horses as though to be guarding the crowd but they were listening. They were listening.

Beloveds, the message today is the same, absolutely the same. Do not judge another. You have no right. You aren't smart enough. You don't know what's in that person's heart. And how can you judge by their actions? How many of you act out something you don't believe in, and if you think you don't, how many of you are absolutely, passionately in love with your jobs? Do you not do what you are told because you must?

Everyone has a point at which their own sacred truth should be recognized and allowed to be.

When you were invited here this day, was there anything upon the registration form that asked you what your religious beliefs were? Was there anything there that said to you, if you are thus and so, you are not welcome among us?

For your world to survive, what has been taught is to be lived. What is in error is to be let go. The most despicable upon the earth is one of the most beloved in Heaven. Those who would condemn themselves have already been condemned, for they did it to themselves... just as Paul did, just as Peter did.

In the days to come when the turmoil is upon your earth, *remember* who you are. Remember the *truths* that you have been presented with, not only from me. Learn to read your Scriptures with discerning eye; there is truth in them. Learn to seek out what is not written, for it can be found. Study the Dead Sea Scrolls. Many of them contain the *truth* of what you only have been handed the error perception of. Learn to recognize that Jesus was a *human being* who chose to bring forth from the within of himself the Son of God, to live it openly, to love freely, to give joyously, to share and to embrace and to bring into life all that he knew of the Spirit Self of him. He got to know God by knowing *himself*.

In his day, any rule that he could break, he did...if it had a point, if it had a good measure of truth in it. Did he do it to make himself famous? No, he never dreamed he would be famous. He didn't come with the idea of being worshiped worldwide. He never came with the idea of being worshiped even in his little towns that he went to. He came with the purpose of teaching and living the teachings that he taught, of making them see how *ridiculous* some of their moral ethics were of the time.

For an example, riding into Jerusalem on a donkey, that was supposed to denote humility and service. Now I ask you a grand truth: How many people in the government of any country anywhere are there because they want to truly, deeply, have no other agenda than to serve the people? Name me one.

Why would one choose to go through with what he went through if it were not to bring an eternal truth into the awakening of the human mind? To restore you once again in consciousness to the truth of your being? He would not have. To what purpose would it be? Absolutely none. Absolutely none.

So, who do you believe in the Scriptures? Who were the true emissaries of truth and light? Who were the ones who truly served and unto this day, truly serve? Who are the ones who *live* what they know to be a truth without judgement, without excluding anyone? Those are the ones that you believe. Those are the ones you listen to and learn from.

Jesus never said, "Fall down and worship me."

"Stand up and follow me."

In the days to come, beloveds, your truth will set you free and your freedom will be observed by others and they will come to you and they will ask you, "How are you free?" and you will have to be able to explain to them, and you will. You will explain to them because you will know from the within of you.

Have you anything to ask of me?

Questions

Participant: Gabriel, would you tell us what Mary Magdalene looked like?

Gabriel: What she looked like?

Participant: Yes.

Gabriel: Well, she was about five foot three or four, somewhere in there. She had dark hair and enormous, very expressive, dark eyes. She had a kind of presence about her. She had an inner beauty. She was quite comely to look at but her beauty radiated more from within of her. But I would say her most redeeming physical feature was the fact that she had these enormous dark eyes that expressed her every thought very clearly, and she laughed a lot. She laughed a lot.

Participant: Just wanted you to know that I really love my job in this life and of course there were people there that made it very difficult but it's okay because I loved my job. Okay, thank you. And also, I just wanted to ask, was Jesus on the cross already when he spoke to the thief? Because I was aware that—I *think* I was aware—that if he spoke to someone, he would release that feeling of being back on Earth, to get to feel the pain. So, how did that occur that he could say this to the thief?

Gabriel: Because he had to occupy the body long enough for it to appear to be a living body. And he was also able to communicate telepathically with the thief. Now the thief only heard a voice. He didn't reckon where it was. He had his own problems, so he didn't look around to see whether Jesus was physically speaking to him or not.

Participant: That's very good because we hear things too.

Gabriel: Indeed.

Participant: Thank you.

Gabriel: And I'm very glad you liked your job.

Participant: Oh yes, I loved my job.

Gabriel: Indeed.

Participant: [Young boy] Hi. Did King Herod order the soldiers to kill children that were under the age of two?

Gabriel: No. No, beloved entity. That was a myth of long ago; that was an Egyptian myth. And when they saw fit to write the story of Jesus' life, you know, they eliminated all of the good parts and brought in what they thought would sell, as it were, and that was one of the myths that they employed, was that.

Herod had no fear of Jesus because Herod felt he was...*if* there was indeed a Messiah coming and it was of the Essenes, that was of no bother to him because he knew the Essenes to be a rather...or thought they were a rather peaceful people, so he felt no threat from them.

Participant: Okay, thank you.

Participant: I was recently reading a book about the Dead Sea Scrolls. It's fairly controversial. It's by a woman who is a Dead Sea Scrolls scholar who has re-dated some of the materials on fairly convincing evidence to show that the important documents about the Essenes actually were written slightly after the time of Jesus and before the fall of the temple. Other scholars believe it was before Jesus was born and her theories, or what she's written, is very similar to what you taught today...talks a lot about Jesus' involvement with the Essenes and Pilate's and all this. Also talks a lot in the documents about the Essenes. They wrote about...I think they called it the "righteous teacher" and the "evil priest." There was a political battle. It was all hidden and she also talks about how it was all in code. And I believe her argument was that this was written after Jesus left, basically, and that the evil priest was Jesus in that the people still at the Essenes were sort of mad at him because he had gone out into the world...

Gabriel: Indeed.

Participant: And the "righteous teacher" was someone who...

Gabriel: Who followed the code. That is true. After he left, those that had been opposed to him from the onset thought that it would not be well for what he did and what he taught to be looked upon with favor in the generations to follow. And so they wrote *their* version of him.

Now another thing you must remember, that when the initiates came into the Essenes, when someone was initiated in there, they went before a council, and part of the purpose of the council was to question the advocate very thoroughly to make sure, number one, that they were not a Roman spy, and number two, that they really, truly understood and believed and embraced the belief systems that were taught there. And so, they had a panel of priests that would come and the panel that represented the Holy of Holies was called the "Panel of Gabriel." I'm not flattered. (Laughter)

The other panel was called the "Panel of Satan." Now those on the Panel of Satan were not evil people, but they played, as you call it in your day and time, the "devil's advocate," and they would...as the Gabriel group would question the prospective member, the devil's advocate would cast dispersions upon the question and make it appear so the question, perhaps, was not a valid one. Now the purpose of this was to cause the person being questioned to go deep within them and to pull from the wellspring of their own truth, their own Spirit, the correct answer.

Participant: Then it would be accurate to say that some of these documents were, although slightly in code, they were discussing the life of Jesus and *his* connection with the Essenes...

Gabriel: Oh, indeed.

Participant: ...and they weren't all written before he died.

Gabriel: No, they were not written before he died. A lot of them were written afterward and greatly slanted. Now, some of them are written in truth. There are gospels by Mary Magdalene. There are gospels by Philip and by Thomas that are... Mary Magdalene's memoirs, so to speak, told a lot of things but the Church suppresses all this. Some of this stuff is in the archives of the papacy and will not be known for a long time, until the papacy collapses, which it will.

Participant: Thank you.

Gabriel: It always sounds...Beloved Woman is always saying to me as she listens to this, "It always sounds like you're after the Catholics." Well, I'm not.

Gabriel: Beloved entity.

Participant: This morning when I asked you the question about Mary and you answered, there was some question whether...which Mary we were talking about.

Gabriel: I was talking of Mary Magdalene.

Participant: Yes, we decided that. I would like to also ask about his mother, Mary.

Gabriel: Mary knew as Jesus grew into adulthood and she watched him go out and, in her mind, begged to be bumped off—oh, those weren't her words, those are mine—but she saw in him...first of all, she recognized that he would never be accepted in the Essenes as in the Davidic line as inheriting the throne, as it were. She realized that wasn't going to happen. And she also realized that his very actions, the breaking of the code and the doing things contrary to their belief systems, was not going to make him find favor with them very much. And little by little, she began to remember the purpose of his coming, and she also began to remember the ending of it. So she knew. Without knowing, she knew

Participant: But she did also experience that on a human level?

Gabriel: Oh indeed, she did. Indeed, she did.

Participant: I also wanted to ask why they chose that Jesus be born...not in...

Gabriel: Illegitimately?

Participant: Yes.

Gabriel: It set the stage for all the rest of the stuff. If Jesus had always followed the rules, who would have ever heard of him? No one.

Participant: I want to thank you for today.

Gabriel: Indeed.

Gabriel: Well, I guess you're next.

Participant: Thank you. Could you give us some other examples of the interpretations of Scripture that have been misinterpreted by the code you mentioned today, please?

Gabriel: Oh, indeed. One of the things that you will read in your Scripture is that, "And it came to pass." Now that was a code phrase which meant, "It is finished. It is completed. We have accomplished thus and so."

Another one is when they refer...they don't always refer to the Romans by name. They don't always say, "The Romans did this or that." They wouldn't have dared. So they gave them code names depending on which sect you were talking about as to what the code name was. But they frequently referred to them as "lepers." (Laughter)

Participant: Makes sense.

Gabriel: Indeed, and when they say, "And Jesus healed the lepers," that was always construed to mean that Jesus answered them in a way they could not lay hand upon him.

Participant: Right. Is there a document that explains the code so we could get in tune with how they were writing?

Gabriel: Well, the Dead Sea Scrolls explain a lot of it. Look into them and study them.

Participant: Can we get tickets somewhere to go to see these?

Gabriel: Oh, I don't know how you get them but I know they are available—some of them, not all of them. A lot of what was discovered was so contrary to what the Church had manufactured that they buried them down into the archives of where the Pope dwells, and they won't be known probably in your lifetime.

Participant: Okay, thank you.

Participant: [Young boy] Right now, do you know where Jesus is?

Gabriel: I sure do. (Laughter)

Participant: Could you please tell me where he is?

Gabriel: Where is he?

Participant: Yeah.

Gabriel: He's standing right about there.

Participant: Really?

Gabriel: Really. You don't think he'd miss *this,* do you? (Laughter)

Participant: Beloved Gabriel, I get a very deep sense of how in so many ways that Jesus broke the rules to get us to break out of *our* molds...

Gabriel: Indeed.

Participant: ...and all his physical actions and his working in both a very turbulent time and a time when there are many rules and expectations, and his manner of breaking them had a purpose in each step. And in your prior teaching of the consciousness that he went through beforehand—of going through Joshua and things that we might not associate with someone who did what he did—and I'm wondering if almost the level of consciousness that he was at, when he made the decision to do this whole process, if at *that* level, he's kind of a rebel in that regard.

Gabriel: He is because he chose to prove that the physical body is ever under the dictates of the Spirit, and you can do whatever you want with your body and it must obey the Spirit. He had his killed and brought it back to life. I think that's pretty good. (Laughter) Truly.

Participant: Thank you.

Participant: What happened to Mary Magdalene? Did she ever get married? Did she...?

Gabriel: No. After Jesus? (Laughter) I don't think so. (Laughter) She lived quietly in France, as I said. That was where she finally ended up. She was in Greece for a while and then that became too dangerous and so forth and she finally ended up in France because they really couldn't reach her there. And she lived to be sixty years old and just quietly passed away.

Participant: Thank you.

Participant: I'd like you to clarify a few things. I'm not sure about the Scriptures anymore after what you've told me today. You said that when the apostles were waiting for the Holy Spirit, they thought they were going to have a visit from Caiaphas.

Gabriel: Mm hmm.

Participant: Now Caiaphas...

Gabriel: Boy, were they surprised.

Participant: Right. Was he not the chief priest, Caiaphas? Was he not the one who delivered Jesus to Pilate?

Gabriel: Caiaphas was a very shrewd, shrewd, shrewd man. He wasn't a bad man; he was just a very shrewd man. And he *knew* how to play politics very, very well. He also was a highly regarded member of the Essenes, and he was one of those who would make decisions such as to hire an assassin and so forth like that. He had acquired a kind of an authority about him, somewhat judgmental, but nonetheless an authority about him. And he ruled for quite a while.

Participant: So, it was the Essenes that delivered Jesus to Pilate, who was again, an Essene?

Gabriel: Oh, we're going to go into that another time. I don't want to hand everything to you on one platter. You're going to use a saturation point. I think I've given you a lot today, do you not?

Participant: Quite a lot.

Gabriel: But we aren't over with the story yet.

Participant: Okay, thank you.

Gabriel: But suffice it to say, what you've had today is sufficient for your understandings.

Participant: The question is about lessons, that we come to this earth plane for lessons, and that Jesus wasn't spared from that and that one of the lessons was patience and you had brought that out in a previous story. I have a curiosity as to what some of his other lessons were, as well as the lessons Mary Magdalene came to learn and maybe some of the things that are obvious, and maybe not so obvious, such as Barabbas being chosen to be the assassin and at the same time, being the co-crucified person. I just have this curiosity about...I wonder what the lessons were. I mean, granted...alright, I'll just shut up. (Laughter)

Gabriel: What the lessons were for Jesus in this you mean, as opposed to the lessons he was bringing?

Participant: What lessons Jesus was to learn from the earth experience. What lessons Mary Magdalene was to learn. I'm looking for examples of: we're all here learning our lessons and that, as we learn the truth that you're bringing to us, how we can practice those and embody those in our everyday lives. So does that question make sense to you?

Gabriel: Indeed. The lessons that he came to learn were I would think probably quite comparable to what all of you are learning. [Gap in recording] ...he had to learn was how to use his power lovingly.

You know, he had a bit of a temper. He could get angry and it depended...it didn't always take a lot to make him angry. You recall how he withered a tree because it bore no fruit? He was hungry and he went up to a fruit tree and there was no fruit. It was just a lot of leaves. Well, that was the end of that tree. (Laughter)

He learned...he learned patience in dealing with people, and that was one of the things that the disciples taught him, was to be patient, because if there ever was a lot that could try your patience, they were it. (Laughter)

He also learned...he had said once, "He who does not leave father and mother and follow me is not worthy of me." Spoken by someone who had not fallen in love yet, but once he fell in love, he understood how people found it difficult to leave people they loved.

That was something. He had never grown strongly attached to anyone, although he had a healthy love and respect for his parents, for Mary and Joseph. He adored Joseph. But he traveled so much as a youngster and he was away from them a great deal of the time and more or less in the care of whoever that he didn't have a strong bond of family, really. He didn't. And he felt at that time that the only thing was to seek the path of truth, the path of Spirit, and you should never let anything cause you to want to get off it at all.

And then he met Mary Magdalene and that changed things a little bit in his understanding. And he recognized that when people love someone, you don't just walk away. You hope they will come with you when you make visits and you come back and forth, and you bring them up through love. And that was one of the things he had to learn.

One thing about Mary Magdalene: she was no pushover. She loved him completely but he couldn't tell her what to do, and that was something else he had to learn. Can you imagine being married to someone who says, "Well, you have to do as I tell you because I am the Christ? (Laughter)

Participant: Greetings from the 3D illusion again. It seems to me that you have to have a certain amount of virtue to get to a high level of metaphysical and spiritual mastery.
Gabriel: Indeed.

Participant: And I know the Essenes did some pretty high-level things...

Gabriel: Indeed.

Participant: ...so I'm wondering how could they still hire assassins and be able to do that?

Gabriel: Well, don't judge all of the Essenes by a few. There were Essenes who held ardently to the truth, who would have had no part of an assassin. Most of them felt that way didn't dwell where there were those who did. There were groups of Essenes up in the hills that lived extremely spiritual lives, very spiritual lives, and would have never considered slaying *anything,* let alone another human. So don't judge them all by Qumran or any of the others.

Participant: Okay, thanks.

Participant: Greetings. When you quoted to us, "Those who seek to be first will be last, and those who think they know will come to learn," were you giving us a little bit deeper lesson with that?

Gabriel: Oh, indeed. Absolutely.

Participant: Would you say it a little more clearly?

Gabriel: Those people who think... Let me put it in the context of your world. The highest person in your land here would be your president, would it not? Would you say he is totally without sin?

Participant: No. (Laughter)

Gabriel: Oh, I'm not judging him or anyone for that matter, but there are people who are in high positions who feel that the position they are in gives them an added advantage in the realm of Spirit or in spiritual truths and things, and those who would place themselves first are usually those who end up last.

Participant: Okay. I thought maybe you were warning us about not being too sure of ourselves.

Gabriel: No, I want you to be absolutely certain of yourselves. I just don't want you to dwell in the ego or to take a holier-than-thou attitude.

Participant: Okay. The other thing you said was that all living things have a right to be just as they are.

Gabriel: Indeed.

Participant: As a parent and as a teacher, and many of us are, that could almost be a hands-off...you know...

Gabriel: Oh, no, no. You teach children values and you teach them right from wrong, obviously. You're not going to tell them it's alright to go out and slap somebody in the face because they do something they don't like. You teach them values but you don't try to mold them into your image and likeness. You let them be who they are.

Participant: So you have to discern the difference between changing someone and guiding them?

Gabriel: Indeed.

Participant: Okay, thank you.

Gabriel: That is very well put.

Participant: Is there any relationship between Mary Magdalene and the Black Madonna?

Gabriel: Oh, yes. When she went into France, they... Now don't forget, the reputation that was built around her, mostly after her death, was that she was a harlot because the very fact that the Messiah could have married was unthinkable. They couldn't allow that story so they had to discredit her. They had to do anything that they could to make it appear that she had absolutely no worth.

The other thing was, the code of dress among the Essenes was black. That's where you get in the Catholic Church, all the priests and nuns used to dress in black. I don't know if they still do. Do they anymore? They do? Well, the idea behind it came from the Essenes. And they had two choices: they either had to raise her up and venerate her, or they had to completely discredit her.

Now, they were divided in France as to which they should do, and there were those who decided to venerate her and those who did dressed her in black and called her the Black Madonna. Actually, much of what is attributed to the Virgin Mary, as far as adoration is concerned, actually originally started out directed at Mary Magdalene and then was switched over.

Participant: So the images that we see in some of the churches, the Black Madonna, is really Mary Magdalene.

Gabriel: Is Mary Magdalene. It was done, actually, it was done to discredit her, to paint her as the "bad woman," as it were. But there were those who supported her and so they turned it around. They took the "black" part, which was meant against her, and transferred it over to the black garb of the Essenes, of a high order of Essenes. Had her decisions in life been different, she could have become a high priestess in the Essenes, but she had to choose that or Jesus.

Participant: Gabriel, without asking for information that would fill another seminar, can you tell us more about Mary Magdalene in France?

Gabriel: In France?

Participant: Yes.

Gabriel: She lived with Joanna for a great number of years. Now, Joanna was older than Mary Magdalene and so Joanna passed on quite a number of years before Mary Magdalene. Those who came to hear Mary Magdalene, those who knew who she really was and came to hear her and learn of the teachings and so forth, most always looked after her.

She took it upon herself to teach as much as what she could of what *he* had taught, and as she got older...she was not well. For one thing, she didn't desire to be upon the earth. She wanted to be where *he* was. So it didn't take a whole lot to get her to make a transition. She wasn't...another person would have well survived her illness but she didn't. She chose to use it as an opportunity to get out of here.

The other thing that she did, she was quick to...she wanted to keep, to perpetuate the teachings, the learnings, and so forth, so she would gather little groups about her, especially women, and teach them and they, in turn, went out and taught others and so on and so forth. At that time in France, while she *lived,* she wasn't regarded with too much one way or the other. People knew of her or they didn't, as the case may be, but after she died...by that time Christianity had gained a foothold as a respected belief system. Then, as is often happens, the value of the gem is not known until it is lost, as it were. Then they began to investigate and look into her life and into her teachings and they began to realize she was a person of value, and they regretted greatly.

Now there are many shrines and cathedrals in France and various places—I don't know the names of these places because I don't bother myself with earthly names—but there are many cathedrals built to Mary Magdalene.

Participant: Is Joanna among us now?

Gabriel: Joanna? Upon the earth? I don't know. [To Tinkerbell] Where is Joanna? No, Joanna is not on the earth now. She was a bit ago, but not now.

Participant: Okay. That was just a matter of curiosity.

Gabriel: Indeed.

Participant: Gabriel, earlier when you were talking about the Essene code, you said that the Father was the highest priest of the wisdom part and the person who makes things run right was referred to as the Son. Can you say again what the Holy Spirit of the Word was in the code?

Gabriel: The Holy Spirit was the person who taught and who saw to it that the teachings were followed and so forth like that. Now you know, they used names that had relevance to the Jewish people, names of Abraham and Moses and so forth, because the people could relate in their minds to these people who brought forth, what they felt brought forth, the Jewish faith. So they frequently gave them names such as the group known as the Gabriel group. There was a Michael group and so forth. Michael took issue with that even more than I, but we let it pass. (Laughter)

Participant: Was there a group called the Cohans?

Gabriel: Mm hmm. Yes, there was.

Participant: What was their role?

Gabriel: They were workers. They did a lot of work. They did a lot of building of things and they built them always with a sacred intent. They were the ones who went forth and made places for the Essene groups to dwell. They worked a lot in that way.

Participant: Okay. In many cathedrals, especially in Italy, you see the dove as symbolized with the Holy Spirit now, was that...?

Gabriel: That stems from the statement of John, "And I saw the Holy Spirit descending as a dove upon his head. This is the Messiah."

Participant: Okay. I was just wondering though, was that the...I'm trying to relate that to the Essene code.

Gabriel: Oh, that wasn't in the Essene code.

Participant: Okay.

Gabriel: No, John did not belong to the Davidic part; John belonged to the Judah part and so John's concepts and Jesus' concepts were a little different.

Participant: Okay.

Gabriel: But no, that had nothing...that was from John within.

Participant: Okay, thank you. And one other question: I think...I just want to clarify because I think you answered this in your remarks earlier, but the fact that in the code or their ritual that it had to be you conceived every four years or that it had to be conception in December and birth in September, that was all very arbitrary as it turns out?

Gabriel: Indeed, it was. It was a control factor. Plus, it was much more convenient to teach children all of one age than it was to teach children that were of various ages. They didn't have a lot of room. Their confines were rather small so if they had six or eight children all of one age and then in another four years, another six or eight children all of one age...

Participant: So it was just practical in that sense.

Gabriel: It was practical.

Participant: There was no significance of being born in September or whatever?

Gabriel: No.

Participant: Thank you.

Gabriel: Well actually, the idea of coming together, a man and woman consummating their marriage or whatever you call it, in December came from an old paganistic belief system in which that was the rite of winter, and all things conceived in the winter were considered to be sacred and holy in some way.

Participant: Thank you.

Participant: Gabriel, you mentioned something that just had so much meaning for me when you said that Jesus said, "Stand up and follow rather than fall down and worship."

Gabriel: Indeed, he did.

Participant: And...thank you. I wanted to share with you and the group a little situation that happened in New York recently, a couple of days ago. On the street there were two very young, attractive men that put up an easel and started to do magic tricks, and shortly after their first rope trick, they started speaking about the Bible and they drew a pictograph of God and man and a thick line in between. And then they wrote the word "sin" on the paper and the word "sin" very quickly became a very big part of that paper. And one of the young fellows walked over to me and said, "Do you believe in sin?"

And I had my groceries in one hand and something in the other and I said to him, "Well, I don't necessarily believe in sin, no."

He said, "Well, do you believe that you're going to make it to Heaven, and do you believe in Hell?"

And I said, "I feel that those are states of consciousness and I think I've been in both of those places." I said, "If I stand here and I regard you with love, then I'm in Heaven, but if I stand here and regard you with judgement, then I'm in Hell." And it just kind of came out and I felt like all of this energy was just moving through, you know.

And the guy stopped and he looked at me and he said, "My God, where did you hear that? What books did you read?"

And I said, "It's not really a book that I've read as much as it is a life experience and a feeling that I have." And this was the first time that I was ever dismissed by a Bible salesman on the street. (Laughter) You know usually you stay there, but he just couldn't wait to get rid of me. It was really wonderful and I want to say thank you for that.

Gabriel: (Laughing) Indeed, but you don't need to thank me, beloved entity, for that came from your own Higher Self.

Participant: Thank you.

Participant: I wanted to ask you if Mary Magdalene had had any other earth lives until now, between then and now?

Gabriel: Oh, yes.

Participant: Oh, she did?

Gabriel: Oh, yes. Learning, learning, learning.

Participant: Is she ready to ascend?

Gabriel: Not quite.

Participant: Oh, okay.

Gabriel: Not quite. She has a bit to go.

Participant: Beloved Gabriel.

Gabriel: Beloved woman.

Participant: I wondered, with the Essene children being born under one or two astrological signs if this made a difference in their relationships with other people, with all these children being born under the same signs with the same particular traits as opposed to being across the board where they...

Gabriel: Well, actually they were born under *two* signs because the delineage between the signs comes in the middle of the month. Now the other thing too is there were three calendars going on—the Roman calendar, the Jewish calendar, and the Greek calendar—so depending on the sect of the Essenes as to which month they were actually born in, some of them were born in August and some were born in October, depending on which calendar that particular group came under.

Participant: So does that mean that these children had the same temperaments?

Gabriel: No, they were quite different. There is a whole lot to it that I'm not going to go into such as ascending signs and your moon signs and all that sort of thing, plus your past life experiences and what you've come to do and what your choices are.

Participant: I have one other question. Did Mary Magdalene have any particular friends when she was in France that might have been named Rose Marie or Rosemary?

Gabriel: I don't know. I would have to search and find out.

Participant: I just wondered. This name came to me and I didn't know if that was a particular friend of hers or why...

Gabriel: I don't know. I shall find out though. I shall find out.
Participant: Thank you. Bless you.

Participant: Has Mary Magdalene reincarnated to teach us?
Gabriel: Oh, yes
Participant: During our lifetimes?
Gabriel: Yes.
Participant: Okay, thank you.
Gabriel: Any others?

Participant: When you spoke about in the days to come, I'm assuming that you mean what you've been teaching us about the religious and political upheaval here in our country and so forth?
Gabriel: Oh, not only in your country, beloved woman, in the world...in the world.

Participant: Gabriel, is it true in the Scripture where it says that Jesus went many times to be alone and to meditate and just separate himself from the disciples? Were you in contact with him at that time?
Gabriel: I have traveled with him for a very long time. He always sends me forth to make the places straight, as it were, to prepare the way, and I gladly go.
Participant: Thank you.

Participant: Would you discuss or talk a little bit about Mary, the mother of Jesus' life, and his brothers' and sister's life after his crucifixion, or is that another seminar?

Gabriel: Well, that's a whole other seminar, but Mary lived with the Essenes. She was well cared for, well loved. There was one thing about the Essenes...they never...just because they didn't approve of Jesus didn't mean they didn't approve of Mary. They loved Mary. They knew her and they knew she was a very loyal and faithful person and very true to the belief system, and they treated her very well. She lived with her children; sometimes with one, sometimes with another. She lived with John for a bit until his callings took him off and around and about, and then she went with her children. But she was kept very well in the community of the Essenes, very well.

I'll get into the others a little bit in another seminar because it's too lengthy to get into and I wanted to allow you questions to ask for this time.

Participant: Can I also ask...? There are four gospels and you've talked about John. What about Luke? Where does he figure in? What's fact and what is fiction?

Gabriel: Well first of all, they took one gospel, the Gospel of Mark, and they rearranged it to suit themselves—they, being the Church fathers and so forth—and they sort of put together the rest of them around the Gospel of Mark.

John, however, is written in a totally different vein, if you will notice. John approaches everything from a spiritual aspect. The others approached it more from what he did and what he said and the events of the times—a little bit of history, not a lot of history—but the Gospel of John, it comes truly from the Spirit, and even that they altered a little, left things out of. The Gospel of John and its original contents spoke much of the marriage of Mary Magdalene and Jesus and of the life in the commune and so forth, like that. They took all of that out.

Participant: May I ask another question? Somewhere I remember hearing about a Council of Nicaea way back, which decided what teachings would be acceptable and what not.

Gabriel: Oh, indeed.

Participant: Is this where...?

Gabriel: This is where the truth got muffled.

Participant: Okay, thank you.

Gabriel: They put a gag in the mouth right and proper there.

Participant: I'm really struck by the portrayal...I think the portrayal of the people intimate with Jesus has been so significant because over time or in our perspective of the apostles, and even of Mary and the Essenes, has been so glamorized through movies and even the Bible that we could make an assumption that they had somehow some greater knowledge than we have now and a higher level of consciousness than that of ours.

Gabriel: Not at all, no.

Participant: So this is very striking to see that and that we, in fact, now know the outcome and they didn't even know the outcome, so that we today...

Gabriel: You are further advanced by far than most of them were at that time.

Participant: That's kind of nice to know. (Laughter) But...

Gabriel: Oh, you think it's nice for *you* to know. (Laughter) You must remember, beloved woman, that the whole thought, the whole consciousness back then was very, very different than it is today in your world. It was stifled. For one thing, the people had no *freedom* of thought. They dared not express a new idea or new thought for fear of their life.

They were always an *oppressed* people, a people that were under the rule of someone who forced *their* ideas and *their* concepts *upon* them. And so, for them to embrace something new, they fought against it because they always took the new as to be somehow going to replace the old, and they *treasured* the old. They treasured the old. The leaders Abraham and Moses and Jacob and all of them...these were venerated prophets. These were the ancestors to be looked to and honored and revered, and when anyone came along with a new idea that didn't bring all that *into* it, they feared greatly that their *whole* tradition and therefore their whole history and their whole life would just disappear into a nothingness. These were a people who had so little time of freedom that their whole life was built in fantasy because the real life was too hard to bear.

Participant: So...but from your telling of the story now, it seems to me that Jesus wasn't accepted. I guess I thought that he spoke more than I'm getting the impression now that he did, that he was more well-known, and that he was expected...I mean, I thought he was expected...

Gabriel: Well, they expected a Messiah. They just didn't expect it to be *him*. They were expecting, as I said early on, beloved one, they were expecting someone to come in and overthrow their enemies, whoever their enemies were at the moment, because they had come under such rule. Rome was just *that* rule of *that* particular time but there had been, right from the very onslaught, there had been the Egyptian rule and all of that, all of the history.

They were wanting someone to come. Now you must remember, the teachings of John the Baptist, they were of... John's teachings were in this wise: That only the active God, only the hand of God, could ever liberate the Jewish people, that there would be no earthy thing take place that could *save* the people, as it were. It had to be through some heavenly intervention. So they were expecting that a bolt of lightning...they were expecting the parting of the sea, the...all of the things that had been perceived of to have happened in the past, and they were expecting some kind of phenomena to come and wipe out Rome and free the Hebrew people and allow them to live.

Now that was *John's* teaching. Because John was an Essene, a lot of people believed him. That was his teaching. That was where he was coming from, as it were. Now along came Jesus, and Jesus was not the man who was going to wipe out Rome. Instead of coming in with an army, he come in to teaching peace and brotherhood and love and acceptance and taking down barriers and all this sort of thing.

John came from the Judah aspect of the Essenes and they were a very...they allowed themselves no joy. They dressed in clothing that was harsh and coarse to the skin. They ate only certain foods. They did not allow themselves laughter or merriment or singing or anything of that sort. They came from a very hard place.

Now, here came Jesus...singing! He'd walk along the road singing to the top of his lungs, and he liked to associate with so called sinners. He'd have a banquet. He ate. He drank. He'd have a glass of wine with his meal. He enjoyed children. He'd get out and run and play games with children. He did all manner of things that John looked upon with concern because...

John knew in his heart that Jesus was a liberator, but John didn't understand in what *manner* he was. And John perceived Jesus to be, indeed, a rebel. A beloved one, nonetheless, but a rebel. And so John's whole teaching was based upon an external act of God that was going to come down, part the river, the Romans were going to be drowned, and the Hebrew people would be established.

Now, John knew in his heart, here was the Messiah, but what was he *doing* for heaven's sake? He couldn't comprehend Jesus' freedom. Jesus *loved* life. He *indeed* loved life. He liked to sing and to make merry. He was a great one to get in with a bunch of people and laugh and talk and tell stories and have a grand time, and this was totally opposite of John.

Now, Herod, Herod Antipas, he kind of liked Jesus. He thought he was pretty neat because Herod was a great reveler, you know. Herod would throw parties that lasted for days. So here come a religious teacher who said, "Party!" (Laughter) Well, he didn't actually say that but... So Herod Antipas thought, "Oh, this Jewish man, he's alright. He's not going to cause any problems because he thinks like I do." That was his reasoning.

John come saying, "Thou shalt not"; Jesus come saying, "Why not?" (Laughter) And there was the difference. There was the difference. Have I answered you?

Participant: You have. So the last question then is: From this ordinary life, from this wonderful ordinary life, how is it, and from this misunderstanding of it, that 2,000 years later, we remember?

Gabriel: The interesting thing is, the life structured by the Church for Jesus—which was begun with Paul, who got a *totally* distorted idea of Jesus—that has been taught and believed in and taught and taught and taught until everyone is so *steeped* in it that they never got to know the man. They never got to know his teachings. They never got to see who he really was.

And now, in this time, when the Christ Spirit that has been grounded on the earth for 2,000 years is now *emerging* in its *fullness,* you've got to get to know the man! You've got to see that he was like you, that what he did and what he learned and what he became is *possible* for *everybody.* Jesus *never* said, "I have done this but you'll never make it." (Laughter)

"What I have done, *you* can do, and greater things yet than these!" He'd be the first one to cheer you on, to say, "Go for it!"

But they never allowed that part of the man to be known. They had him depicted as the sterile, solemn, suffering Messiah. Never happened. Never.

Participant: So he overcame it anyway.

Gabriel: He overcame it anyway. But the thing is, beloved woman, despite what the Church built, the truth of the Christ won out and *that* is what *holds* the people. That's what brings the people. It doesn't matter what religious faith you are; you know that somewhere in under all of that there is a life that is *beautiful* beyond what you could even imagine.

If he were physically present in this room, the love that he would give forth would capture you all. It would transform you...because he loved life and every aspect of it.

Participant: Thank you.

Participant: The secret order that the Essenes had, like with learning and their teachings of everyone at that time, is there any connection in this time of our life? There are groups who are called the "Masons" and they're very secretive. In fact, when they initiate someone in their group, they're told not to tell because, you know, like death will come to them or...I'm just saying that. Is this a connection from the Essenes from that era of time to today's...?

Gabriel: It is a borrowed one. That originated in France.

Participant: Yes, and now in France, they're making women initiate in their Masons' thing—and they have them in Canada...they came to Canada to initiate—but they're from France.

Gabriel: They are from France.

Participant: And they do that initiations where it's secret and do certain things and you are not to *talk* about it, but I don't know. I don't think they're learning anything. (Laughter) I mean, myself. I mean, I'm sorry.

Gabriel: You don't think they're learning anything, eh?

Participant: No, I don't... I'm not judging. Oh, that's judging. No judgement.

Gabriel: Do you know them well?

Participant: No, I don't. This would be revealing, but I happen to have some involvement with the women in Canada to be initiated so I know what is gone through it and it's a bunch of...but interesting. It was a very interesting time of learning for me too, you know. So, revealing and all this is baloney, but I'm just saying, is there a connection with the Essenes because I feel I was an Essene at that time. I don't know...just a feeling. I didn't want to connect with the Masons. Okay, thank you.

Oh, one more thing...the thief. Who heard this? Was the voice loud? If it was...because...?

Gabriel: There were those near the cross who heard the voice.

Participant: Near the cross...who heard...maybe the thief...heard the thief because he couldn't speak, right? I didn't want him to speak because he would feel the pain.

Gabriel: He heard the voice, not reasoning in his mind where it came from. There were others who heard it too.

Participant: Okay, good. Thank you. I wanted to say that just in case.

Participant: Greetings Gabriel. We were taught to worship the Christ. How do you want us to approach him today?

Gabriel: First of all, to "worship" means to honor, to revere and to honor, and you revere and you honor the Christ within *you*. You love Jesus as you would love a very dear, dear friend but you honor the Christ in you as you would honor the Christ in him and as *he* honors the Christ in you.

Participant: So look at him as a friend.

Gabriel: Oh, indeed. Absolutely! He would not... He's not comfortable with this idea of being thought of as a kind of God because he knows he is no more God than you are, and yet you *all* are God. So there's that difference.

Participant: Gabriel, this maybe a broad question but I just came back from Indonesia and in Indonesia, many of these wonderful, loving people—and they are people of the heart—are Islamic. They worship Islam. Did Mohammed have a spiritual relationship with Jesus? I mean, was he kind of connected so that this... I mean, they are the largest religious group in the world today and they pray five times a day and they have... I mean, there's something *wonderful* about what is part of their religion, but I really don't know what Mohammed... where he was at as he began...

Gabriel: He was bringing in a kind of truth. He was introducing a higher...an ideal of something beyond what the five senses can bring.

Participant: Right.

Gabriel: And he took that truth and he brought it forth. He taught it and he taught it and he taught it. The difference being that Jesus was a very *free* person and Mohammed was not. But, as to the teaching of the Islamic belief system, there is a lot in there that's very valid and very true.

Participant: Good. Thank you very much.

Participant: All of us that walked the earth at that time, at the time of Jesus, it must be somewhere in our memory bank, the truths also.

Gabriel: Indeed, it is. You know, first of all, your biblical history is so distorted, so changed, that it's hardly recognizable. So much of it is left out. So much of it is hidden away in the archives of the Vatican. You have *volumes*—written in Hebrew, written in Greek, written in Arabic—of the things that happened, not only to the man, Jesus, but to all the people back then. But, it isn't the story that the Church manufactured, and I'm not talking about one church; I'm talking about *any* church. That is not what they wanted the people to know.

You must remember, the paganism that was rampant upon the earth at that time was part of the reason why things got out of hand. The Hebrew people were the only people, with the exception of one group of Egyptians who accepted the idea of *one* God, but even *they* had the idea that God was the God of wrath, that God would give and God would take away, God would slay and God would do this and God would do that. They had no idea of the *love* of God. They saw God as someone you feared, someone you placated, someone you begged of, and in that wise, their belief system was very paganistic. All around them, in Syria...all of the countries had their own paganistic beliefs.

Now along comes a man who grew up among them and he's going out and he's proclaiming some new truth. "Well, is he not our neighbor? Where did *he* get this stuff from?" They were hard-hearted in the sense that they wouldn't open the chambers of their hearts and let that truth flood in.

This was not the God of Abraham. This was not the God of Moses, this loving God, this forgiving God—love your neighbor, forgive seventy times seven, share what you had, do not divorce a wife. The reason that was was because divorced women had no recourse if their families were dead. They had no way to earn a living. Most of them ended up either starving to death or entering into prostitution. So to divorce a woman back then was to sign a death sentence to her. The Master Jesus knew that. That's why he said, "Do not divorce," because he knew the woman had no chance of survival whatsoever, and if there had been children, usually they were taken from her and given to his parents to raise. So here was a woman cast out with no family, her own children forbidden her, so of course he's going to teach, "Do not divorce." He was a man of compassion. He loved everybody. He wasn't going to single out women and let them be treated in that fashion.

But all of this is taken out of *context*. He lived in a very harsh land, an unyielding land. The Hebrew people were free such brief, little periods here and there, they didn't know *how* to deal with freedom. They didn't know *how* to live in a democratic manner so they had all these arbitrary laws and rules and regulations that were set up, always, ultimately, for the benefit of the wealthy.

You must remember, they lived by the caste system. There were those high up who didn't work, who took money from the ones in between, who in turn took money from the ones on the bottom. Now Jesus was born into that caste that was on the bottom. He was born into poverty. Mary Magdalene, she was in the middle. She wasn't up there but she was in the middle.

Now the other thing: She was of the House of Judah and had not the right to come into the Essene community in which Jesus was a member. He was of the Davidic...of the King David part, and these two were...I won't say warring—they didn't make war—but they didn't agree. They had *their* rules, they had *their* rules, and they were not necessarily the same.

So number one, he was very busy building for himself a reputation in order that he might lead the people into learning that you don't need all these "thou shalt nots," as it were. And then, he has the audacity to bring a Judah woman over to *his* compound and ask that she be admitted! Well, I mean everything he did had a purpose behind it: *to break the old and allow in the new*. And that's why he did the things he did. Never to harm. Harm no one, he taught. That was unheard of.

The Essenes were a very political people. They had their hierarchy. Men vied for the top place to be called "Father." Where do you think the Catholics got the term from?

The women, during the time in which they were not allowed to be with their husbands, were regarded as "sisters," all of them were regarded as sisters. That's where the term in the Catholic Church came from, "Sister." They were women who lived a celibate life. The women who were with child lived in a different place. They lived in a different house. They had different duties. The women who were barren were the workers. They were next of kin to the slaves. They had no rights whatsoever. They did all the hard work. That's why it was so terrible for a woman to discover she was barren. That's why you will read in your Scriptures that for a woman to be barren, she would rather be dead. It totally took away every right that she could ever imagine.

Children were the key to being accepted for a woman if she could bear children, and if she could have sons. Now you must remember, back then it was the belief system that the *woman* determined the sex of the child and a woman who bore only daughters was considered the next thing to being barren. Sons were the important thing and if the first born be a son, then the woman was venerated. She had a son. She gave her husband a son. She was considered a treasure, a great treasure, but a woman who did not bear children, she was treated cool— polite, but cool—but was never included in the inner circle. Her life was very lonely.

Now if her husband was of a mind to not divorce her—to let her live, as it were, as it was termed—then she had some measure of hope that perhaps one day, like

Sara, God would open her womb and allow her to conceive. But they didn't know about the cycles of procreation back then. They didn't know that some women will not conceive a certain time of year. Some women have their...I don't know your term when they are fertile...

Participant: Ovulation.

Gabriel: Ovulation, that is the term. They didn't know that some women, although they ovulate every month, do not always conceive, that ovulation might pass by if there is no sexual activity at that time and she would not conceive. They didn't know those things. They had not a clue that when they limited the women to sexual activity only in the month of December, they were automatically declaring certain women to be barren. Probably if those women were sexually active a different time, a different month, they would have borne children, but they weren't allowed.

The Master saw the stupidity in these rules. He saw that life is a treasure, life is beauteous, and what transpires between two people who love one another is a very wondrous thing. But he couldn't make *them* see that. They didn't *want* to know that. They didn't want the world to know that these astute Essene men often left the compound and went into the villages and took up with prostitutes for a night or two now and again. But they didn't go back to the compound and say, "Well, guess what I did last night?" (Laughter) It was kept very quiet.

Now the women, on the other hand, were not allowed such freedom. A woman had to live a very chaste life. The sins of men were frequently overlooked; the sins of a woman were never forgiven, ever. Some of the Essene communities refused to allow a woman to speak to a man who was not related to her or married to her. She couldn't even lift her eyes and look upon his face as he passed, and if she did and she was caught, she was considered to be an adulteress. Just the exchange of eye contact was considered to be absolutely adulteress.

How could there be joy in God and happiness and love in a place where you were forbidden the very nature of your being? There could be none, absolutely none.

A man did not touch his wife in public. He didn't reach over, take her hand, put his arm around her...nothing. He walked with her behind him and he never looked upon her in public.

That is why when Jesus would grab Mary Magdalene and kiss her on the mouth...oh, well, that was the most horrid of things and that's precisely why he *did* it, was to show them that God did not send a bolt of lightning out of Heaven and strike the two of them dead. But the people didn't understand that and that is why he took her out of there into the hills where they could live as they were meant to live, normally.

It is difficult for you to think of these people as real people because they are names in a book. They are faces you have never seen. You read what is written upon the printed page and it's like a fairy tale or a storybook. But these were living people with living needs, living feelings. They made their mistakes. They had their joys, their sorrows, their illnesses, their deaths, their agreements, their disagreements, their wars, their famines...just like you. Just like you. And so did Jesus, just like you, because if he hadn't, he could *never* have done what he did and have it mean anything.

When you think of him, think as you would think of a dearly beloved friend whom you love and trust. Think of him as one who has gone before you and prepared the way, who has said, "Here, this is how you do it. This is what must be done," because that's what he is. He is the ultimate teacher of teachers. He is the Son of God just as you are the Son of God, and he learned just as you are learning.

He had his loves. He had his days of feeling down. He had his times of questioning the very core of the purpose for which he came. He had his times of being depressed and thinking perhaps he had made a mistake. He had his times of feeling that he failed. He was a person who knew God but who walked as a man.

Some of the things about his life can't be told now—but they will be told—because you wouldn't understand it. If you had trouble with what was presented Saturday, then anything more in depth than that would turn you away. You wouldn't come back to listen. You wouldn't want to know.

The only one you worship is God. You do not worship your saints, as you call them, and the Master Jesus does not want to be worshiped. Loved and welcomed as you would a dearly beloved friend, but not worshiped, not at all.

Participant: I know that there's been such a big change in what I'm doing, and in all the years that I was a religious Jew, I always felt the connection with God but I never felt it in the temple; I only felt it through the music but I never felt it through the words because I felt like I needed an intermediary in order to feel his presence, and that's changed so dramatically for me that I go for walks with him now.

Gabriel: And isn't he a wondrous companion, indeed?

Participant: He holds my hand.
Gabriel: Indeed. Indeed.

Participant: Welcome Gabriel. I'm really glad you're here. I unfortunately missed—this is like the first one I've missed in years—the Saturday session. And when I was told Jesus and Mary Magdalene were married, I was delighted.
Gabriel: So was he. (Laughter)
Participant: Yeah, I bet! So I guess my Catholic paradigm isn't as deep in me as in some others because I think it's a wonderful thing that he had joy in his life. So often, what we hear is the suffering and the anguish, and I know that there have been times that I've felt *guilty* of the idea of "he suffered for us" concept. In light of that, I was thinking of some of the other things you mentioned that were traditions in that time and another participant just said about traditions coming through. I have a sister-in-law who is expecting their third child and she has this compelling desire to give my brother a son, and it's like he is now holding this disappointment because they had a test say that it was a girl. He has two daughters and he loves them dearly but there's this something that interferes with their welcoming this child now into the world because it's probably a girl. And some of us would like them so to get off it that we've decided it's a boy anyhow. And we'll all be so grateful that it's a healthy child. How do we help people get off this old stuff that isn't such a big deal anymore?
Gabriel: When they are so ingrained in something like that, the only thing you can do is to encase them in light, ask that God bless them with an open understanding,

and just always project to them the light and the love. That's the only thing you can do. Words mean nothing.

Participant: I've been reading a book, "The Essenes and Jesus Christ," and it's written by a person, Dolores Cannon, and in the book, she's a hypnotherapist and she's taking an entity back into one of the past lives as an Essene and the Essene's name is Suda. Suda said, and I hope I'm quoting this correctly, that there was an equality in the Essene community between men and women. And this community, as I understand it, was in Qumran also and I'm beginning to wonder, was that equality based on a comparative basis as compared to the other Essene communities? So that's what he meant when he said "equality."

Gabriel: Yes, because you see, beloved entity, contrary to everyone's belief, everyone thought an Essene is an Essene is an Essene and that isn't so. They all...just as your religious groups this day differ even within a single denomination. There are priests who teach this and priests who teach that, yet they are both Catholic priests or Episcopal priests or whatever. So it was with the Essenes. Each group had their own rules and regulations, their own code, as they called it, and some of them were much more liberal than the others.

Now the ones who were comprised mostly of very poor people without a great hierarchy, those were the ones where equality was most often practiced. But when the wealthy ones came in, then equality disappeared.

Participant: I have another question: People from the House of Ur—again, this is still that channeling—they said from the House of Ur is a culture group, not a place, and in this culture group belonged Abraham and the three Magi, I think called them. Is that true and if so, then it seems as though the House of Ur, that culture group, was highly evolved as compared to other members of the Essene community?

Gabriel: Some of them were. Now most of them practiced a form of what would be termed in the outer world as "magic" and that's why they were called the Magi.

Participant: Okay.

Gabriel: Now, the thing is that it depended upon which group they were in as to which type of magic they used.

Participant: So there were several houses.

Gabriel: Oh, indeed. Indeed. When you say the House of Ur or the House of Abraham or the House of David, you aren't referring to one single place. You are referring to a loosely knit belief system. And there has to be someone in that group who is a direct descendant of either Abraham, Moses, of Ur, whatever. Now, some of the poorer communes, the common people, as it were, who had no claim to a kingly line, blood line—such as the Davidic Line or the Abraham Line or anything of that sort—they would choose a name that had meaning to them within themselves and they would be of the House of that.

Now most of the Essenes followed either Moses or Abraham or David or some of the...Joseph—Josephes, as they called it, and there were other groups—but they had these groups and there was always at least one family, if not more, who could trace their ancestors back to that particular prophet or teacher and that is what they based their teachings upon.

And that is why it was so difficult to get them to change, was because ancestors were *worshipped*. Once you were dead, you were the Holy of Holies and to deny an ancestor proper worship was unthought of. They would no more have blasphemed the name of Abraham or Moses than anyone of a high Christian caliber today would blaspheme the name of the Virgin Mary or Jesus. So, you have these traditions that are followed, one after the other, and they don't vary. They don't change. They stay within that code as it was called.

So what you're getting is that particular House of whoever, *their* code, how they lived, and they varied one right next door to the other. They varied.

Participant: It was also said that in this community, that their scholars had written these scrolls and these scrolls had been sent to various groups throughout the world so that they would be recorded, so that the Dead Sea Scrolls are not *only* in the Vatican. It would seem to me that they're all over the place.

Gabriel: There is quite a few of them in Egypt. There's some in India.

Participant: Okay.

Gabriel: The ones in Egypt... There are places, tombs—places, some of which are long covered over with sand and buried very deep—but in them there are written scrolls. A lot of them have been translated and written in the ancient Egypt, Egyptian words and so forth. But all of the Essenes did that. They all sent scrolls to various places of the earth to be hidden. They were a very secretive group. But they did, for the most part, mostly, they cooperated one with the other, especially in things of recorded history and belief systems.

Participant: So then those graves, the pyramids, and the practice of the Egyptians burying their kingly people or their queenly people, according to this channel—and I think I'm remembering it correctly—this was a deceptive thing because that wasn't the important thing at all. It was those scrolls; it was that written information that was incredibly important.

Gabriel: The grave, as it were, the sepulcher was made and in the very bottom were placed the vases and the containers with the scrolls in. Over that was placed a layer of dirt. Then treasures were placed—riches, jewels, money, whatever. Then over that was placed the body. Then over that was placed food and elements that they...cooking elements and so forth that they might need in the next world. Then over that was placed the family pet, whether it be a horse or a cat or an ox or whatever—whatever was treasured by the person buried there. That creature was also mummified so that when that person got to the other side, they had everything they ever needed to continue life. And usually grave robbers only went as far as the jewels. They never went further. So the scrolls were very safe. Very safe.

Participant: Well, if this is true about the Egyptians, with some of the mummies that they have found, they never found any of these scrolls in the sarcophagus?

Gabriel: They did find some but they were usually, and no pun intended, spirited off before anyone could know of it. Now, it depended on who the archaeologists were, to what country they belonged, whether they were of England or of Australia or of your continent here... depended on where they came from as to where they took them. They were worth a great sum of money.

Participant: Have they been translated?

Gabriel: For the most part, no, because then they would become public. But in time, they will be. In time.

Participant: I think you told the gentleman Saturday that it wouldn't be in our lifetimes at all. It would be some time in the future when all this would come out.

Gabriel: That is true. Some of the earth changes will unearth some of them. You even have some here in your own country.

Participant: Buried?

Gabriel: Indeed. In the middle, in the plains, where the plains are, and there's also a mountain range in your country here, a very large mountain range in the west. There are caves there that are covered over but will be opened when some of the earth changes take place.

The land on the top of your globe used to touch and one could walk across where now there is a sea, but that was not always so. And so the peoples frequently would cross over what is now ocean by simply walking, and these scrolls were taken by *trusted servants*. Trusted Essenes would travel for thousands of miles, sometimes on foot...took them years to take their treasures and put them in what they perceived to be a safe place.

Participant: For future generations, I assume?

Gabriel: For future generations when they, themselves would return and bring them to light.

Participant: Ah, a method in their madness.

Gabriel: Indeed.

Participant: One other thing. Some of the Arab nations are still of the same belief system as it was 2,000 years ago as far as women and the garb that they must wear and walking behind their men and not being able to raise their eyes. They haven't changed in 2,000 years.

Gabriel: Oh, more than that. More than that. These belief systems go back 5,000 or 6,000 years, back way before the common area, as you call it.

Participant: In this lifetime, I'm from a Jewish background, and I just want to clarify something that opened up for me on Saturday. I was always raised believing that the Jewish people never accepted Jesus as the Messiah because he wasn't. And on Saturday when you explained about the people at the time thinking a Messiah would have taken all the Romans out of there and relieved them of that rule and therefore, they didn't really accept Jesus as a Messiah, it really opened up for me that I *could* accept him. There's been such a blockage, a block in the Jewish people, at least the way it came to me, their beliefs about accepting this man...that understanding the truth of it all just totally dissolved that blockage. Am I making sense? Because I think what I understand now is that the whole concept of a Messiah and a Savior was all bupkis anyway. It was just created afterwards by the Church, whatever.

Gabriel: Actually, there was a belief in a Messiah. However, it is an old, mythical...it comes in your terms of what you would use today as a myth, like a fairy tale. And the purpose behind it being, the people never believed that they were in control, the Hebrew people, because they never were—someone always had them enslaved— and so therefore the idea of a control coming from within themselves was...they couldn't conceive of that.

So there was always this feeling that God was going to strike dead their enemy because it would have to be an external force and the only force they could perceive of, more powerful than whoever had them captive at the time, was an act of God. It had to be an act of God and that was the *only* thing that they could accept. Coming from a man, it would have to be a man who had *power,* and he would have to have power because he was the *chosen* of God, just as Abraham had been chosen, just as Moses had been chosen, and Josephes, and all of them. So, this man had to be a chosen one of God and he had to come with *great power* and able to strike down the enemy.

Well, here comes a neighbor. Here comes Jesus, who grew up among them, lived among them, born among them, and he's preaching this "love thy neighbor" business. Didn't work. (Laughter) Didn't work. So, the whole idea of a Messiah is traceable back in your Hebrew history—very, very far back—but it was the thinking, the consciousness of the people, that produced the idea of a Messiah.

When things were at their *worst* for the Jewish people, when slaughtering and all manner of things... You know, they went through terrible, terrible, unspeakable things. If you were to liken it to what Hitler did to the modern day Jewish people and add to that *centuries* of time that that same thing went on, then you would have a good idea of what the Jewish people went through.

And as quickly as they would get in with someone who treated them not too badly, someone would come along and get rid of that one and take them over and do even worse things, so there never was a time when their freedom was a realization. It was always a dream, a "Wouldn't it be nice if...? Won't it be nice when...?" That is why they are so sorrowful. That is why they are so lamenting. Have you ever watched them pray?

Participant: Yes.

Gabriel: Is there joy?

Participant: No.

Gabriel: Indeed not, for the sorrow is born into the centuries behind them and they carry it forth like a banner. Now here comes this audacious young man, laughing and speaking with gentiles—the unclean, the uncircumcised, the unknowing! *Well.* And he's going to be called the "Son of God"? I don't think so. And so, of course they could not see the value of what he was teaching. He was teaching them freedom—break down the barriers, join, become one, unify—and then we will go after Rome. No.

One belief system argued with another belief system. They spent more energy standing on the corners arguing over the Torah than... If they had put all that energy into unifying, they could have overridden Rome or the Syr...everybody. But they didn't. They fought among themselves and they still do. They still do. If you want a good argument, hear it, listen to two Jewish women, and that's a grand truth!

Participant: That's true. So, what I want Beloved Woman to know in a very, very deep and profound way, the information that she was able to bring forth on Saturday potentially can break down tremendous, tremendous barriers because there's a real opening here to dispel these blockages that you talked about that had been so deeply ingrained for centuries. I guess I'm just feeling that very personally within, that freedom within, because it no longer has to be sought from without. Thank you very much.

Gabriel: You are very welcome. Guess that's it? A prayer...

Prayer

O Thou life, Thou love
that manifests Thyself in all forms,
O Thou to Whom I honor and give reverence
and devote my life and energy,
From Whom I have come forth at Thy bidding,
to do Thy bidding,
for these, Thy children,
Whom Thou has given unto me yet again,
I give Thee thanks.

I thank Thee for the presence of the Master,
who comes with love and joy
to be with these whom he loves.

I thank Thee for this time in which I have been allowed
to be the vessel of Thy truth,
And I thank you for Beloved Woman,
who has allowed me the use of her vehicle.

Bless them, Father God, into the light of truth
and into the love of Thy presence.

And so it is.

Living the Christ

January 17, 1998

Lesson

Master Jesus: Peace be to you, Children of God, brothers and sisters in the light. My heart is full of joy to see your faces, to be in your presence, to feel your love, to feel the bonding that comes in fellowship one with another in the presence of God.

I have long awaited this day in which I might come and gather with you here. My desire is not to speak of how I lived...

John, good friend. Indeed! [Hugs and pats on the back a participant who was the disciple John.] Indeed! Good friend! Man, it is good to see you and touch you in form! My best friend! My best friends.

Much of what I taught upon the earth has been greatly misconstrued and it has troubled me all this time that so much of the truth of it was left behind and was molded and made into what mankind thought should be said. I have come in so many forms to so many people in so many ways to try to make right what was made wrong, and my desire this day is to straighten the crooked places that the truth of what I brought might be fully understood and *lived* and not bound by the old ways.

In order to understand why things happen as they did, you must first understand the Law of Vibration. When you ventured forth upon the earth in form, you came in at a very low frequency, and by that I mean you were not fully conscious of the form and the earth upon which you dwelt. Your attention was still held in the Spirit because it was from the Spirit that you came forth.

So as a result you became bonded, one with another, for you felt that in this *new* place, this *new* sense, this *new* adventure, you needed to be held together. And so, what began as your connectedness to the God within you—to the Father, to the Mother God—became transferred to family unit and the family, finally unto the clan and to the groups, the tribes, if you will. And this was done to the exclusion of anyone else.

Because you felt you had to keep pure, you never allowed others in, and it was a common practice within families to intermarry—brothers to sisters, cousins to cousins, even mothers and sons and fathers and daughters. It was a common practice and the reason being that you firmly believed that the Spirit of you was contained in the blood. That is one of the reasons why blood sacrifices became so popular, was because it was a method that you chose to use to express your complete sacrifice.

This held your consciousness in a tight fist and it did not allow anything new to come in. In physical form, it was represented by no intermarrying within one tribe and another. The tribes held themselves separate, even if they were not at war. It was not an acceptable thing to marry outside of your tribe, and as a result of that, there came about a vibration upon the earth that was exclusive. It was held so firmly that one did not take in anything or any*one* from the outside, that one held only to the *old* ways, to the *old* truths, to the ways of the ancestor.

Now at that point your consciousness was so bound into that that you had memories that belonged to your predecessors; your great grandparents' memory was very vivid and alive in your consciousness because you never reached for anything new. You ever, always, always looked backward. Because of this, the consciousness of the whole human race did not progress. It stayed always the same, always the same...abiding, abiding, never moving.

Now this went on for thousands of years—marrying within the tribe, always within the tribe, and if anyone had the audacity to go out and marry outside of the tribe, they were ostracized, they were never welcomed back, and if they tried to come back, they were slain. Because it was believed that the blood must be kept pure, it *excluded* growth.

This is why, in the Old Testament, the people of the time took the name of the lineage. It would be James, the son of David, the son of Abraham, and so on and so forth back. It was *always going backward, never forward.* And so it was that there came onto the earth this *rock hard consciousness* that held and bound the hearts of all humankind. This is why cruelty was such a common thing and not thought anything about. It didn't *occur* to anyone to be kind or loving because they always looked back and what was done then was done now.

This could not go on. How would you grow? How could you come into light if you never knew there was a light? The shadow upon you at that time was very dark and deep and that is why you will read in your old testimonies—your Old Testament—of the arduous task of the leaders to get the people to *move*.

Symbolically, the wilderness that Moses walked his people through was the wilderness of "never taking in anything new." They tracked over the same land again and again and again because consciously, that's where they were at, always in the land of the barrenness, empty space that represented their internal outlook.

Moses symbolizes the law. He was the one who came to awaken within the people the realization that they must not continue on in this way. There had to be an upsurge.

Moses knew there was one God. Moses didn't understand God, but he knew there was one God. And knowing the way people of his times thought, he knew he had to bring them out of the worship of idols and into the recognition of one all-pervading, loving presence. But Moses himself was bound by the old ways. Moses himself honored ancestors. Moses knew but couldn't produce what he knew. This is symbolized by his stuttering. It was difficult for him to speak because he could find no language, no words within his language, to express what *he knew* and therefore he found it difficult to bring out *into* the consciousness of the people those things which he knew to be a truth.

So Moses took himself up to the mountain. Symbolically, the mountain is the highest place of spiritual contact that one can attain to within the unit of their understanding, within the unit of their present understanding. And Moses went up to the mountain.

Because Moses was so integrated into laws and rules and regulations, his perception of the truth of God came as rules and regulations, and thereby he came into bringing forth what you have come to call your "Ten Commandments."

Particles of truth in each one, but the totality of the truth of them is lost and symbolically, the outpicturing of Moses's own consciousness, these were cast in stone. Cast in stone. Could not be changed. Could not be moved. Could not be altered. Could not grow and take in more. Cast in stone. So the consciousness of the people and of Moses was cast in stone.

When Moses came down from his Higher Self, back into the everyday world, he found the people not following his instructions at all. They had gone...they had reverted back, as ever they had done, they turned backward, looking backward, and he found them building idols, living almost animal-like with no concept of the beauty and the truth of the God within them. So angry was he, so *frustrated,* that all of this work, all of what he knew, could not be forced upon them.

He did a symbolic thing. He smashed the tablets. Outwardly, that was the manifestation of what was going on within Moses, to smash this rigid, unyielding, unmoving, un-allowing attitude. Moses had the idea, "This must end. More must come," but he couldn't quite bring it forth. Not quite.

So he went up into the mountain again. Now each time that symbolized that he went in his consciousness and grasped a higher truth, but in trying to bring it into form, it became hardened again. And so consequently, the consciousness of the people remained nearly the same. There were so few among those who followed Moses that truly wanted to grow. They wanted a better life, but they didn't want to do anything to get it. They wanted some God in the sky to hand it to them. They didn't want to have to break the stone of their own hardened hearts and learn to love and to move forward and to take in and to grow.

Every time they encountered another tribe, it was war perhaps. What if they come after us? There was never peace among them. And all of Moses's efforts, out of all of those efforts, just a few grains of sand was all he accomplished because the consciousness was so locked into that. Now, in all of the years that followed, that consciousness did not move. It still was locked into the *old* ways…"Thou shall not." There is nothing more limiting and binding than "Thou shall not." How can you grow if you can't, if you're not allowed, if you are prohibited by your own internal guardian that says, "Thou shall not"? *Inside is this freedom,* but nobody knew it. Nobody knew it.

Now, we come into an era in which this consciousness just swirled around and around. It didn't grow. It didn't change. It just swirled, begetting its own, begetting its own, and never coming forth into the new light of truth and growth.

The symbolism behind the Roman rule of the Hebrew people was the outpicturing of the consciousness of the times. There they were, in bondage to who? To themselves. In bondage to their own thinking of constantly looking backward. So many symbols, *so many* messages came through that they didn't get. The story of Sodom and Gomorrah. The woman who looked back and was turned into salt. Whenever you rely upon the past to be your vehicle of truth, you are turned into salt.

It is in the present moment that truth abides, not in yesterday, and tomorrow hasn't come. You only have the now of it. And these people did not want "the now of it" because the "now of it" was a terrible existence, and so they longed to be free but they didn't even know what freedom was. It was a myth. It was a kind of an abstract idea, a "Wouldn't it be wonderful if…" But they didn't know freedom. And so conqueror after conqueror came, always binding the Hebrew people, always "Thou shall not," always keeping them from their full expression because within themselves they had bound themselves so tightly to the past.

The conditions upon your earth were not unlike the conditions of the last…this past century of oppression, of war, excepting they made no movement forward. None. And even when I came, I was not accepted…not accepted. Why? Because I broke every rule. I broke every rule. I loved. I loved openly. I loved freely. I cared about people. I didn't care if it was the Sabbath; if someone needed healing, so be it…"Be healed." I didn't follow the rules of the synagogue. I didn't follow the rules of Moses. I didn't follow any rule except the internal rule of the voice of my Father within me. And because I came, inviting the uninvitable into my home, into my presence, to my table to eat…that was unheard of. That was not acceptable.

I loved my wife. I had no problem kissing her on the mouth in public! How *dare* I? How dare I? Women were not equal with men but they were to me. I purposely would bait the Pharisees. When a group would gather to hear me talk, I would take the lowliest of the women and I would say, "Come, sister, sit beside me," and I would touch them…touch them.

A man did not touch a woman in public. A man did not speak to a woman in public. Women were nothing more than possessions, someone to bear your children, cook your meal, and speak to you when you asked them to.

I delighted in women! They're an interesting lot, you know. (Laughter) They know things. They're warm. They're loving. They're generous. They're caring.

It is a time when love was not expressed, not felt, and here came this audacious, itinerant speaker who went out and clasped an arm around a friend, who liked to laugh, who enjoyed a good joke. If you don't think so, ask Peter.

Peter was a staunch man, narrow-minded, stubborn. I had great sport with Peter. (Laughter) Peter didn't like women. As he said to me once, "I have two at home. I have a wife and her mother and they make my life unhappy." (Laughter)

However, Peter was a good representative of the thinking of the times. Peter was the kind of man who was outspoken; you knew what Peter was thinking. There was no guile in Peter. He said it. He wasn't always correct but he spoke out what he felt. Peter was honest, if nothing else.

But typical of the thinking of the time, Peter looked backward into the past. He looked, as they all had done through eons of time, to the old masters, the old teachers, and it was difficult for Peter to take in the truth of the present moment.

I was walking along the street with Mary Magdalene one day, holding her hand and we were laughing together, and Peter stepped out of an alley, he grabbed me by the scruff of the neck, he held me, and he said, *"What are you doing!?"*

I said, "Well right now, I'm standing here, looking at you, and wondering what *you're* doing." (Laughter)

He said, "You're *touching that woman.*"

"I *like* touching that woman." (Laughter) She was nice to touch. I said, "So I am touching with this woman. What of it...is it to you?"

"What will people say?"

"I don't care!" I don't care because in my heart, in my soul, I knew the love of God and I knew that I could touch that woman.

People think that to follow God you have to restrict yourself and be narrow and not allow and not do and not be. God, to be expressed from within, is a freedom that you have yet to come to know. It is a freedom of love, not a freedom to go forth and hurt, but a freedom to go forth and love whomever you will. Whether they love you back or not has absolutely nothing to do with it. Most of the people that I loved didn't like me...not at all. And oddly enough, the people who one would think *wouldn't* like me were the ones who loved me the most, namely Judas. Judas loved me dearly and paid for it with his life.

Within every human being, there is a living Spirit that is the truth of your being and that Spirit is the Child of God of you. That Spirit in you is pure and holy. It knows no sin. It knows no error. It knows nothing of anything that would make you *bad* or *wrong* or not what you should be, for that Spirit is cast perfectly, absolutely perfectly, in the image and likeness of God.

Around that Spirit you have the personality that you yourselves have created, and that personality is the Roman soldiers around the Hebrew people, if you will— the limitations, the bounding, the "Thou shall nots." Because you have this holiness within you, because you are a sacred, precious emanation of All-That-Is, you have this truth laying latent there.

Do you know what a sounding fork is? In music, it is that which is struck and its vibration sets a tone. Interestingly enough, if you were to take two of these and you were to lock one away and strike the other, the one that is locked away would reverberate with the tone of the one that was struck. It would respond in kind to the vibration of the first sounding fork. And you can prove this to yourself. Get two and try this experiment and you will find that the second responds to the first. Why? Because within both of them is the same quality. Within both of them is the same Spirit. And when one Spirit lifts up and *speaks out loud,* the Spirits all *must* respond.

Now, I'll tell you something about the spoken word...it is *power.* Why? Because it is an energy unto itself. It will *call to* the feeling nature of anyone who hears the words. When you hear words, something inside of you reacts to that, do you not? You either agree or you disagree or you don't care or you care greatly, but it is the spoken word that brings forth the reaction.

Now, within you is the same Spirit that is in me; lying asleep, curled up in the boat of your consciousness is the Christ. I was the sounding fork. I came forth and I *spoke!* And the words that I spoke 2,000 years hence are still making people react. They either hate me or they love me, but they have some feeling, some one way or the other. They are either for me or they are against me. They either believe in me or they totally disbelieve in me, but there is nothing that brings a person's reaction out quicker than the discussion of whether or not I ever existed and if I did, was I indeed born of a virgin and was God really my father and who was Joseph and how could I, this man of sorrow, which I *never* was... (Laughter) I loved life! How could you love God and not love life? How could this person go about healing and raising the dead? The controversy over the life of the man rages on still. Why? Because I spoke a truth and it resonated throughout eternity and it will always resonate because I spoke with the voice of Christ. I spoke with the authority of my Father. Everything I did, I did because I was told to from the God within my breast...*everything* I did.

If I said or did something that was not acceptable to the times, the scribes who followed thereafter merely eliminated it. None of the words that were written about me were written...I take that back. Only a few of the words written about me were written from the truth of the being of the writer. The others wrote what would be *acceptable*...what would be *acceptable*.

Of the twelve who followed me, there was only one who truly understood the spiritual significance of what I was doing and that was John. The rest of them got little bits and pieces of it, all strangely mixed with their previous concepts of what God and man might be, of the relationship.

And then you have Paul. Paul had many demons within him and because he had many demons within him, he was a fighter. Paul was a persecutor and he persecuted none more than himself. He took what *little* he knew of me—and he did know very little of me—he took it and he made it into what *he thought I was*. Paul and I met once.

Paul dwelt in fear—fear of being discovered, fear of not being acceptable—and so he took the offensive. Paul was bold. He was a small, wiry man with piercing eyes and a dominant air about him. Paul was quite fearless, but he was fearless out of fear. His very fear gave him courage. Because he couldn't love, because he hated so much, that made him bold.

Now, he came in an encounter with me and all of his so-called boldness melted away. Here was a force he couldn't reckon with. Here was a force he couldn't order about. Paul was a powerful man. Paul was highly thought of. He was regarded *quite well* when Rome… For many years Rome considered Paul an ally because he persecuted. They would say to Paul, "Go kill," and Paul went and killed or had them killed. Paul stood by smugly while they stoned Stephen, thinking, "Chalk one up for us."

But then, Paul's fears had to be brought out because in Paul, that fearlessness turned to the right, could be an ally for the new truth, for the good news. But you didn't walk up and reason with Paul because Paul was a know-it-all. Paul knew it all; you didn't tell Paul anything. If he didn't already know it, he pretended that he did and he dismissed you…and then investigated quietly on his own. Paul never admitted to anyone, "I didn't know that," so one had to get Paul's attention. You know, there is nothing like putting a man flat on his bottom and standing over him to get his attention. (Laughter) That will do it every time.

But Paul had to deal with his own internal demons, one of which Paul lived in great fear, that it be found out that he was homosexual. Paul didn't know what to do with that. He hated it. He hated himself. Because he had such self-hatred and self-loathing for himself, this is why he could go and kill. You have to hate yourself so completely if you are going to be in a position to slay another.

Now, when Paul and I encountered one another, Paul was on his way to Qumran. Paul wanted to infiltrate the Essenes, for he felt he could do his best work there, but I intercepted him.

I saw in Paul a great light, a light that if it were liberated in truth and in love would be a grounding force for the good news, but Paul had first to release and let go of his fear. How do you counteract such *deep* fear? With a deeper love. With a deeper love.

So first Paul had to be made to realize that he was not the all-conquering hero. He encountered a force that he couldn't order about, that he couldn't run away from, that he couldn't escape, because it *held* him. And there he was at its mercy. Then Paul could listen. Then Paul could not walk away and say, "I already knew that."

Here he was, his horse long gone on this little narrow mountain path...just him and me. Part of it was shock therapy because Paul knew I was dead and yet there I was. Part of it was a total disbelief facing his total disbelief, facing the truth that there is life even after the body has been lain away and that there is an abiding love that can take a man like Paul, who quivered on the ground, "What do you want with *me*?"

He wouldn't look at me at first until I commanded him to and when he did, he said, "Don't slay me. Don't slay me."

I said, "Paul, look at me. Do I look like I am about to slay you?"

And he looked at me and he felt love. For the *first and only time in his life, Paul felt love.*

When a person is so full of self-hatred and so full of the damnation of the ages that was preached to him and taught to him and in his blood, when love first is encountered, it is a completely debilitating power that comes over the person and from the very Spirit of them outward, it wrecks havoc. It takes away *everything* they have ever believed in. All of Paul's belief system, that which was bred into his bones, was on trial here on that mountain path. Everything that he had thought about, believed in, taught, did, stood before him absolutely helpless and in its place was a power, not of the sword but of the soul, not of hatred and of conquering but of love and acceptance, not of condemnation and judgment, of which Paul was full of both, but of forgiveness and truth.

And as we met, I watched the fear, the hate, every false and untrue thing of this great light fall away. Even as his horse clattered off over the stones and down the path away, so did Paul's fear, so did his judgment and his condemning thoughts. And he lay there looking at me, and he said, "What would you have me do?"

I said, "Well first of all, they're not going to let you in that ashram. They are not going to let you in because you are Paul and they know who you are."

He said, "What would you have me do?"

"The only way they're going to get you in there is if you are in need, if you are totally, absolutely helpless and absolutely *no* threat to them whatsoever."

And he said, "But I have no horse. I have no weapons. I have nothing. I can't hurt them."

I said, "But you can see them and you can name them before the Roman magistrate."

He said, "What would you have me do?"

I said, "I would have you be blind, then you can't identify anyone, can you? You can't point a finger and say, 'That man was there.'"

He said, "So be it then," and Paul was blind.

Now, one thing about the Essene community, they were loving, helpful people. "Come on in and let me feed you, clothe you, give you a place to rest, heal you, take care of you." This was their way of thinking. So when Paul approached, at first there was fear. They peered out at him and they saw no army with him, no soldiers. Here was a man groping, calling out, "Help me! Help me!" Ironically, it was the women that took him in. Paul didn't like women. They brought him in and they set him down, and then they sent for the healers.

Now in the meantime, of course, angels had gone into Qumran and prepared these people for the visitation of Paul. The reaction is rather interesting. When the angels came to the seers and to the prophets and they said to them, "We are sending you Paul of Tarsus..."

"What? Are you out of your mind!?"

"Do you believe that God would send you anything that is not a blessing?" Oh, that was a tough question. (Laughter) There was a tough question.

Their instincts, their way of life, their way of believing said, "Of course not," but the human side of them said, "You're sending us *Paul!?*" It was a battle, and herein came faith. "Do we believe what our senses tell us, which is to run, to block him out, to not allow? That is looking backward. That is going back to the old ways. Or do we open the gates, the doors of our hearts, the windows of our mind, and do we take in this man, for God has spoken and we must listen?"

And so, they took in Paul. And they kept him there and they taught him *their* version of me, and they taught him mostly about himself, that he was a Child of God, that any honors or decrees that he had from Rome had no value at all in the realm of the human heart.

In the realm of the soul, there is only one criteria to be met and that is to love and honor yourself and all your fellow human beings—to love God, to seek God with *all* of your *beingness* and to love completely and without conditions. And this is what they were teaching him, as much by what he *felt* there as by what he ultimately began to learn.

When the human Spirit hears the sounding fork of truth, of absolute love, regardless of the personality, regardless of anything else, there comes the response, "Yes, Father, I am here. Yes, I am," and *in* that response, in that moment, that sacred holy instant of truth, the Son of God has come home. Paul heard the words, Paul felt the power, and Paul came home.

As with all humans, at the moment of the encounter, there is this absolute dedication, this absolute, complete commitment that is made and truly, truly felt.

But as with Moses coming down from the mountain and going back into the hordes of people, so coming from the encounter and back into the world, the encounter is sacred and holy, but *living* it becomes the difficult part. Because now you are facing your ancestors again. Now you are facing the old rules and regulations, the old laws of Moses, the old ways of Abraham. Now you are facing everything around you that tells you, "Thou shall not."

And yet, burning within you is this "Yes, you can," this knowing, this loving. And so there are two voices that besiege you: one, the voice of truth; the other, the voice of the past. Because you are conditioned to listen to the past, because you are conditioned to *old ways,* the voice of the past becomes louder and louder and louder and the ability to follow what is within becomes weaker and weaker.

And so Paul, like everyone else, vacillated between the *old* beliefs and between his new encounter. I tell you these things because I want you to recognize that in you is the second sounding fork. In you is that aspect of *response* to truth and to love, whether it be from my words or whether it be from something else; it doesn't matter. When you *hear it,* you will *know it* and it will awaken in you something that you have to follow. You have to follow! You cannot deny it. It will take you where you need to be. It will open for you your own internal truth, your own *ability* to be all that you can be, and then side attractions can't hold you.

Paul went forth and did mighty things! Some of them quite in error but nonetheless, he never faltered. He never stopped to think of his own safety. He just went and he did it. Albeit a lot of the things he did were not what, perhaps in the truth of Spirit, should have been done, but nonetheless he did it with a great conviction.

Every particle of the human Spirit is longing to be free of the limitations that the personality has placed upon it. It is the personality of you that is fearful, the personality of you that is judgmental and condemning, and none so more than toward yourselves. It is that aspect within you that is free that you deny. Now is the time in your time...this age upon your earth is calling out the spiritual, calling forth the truth, calling you to love, love, love, love yourselves, love God, love each other.

Have you noticed that in the last forty or fifty years of your earth life how things have changed rapidly, rapidly, rapidly, rapidly? More progress has been made in the last thirty years than in the previous hundred years upon your earth. Now people of any faith are free.

I want to speak of the mingling of blood because it will help you to understand many things. As I said, the tribe in the beginning, the tribe held people in its bounds. There was no mixing of blood. They interbred rather than to allow new blood to come in. Now it is symbolic upon your earth the intermixing of blood, which means "the acceptance of." Now go to any country on your earth excepting this one and you will find still the *old clan tribe thinking*. There are not too many countries upon your earth where intermixing of races, or intermixing even of different families, is really looked upon with favor. It is done and it is accepted, but there is always that reserve.

But look at this continent upon which you live. How many pure strains of any race is there here? Only those who come in from other countries. Most of the people born in this continent are a mixture. As this beloved instrument says, she is a grand and wondrous mongrel. There's so much of the *accepting* and the taking in and the allowing going on, and especially in this continent, that it symbolizes it is the outer expression of the *inclusiveness* that humankind's consciousness is finally awakening to. It's finally coming up and into where it will *be* that inclusiveness.

When you meet someone who is different than you, you automatically click into the old tribal way of thinking. You immediately notice the differences between them and you, do you not? You may not express it with drawn sword or throwing them out, but you do make note of how they are different from you.

Behold, I tell you a truth: The day will come when you will look upon others and see *no* difference. You will see them in the light of God, you will see them with the eyes of truth and with a heart of love, and you will find that no matter who they are, you know you love them. You may not like their words or like their deeds, but you know that they are one with you. And that is what will make the difference upon your earth.

Do you seek *peace* on your earth? Is this what you seek? A unity of purpose, a community of love, an acceptance of all people everywhere. This cannot be done with the tribal attitude. This cannot be done by looking in the past. This cannot be done by following *old ways*. This can only come with the inclusion of people and their belief systems and where they are at the moment.

Has someone offended you? Then think, "Do I take that offence to me and do I say to myself, 'I am justified to have anger against my brother'? Or do I think, 'They are a troubled soul and they are striking out at me because of their own internal ill will toward themselves; therefore, I will send them love and let them know that they don't have to dwell in that consciousness'?" There is no justification for anger toward your brother. None.

[Gap in recording] ...and so you have hip and leg and back problems. Some of you feel that you cannot take in and digest and internalize the truths that are flung at you from every direction—for God uses every method—and so you have digestive problems.

Some of you feel that you cannot go forth and spread the good news, as it were, and so you have circulatory problems.

Some of you hold an abiding resentment toward others. You feel you have produced—given birth to— problems for yourselves and your mate and so it is manifested in your children.

I will tell you a truth: There is no ailment that cannot be healed by the resolution of the fear within you. If you dwell in your fear, you will never be well, you will never know truth. If you are afraid to assert your own divinity and to claim it and to live it—I don't mean claiming it by declaring it to your neighbor, "I am divine and thou are not," (laughter) but by living it as a proof—then you will find your ills and ails disappear. But it is easier to remain in the hole with the devil that you know than to climb out and face the challenge of being your own God Self.

It is not easy to live constantly in the God Self of you. Not when you are in the world and the world besieges you with its errors and its lies and its deception. It is not easy to remain steadfast in the truth, but that is what is necessary, is to remain steadfast in your truth.

It is *your truth*. It is yours. No one can take from you your truth; it is an integral part of whom you are. You chose to come upon the earth to experience the challenges so that you might assert that truth and conquer.

People ask why is the earth the way it is? Why is there turmoil and pestilence? Why is there deadly diseases? Why do little children be born to have cancer and die? Why? Because the shadow of fear has so engulfed the consciousness of humankind that you *believe* it. You believe you have great unshakable faith in fear. You really believe that life is meant to be lived as a great challenge and that you can never quite win, and that's what you practice daily in your lives. Your own bodies seem to turn on you and not allow you the sweetness of your lives because you believe that your bodies govern your lives. No, they don't. They are the vehicles you wear while you are on the earth. They should be honored as the temples of God because you are the Children of God and you occupy them, but they are not the rulers of your life unless you make them so.

There is a simplicity in Spirit-truth that when lived, un-complicates your life upon the earth. You become enslaved by *things* and as this beloved channel says, "by *stuff*." She and her *stuff*. I said to her one day, "What are you doing?"

And she said, "I'm sorting through my *stuff*."

I said, "Is that important?"

She said, "Well, it certainly is." (Laughter)

How important is *stuff*? Really, how important is stuff? If a thief were to come and take all your *stuff* and with it, your memory of the stuff, would you miss it?

Audience: No.

Jesus: Would you not just go out and get more stuff? (Laughter) That is how unimportant *stuff* is. And stuff takes many forms. It can be an obsession with your appearance. It can be an obsession with how much money you have or how well you are taken care of. It can be an obsession about the physical health of your bodies. It can be a fear that you will be one day left alone and destitute; that seems to be a major fear, especially as the body goes through changes of becoming older.

You have so many packages of *stuff* that you carry around in your consciousness. "What will become of me? How will I live? I don't want to be dependent upon my children." When the prayers are sorted through by the angels, and they *are* sorted through...you talk about stuff! (Laughter) It is a major job. There are angels who do nothing but sort through prayers, and that is a grand truth.

The vibratory rate of the asking that comes up and I would say probably...how much? [Asking Gabriel] Ninety-seven percent, he tells me, is concern about stuff—my job, my marriage, my relationship, my children, my health, my finances. Every now and then a bright, silver, golden, shimmering light comes up and it is a prayer, "Dear God, help me to be who I am in your eyes." That is straight away gathered up by the angels, but all this other stuff is dealt with in the level in which it is asked.

Now I'll tell you something about prayer. You will get back the answer in the exact vibratory rate of the question. And if that question, if you're asking, if your prayer is said with *fear,* then you're going to get an answer back in that same vibration...one of fear. If your prayer is done with the holiness of faith, then you get your answer back in faith, but you cannot get a pure, clear answer from a troubled, mangled question.

It is the power of your feeling nature that propels your prayer. It isn't the words. It isn't anything but the *feeling* behind the prayer, and most people pray in absolute desperation.

Let me put it another way. If you were very thirsty and you felt your mouth was full of sand and you went to a well and you spat in it before you drank from it, would you not get water that had sand in it? So it is with your prayers. Let your prayers be pure.

If you must ask about stuff, then take the stuff up to the level from whence it came. In other words, are you concerned about a job, your income? That seems to be the major concern upon your earth. Not literally, but figuratively, we have warehouses full of bushel baskets of prayers asking about jobs! But if that is your concern, then you are going to keep that vibration down in your *lack of* a job or your unhappiness with a job.

But let us suppose...what do jobs' income represent? Do they not represent the care that is given for your well-being? Is that not what a job does? Is that not what income does? It allows you to live, by your perceptions. It allows you to live. So let us trace back this job, this income. It has to come from a source that is willing to take care of you. What is the source that takes care of you *ever?* God.

Now, God is eternal; God never not is. So, therefore, what have you? You have an unending, not possible to deplete, forever and ever guaranteed Source. The job, the income, is only the outpicturing, the method by which this Source meets your needs. So, when you pray about your Source, it should be in this wise: "My Father, my heart is full of gratitude for the income that You have expressed to me. I give You thanks, for my abundance is full, overflowing with more to share, and I thank You for this that is mine, for what is Thine is mine always. And so it is."

[To a participant] Are you listening to this, brother? Stop crying. There is nothing on Earth to cry about.

When you go to teach, do not look into the past; there's nothing there for you. Rather, take the present moment and its blessing and speak of that and speak from your heart. Speak of the truth of your beingness and you will find they will ask you again and again and again, "Come and give us of your wisdom." But if you let the past interfere, you will be asked only once.

Why am I not healed? Why am I suffering? Because sometimes it is easier to suffer than to take responsibility for one's own self. Sometimes *fear* makes you think that you aren't capable, but you are.

Every one of you suffers from a great dose of fear. Some of you beat yourselves up in auto-motion accidents and suffer greatly thereafter. Some of you are so at war with your bodies that you believe your body trembles in the fear of life when there is nothing in life to fear. Nothing. Nothing.

Some of you believe that you have to do everything in the world and do it right now. Some of you believe that you have nothing of value to offer the world and therefore must allow others to do what they will with you. Some of you believe you have no internal beauty, no truth to share, when you are a living truth. Some of you believe that you are not worth it when you are worth everything...everything.

Most of you think that you are limited and you could think of a thousand reasons why you are limited when in truth, the only limitation that any of you have is what you believe in. Withdraw your energy from your error perceptions and live the truth of your being and you will find that you are free. This is the truth that sets you free, is living in *who you are*...who you are. If you could know how *glorious* you are. Do you think God makes junk? (Laughter) Indeed not.

Of all of the creations that the Father breathed forth, only unto one did He give free choice. Only unto one did He say, "Thy will be done," and that was us, the human element, the divine Children of God.

To each, he gave a unique blessing: he created each one of us different. Why? He likes variety. (Laughter) He also enjoys watching us go forth and create and create and create, and the only thing he longs for is for us to create beauty in our lives—joy, love, love, love—and when we create opposite of that, then we bring in the Law of Consequence.

Now, the Law of Consequence works in this way: Everything has its own vibration—the element of plant life, the element of creature life, the element of human life, of angel life—everything has its own vibration and that vibration works in this way...

I can do what? Write upon the wall? You allow writing upon the walls here?

Participant: The blackboard.

Jesus: Oh, it is written upon.

Participant: You can erase it. You can take it off.

Jesus: Oh, you let me see you do that! (Laughter) What a wondrous example! Behold, she waves her hand and it's gone. (Laughter) That is what you do with fear! You simply...what do you call that?

Participant: Erase.

Jesus: You simply erase it, eliminate it, wave the hand of confidence and its gone. Now, I write upon this with what?

Participant: Chalk. It's on the table.

Jesus: Alright.

Participant: Use the other end.

Jesus: [Draws a cross] I used to do this in sand. (Laughter)

In all living things, in *all living things,* there is a positive current that comes down and there is a negative current that transverses. Purpose of them is this: In the positive, in the downward, in the positive, there comes in the energy of *motion* and motion is what carries things forth, brings them into a becomingness. When something is growing, it is the positive energy that moves it forward. Now that energy comes from the spiritual Source, the *cause* of it, which is God.

The cross part is the negative, and I don't mean negative in an error way, but the negative as you have been taught is the sustaining vibration that keeps life sustained. Otherwise, life would come, be, and be gone. Form would come and be gone. Before it could fully manifest, it would be gone because the vibration of the positive is an action and it moves rapidly.

This part of it, the cross part of it, sustains it and holds it so that the form can manifest. Now this is true of every living thing. From the Spirit, from the Source, comes the life. From the earth upward...what thing?

Participant: On the table. The silver thing.

Jesus: Oh, I can write with this too?

Participant: No, you point.

Jesus: Oh, just point. I have to judge my distance with this one. (Laughter)

From the Spirit up here comes the Source, the energy. From up out of the earth comes an energy that binds the spiritual energy to form. The sustaining, which is cross, represents the taking in of the energy from the air around you, from the ethers, and this sustains this upward/downward vibration and keeps it level, keeps it so that it doesn't dissipate before it takes form.

All things come into being in that way, all things. The energy comes down, the energy is met with energy coming up, and form is created. Then the cross section *sustains* that form.

Now, you use that in your thinking. We all do. We all do. When you are thinking...when you are creating with your thought and your thinking, you're pulling in the energy from above and you're grounding it with the energy from beneath and you're sustaining it with the energy that goes across it.

Now the energy that goes across it...I'm looking in her brain for a word. I have to use what words she knows. Alright. This energy that comes down from the Spirit and up from the earth needs no intervention by you. Your desire calls it into being and beyond that, you have no influence over it. But you have great influence over the cross piece, the sustaining, because it is in *that part* that your thought, your feelings, your beliefs, influence the form that is being manifested.

Let us say that you create in your thinking...you desire to have an experience. You desire to have an experience of joy so you create in your mind what that experience might be. Now in that, you have pulled in energy from above and energy from up here, from the earth. Now, your belief in how that will manifest is in the energy that goes across it. It is in the sustaining energy that your belief system rests, and how you believe it will manifest is how it *will* manifest because this is what sustains it.

If you built a bridge and you used heavy timbers to make the span from one shore to the other but your belief system consisted of little splinters and that's what you would use to sustain it with, would your bridge hold? So it is with what you create. It's what you sustain it with— your attitude, your feelings, how you *believe*—that determines whether or not it holds true to the original idea. Do you understand that?

When you do healing, you are not dealing with the vertical process; you are dealing with the horizontal process within the concepts of the person you are healing. Basic good health, soundness of body, is already *in* the vertical. That's nature's way of creating perfection. But the sustaining belief system of the individual determines whether or not that perfect vertical line is going to remain healthy and strong or whether it will not be sustained.

So when you do healing, you are working with the consciousness of the individual who needs the healing, and if their belief system does not sustain perfect health, even though you touch them and heal them, they will call back to themselves the ailment again or another ailment far worse.

Do you remember the parable, the story in which a man was brought to me and they said he had seven demons? Well, they were demons only inasmuch as he had seven different ailments the matter with him, any one of which could have caused his demise. I healed him and for a short time, he was fine. But then his old fears came back, his old belief system returned, and he drew back to him all of the negative energy that I had cast out of him. And it, in the meantime, had collaborated and brought in more energy with it and so in the end, his condition was far worse than it was before I healed him because he *added* to the negativity and he brought in with that *more* negativity.

That's why healing must be done in the soul, and only the individual can heal their own soul. A healer can cast the ailment out of the body cells but unless the memory is removed from the soul, those body cells will feed on the memory of the soul and re-enact the ailment.

That's why so many times people come to be healed and they are healed in that moment, but their belief system pulls them back into looking back. They talk about how they *used* to be. "Oh, I was so sick. I had this.

I had that. Nobody knows the trouble I've seen." And in so doing, they have regenerated the old cell memory of the illness, of the sadness, of the sorrow, of the beleaguerment— whatever it is—and they will draw it to themselves and it will be twice as bad. This is why sometimes people are healed of cancer and several years later the cancer returns and devours the body. It is because the transverse process in the thinking and the sustaining has been polluted by negative fear thoughts, old memories that are recalled and welcomed home.

Whenever you are repeating a pattern in your lives...and oh, beloveds, you do repeat. Tinkerbell says it's like eating bad food; it will keep coming back. (Laughter) When you do that, you weaken the structure of your spiritual Source, of your *in*flow. That comes purely to you, *purely,* with nothing wrong with it. But it is the vibrational rate of your thinking that determines how it is sustained, so remember that.

I am to ask you questions? No? Oh, you are to ask *me* questions, I guess. That's how it works? Although I have some of my own, but... (Laughter)

Questions

Participant: Good morning. In our working and all— we've been working with Gabriel for years—we know the fears, the big obstacles, and we've been taught about the Angels of Destruction and whatever, and when those of us use it and we ask the Holy Spirit to come in to fill in all the spots, and then the fear comes back... (Sobs)

Jesus: It is this, beloved woman: it is the fear. I shall tell you what your fear is. [To Tinkerbell] Why can't I do that? I am Christ. I can do anything I want. (Laughter)

Participant: I guess you can't.

Audience: Go for it!

Jesus: Many lifetimes back, you were one of several wives of a man who was crossing the desert, and he realized his journey was longer than he had anticipated and he didn't bring enough food so he selected his two favorite wives and the rest of you he left.

Participant: Okay.

Jesus: And you were left with no comfort, no food, no nothing in the desert; you were left to perish. And when you questioned him as he was leaving, "What will we do?" he said, "Take care of yourself," but you found you could not. There were no resources there. And that left an indelible imprint on your soul that said to you, "I cannot take care of myself. I have no resources," and that fear abides with you still.

Participant: (Sobs) How do you get rid of it, because it's in the soul?

Jesus: I can cast it from you, but you...

Participant: But that's not going to help if I bring it back. I want to get rid of it. (Sobs)

Jesus: No, it isn't, but you have to be willing to let go of many treasures—the treasure of not having to support yourself, the treasure of having freedom to rise in the morn when you will, the treasure of not having to answer to any man excepting your own self. These are things you treasure greatly.

Participant: (Sobs) I know.

Jesus: Are you willing to relinquish them for your health?

Participant: Yes.

Jesus: Now you must remember, it is *your* choice. *I* cannot choose for you. Only *you* can choose.

Participant: I choose.
Jesus: You choose?

[Jesus performs a healing]

Participant: Thank you.
Jesus: In seven days you will see a difference. The difference you will see will depend upon you.
Participant: Thank you.

Participant: Beloved Christ.
Jesus: Yes. (Laughter)
Participant: You got me! Could you help us understand how we could maximize the healing ability of the healing of the soul, of ourselves, and of others? And I'm talking about the energy flow coming up...
Jesus: You cannot heal another's soul. Even I cannot heal another's soul. You can cast out, but it is the soul's determination whether it stays cast out or whether it draws back in the old energy. First, work on yourself, brother.
Participant: Okay, I understand that.
Jesus: You must be willing to let go of your stuff, of your treasures, of things that you love to have.
Participant: Okay.
Jesus: And I don't mean your stereo, whatever that is.
Participant: Okay.
Jesus: Or things of that nature. I'm talking about the internal stuff that you hold on to.
Participant: Okay.
Jesus: You have to be willing to relinquish...and I will not name your things because it is between you and God. When you are willing to say, "I give it all. It is no longer

of import to me. I free my soul in the only truth that sets me free and I accept the will of God." That will free you.

Participant: Okay. Could you repeat that when I go to my seat so I can write it down?

Jesus: Did someone write it for him?

Participant: I want it now! (Laughter) Okay. The other question: You talked about prosperity and abundance and you gave us a prayer associated with, of course, incorporating thankfulness. Would you mind repeating that slowly and wait till I get to my seat? (Laughter)

Jesus: Have you no scribe to write?

Participant: You went pretty fast with that, particularly with the latter part of it.

Another Participant: We have it.

Participant: You've got the whole thing? Okay. She says she's we've got the whole thing so that's good. Thank you very much.

Jesus: I'm glad because I don't know what I said. (Laughter) I'd have to go back into the past and I refuse! (Laughter)

Jesus: Beloved friend.

Participant: Beloved Master, it's good to see you. You told us that much of the things that were written in the Scriptures were not accurate.

Jesus: Oh, indeed. That's true.

Participant: I have a request that when we come back from the lunch break, if you could go over some of the things that were accurate, some of the things that you said that they did record accurately.

Jesus: That should take about three minutes. (Laughter)

Participant: Okay, okay. So they interpreted them in a way that they thought the masses would accept them or what they thought was appropriate?

Jesus: What they thought was appropriate. And also, you must remember the differences in language. Different words in different languages have far different meanings, and what may have been recorded accurately originally would have been lost in translation from one language to another.

The Arabic language, which is what I spoke, was recorded in Greek, which was the common language of the era, even through other...outside of Greece even. Most people understood Greek. How interesting today that if you don't understand something, you say, "Its written in Greek." (Laughter) But the most common language spoken by most of the people back then, even through Jerusalem and everything, was Greek. So, in translating from Aramaic into Greek, it lost a lot of its meaning there. Then when you transcribe that into French and English and so forth, a lot of it was lost, not with intent to lose or to change, but simply because of the language.

Participant: So when we read the Scripture, we should take it how?

Jesus: I spoke esoterically and exoterically; I spoke for the common man, whose understanding was very dull, and I spoke for the learned disciple, whose understanding was greater. So in each thing I said, there was two meanings. Is that what you wish me to disclose?

Participant: Yes, on more or less on what *you* meant.

Jesus: What *I* meant?

Participant: Right.

Jesus: I've covered a lot of that this morning, but I can answer that for you.

Participant: Thank you.

Participant: Hello brother!

Jesus: Hello brother.

Participant: Oh, I want to let go of my mind, just for a moment. [Tosses notebook to the floor] I'm going to pick it up again.

Jesus: Your mind or your paper? (Laughter)

Participant: I guess the paper. I have a question. About this cross here, can you say that the transverse represents the free will and perhaps the vertical represents divine will? Can you see it in that way or...?

Jesus: No. The vertical is the Source. That is not under your command. All command you have over that is to draw it *to* you by your desire. Your desire draws in this energy. Beyond that, you have no control over that. The control you have is in the transverse process because that is...the sustaining aspect of it comes from *you*.

Participant: Okay, I see. Also, you spoke about the energy coming up from the earth. Could that be considered the kundalini energy or that energy that needs to sustain the form?

Jesus: The kundalini would be the finer, etheric form, perhaps, of earth energy, but the earth energy is very much what it says—earth energy. Earth is a living thing and her very nature is to sustain and to give birth and to cause to become, so the vibration from the earth would be that which would cause to become... In other words, the energy coming down would be the material to be used. The energy coming up would be the determining factor of the form. The energy going across would be the sustaining of that form.

Participant: Okay, I see. I have one more question: According to the last time Gabriel was here, one of my buddies here had mentioned something that...I mentioned something to Gabriel about spiritual leaders coming and he said something about, "Why did you kill all of them?" and this person seems to think that I was the one who killed Ghandi and all these other people, although I can't imagine myself doing that.

Jesus: In other words, your question is, "Did you kill a spiritual leader?"

Participant: Yes, like Ghandi or any of these other people?

Jesus: No.

Participant: Okay. I just wanted to straighten that out.

Jesus: Part of his feeling of that is based upon your ethnic background.

Participant: Ah...wow. That's interesting. Okay, thank you.

Participant: I have two questions. The first one is on healing. Gabriel was talking about how sometimes someone will have a toothache and they will work on it all night long and be very frustrated because they aren't able to heal it. And he says, "Well, just go to the dentist." And if we're really in touch with the Christ part of ourselves, why would we need to do that?

Jesus: You don't, if you're really in touch, but name me how many people you know who are. That's why you have dentists, because not many people are in touch with their Christ strong enough to do that.

Participant: It very much depends on the dentist though, and Western medicine, as it is right now, is being questioned because some of it is very good and some of it isn't.

Jesus: What would the dentist have to do with your Christ? Nothing, absolutely nothing. He's got his own Christ to worry about.

Participant: Well sometimes you go to the dentist and come out in a great deal of discomfort.

Jesus: You're bringing it down into form. Get out of there; go up. You have the ability within your own consciousness, your own Christ awareness, to heal. The dentist is working with earth hands, taught knowledge, not working from the Christ. So, the dentist, what he does with his *earth* knowledge, with his *taught* knowledge, has absolutely no bearing on anything but your tooth.

Participant: Right. And suppose somebody goes to the dentist and the dentist makes a mess of the job. That means what's going on inside of them isn't...

Jesus: It means that they have agreed with this dentist to go and have their mouth invaded and persecuted because they believe that they deserved to be invaded and persecuted. And what is the mouth? The mouth is the vehicle of food, which sustains them. It is also their vehicle for communication, which opens the way for them to take in others. So therefore, their problem is that they don't feel that they have the right to be sustained, nor do they want to interact verbally or communicate or open the door to allow others in, so how better then have a bad mouth?

Participant: Hmm.

Jesus: A lot to think about.

Participant: Yes. Well, I don't have a problem with my dentist actually. (Laughter) He's okay.

Jesus: I wasn't accusing you of having any problem in that way. I'm just saying that there is a lot to think about in that.

Participant: Yes. Oh, yes. I mean I personally...and I'm sure everybody here would much rather heal themselves than have to go to...

Jesus: No, they wouldn't because that would be taking responsibility and that's why everybody goes to a dentist.

Participant: Hmm. Or a doctor.

Jesus: Or a doctor.

Participant: Uh huh. Mine is a very spiritual man so I like him very much.

Jesus: Then go.

Participant: So you're saying that we don't actually necessarily have to go to the doctor if we're working from the Christ...

Jesus: If you are connected to your Christ center, you don't have to go to any external force or person for anything. But there is no one upon your earth at this time who's *that* connected.

Participant: But we're getting there, aren't we?

Jesus: I do hope so. (Laughter)

Participant: Because you know, sometimes—and I'm sure everybody here has this—you think that you're making progress and you definitely want to be a light for other people so you *think* that you're making progress and people seem to be...

Jesus: But you *are* making progress.

Participant: But then all of a sudden all sorts of things go haywire in your life and you go, "Wait a minute. Maybe I'm not doing what I'm supposed to be doing to..."

Jesus: Can you think of a life where things went more haywire, as you call it, then mine? (Laughter)

Participant: No, but you were...

Jesus: I was what?

Participant: ...able to heal people, at least temporarily.

Jesus: I was able to heal people when they wanted it, yes, alright. But how does that explain what happened to me?

Participant: You chose it?

Jesus: What is your word? Bingo. (Laughter) I was going to say, "boomerang," but that wasn't the right... (Laughter)

Participant: Bingo.

Jesus: And?

Participant: Then how does one measure one's progress? For example, ...

Jesus: You can't. The only way you can measure—and I don't know too many people who can do this—is to take yourself totally up out of the personality, go completely into the Higher God Self, and take a look at where you are. You can do it that way.

Participant: Through meditation?

Jesus: Alright, you just withdraw your energies from the situation and you go up totally into the Spirit God of you. And then you view the illusion beneath you and you see in the illusion what progress you have made by the dark and light spots.

Participant: That's sort of like asking to see the gift in it.

Jesus: Absolutely.

Participant: And about healing other people... I'm sure it has happened to the rest of these people where you're with someone who is very ill or is suffering physically and you want so much to take it away, even if it's only for a moment.

Jesus: Tell me about it. Unless they are willing to relinquish it, which few people are, you can't take from someone what they're desperately holding on to.

Participant: Frustrating. Thank you.

Participant: I don't know how to think about something. I've had an accident, which could be serious from some points of view of looking at it, but then part of me thinks maybe it's really a blessing. It depends upon how to look at it. It's an injury that has happened to my body and so I don't know how to think about it because a part of me, you know, wonders just where am I in my life, in my life progress, how I should be thinking, levels of thought—one think it this way or think it this way, a higher level or lower level. And so this condition is there, which in some ways, you know, in this physical world that we live in, could be dangerous. It's possible. People do talk about it in that way…"This can be very serious, you know. This may be attended to." But then again, maybe it really is a *great* blessing and just leave it be. Why get trammeled up…

Jesus: Shall I tell you what it is? You needed a space to go in which you could think through and make a decision whether you want to stay upon the earth or whether you want an opportunity to leave the earth. And you still haven't made up your mind so you're holding on to that injury until you decide what you want. When you decide to stay upon the earth, the injury will be healed. They will do what they need to do to make it go away. And if you choose not to stay upon the earth, then you will choose to allow the injury to end your physical life. But the choice is yours and that's why you had it happen in the first place, was to give you this opportunity to slowly think it through, and that is its only purpose.

Participant: Which is also the slowly thing through my whole purpose in being here on this planet in the first place.

Jesus: Absolutely. Exactly. Yes.

Participant: Which makes me confront my work and why I do it and what it's all about.

Jesus: It makes you confront yourself.

Participant: Ah, great. Great. Thank you so much. Thank you.

Participant: Greetings, Master. I was very moved, touched, by the expression of the love that Judas had for you.

Jesus: Judas loved me greatly.

Participant: And that touched me too so I thank you for sharing that. My question was very much concerned with the transverse energy, the support and the sustaining energy that we receive, and I'm wondering, would it be symbolic of the energy that comes in through our arms, that part of us that touch into the world?

Jesus: You could put it that way; the hands, the touching... The hands are your instruments of action in many ways. You do many, many things with your hands. Your hands can heal. Your hands can harm. Your hands can grasp in a greedy way. Your hands can reach out in a holy way. I would think that would be a very good analogy...would be the arms, the hands.

Participant: Then to further clarify this, could you give me clarification as to why one would feel a sense of numbness in one's hands?

Jesus: A numbness in any part of the body denotes a rejection of some situation where they don't want to have to *feel* that way.

Participant: So, it's very much a form of fear?

Jesus: Of fear. You have a great fear of *feeling*. You have a fear of being betrayed. And if you feel, if you trust, if you love, if you give of yourself, then you fear that that will be betrayed and you will be left to sorrow again.

Participant: Okay, that's interesting and I can relate to that. On that level again, why is it coming up at this time?

Jesus: Because you are in a transitional position. You are going from one state of consciousness to another. You are learning. You are expanding and growing and there is that aspect of your personality that *fears* what it will *feel* in that growth.

Participant: So it's not necessarily, just...I guess that part of the ego that says, "This is good that she felt this," but it really isn't. It's a transitional state that I'm going through and it's...

Jesus: Never cast anything out as not being good for you. When the child asks for bread, the Father does not give a stone, and when you ask to grow—which you have, prayed ardently to grow, to go past the past—then you must be willing to walk the path of growth and take what you meet upon the path as a blessing, as an instrument of setting you free from the past. So this is not a bad thing, child. It is merely an experience and nothing else.

Participant: Okay, I give you thanks for those words. They are very encouraging. Thank you.

Participant: You have not been a part of my tradition.

Jesus: Oh, I know. Even though we are kin under the skin...I was Hebrew too, you know. I had a Jewish mother like you. (Laughter)

Participant: Was she a good cook? I think that...I'm so touched by all this, I can't stop shaking. I think that what's happened to me has been so dramatic; I've had the highest moments of my life and some of the lowest moments of my life. And last time you were here, you talked about the ability to be able to heal but then people bring back what they try to give up. And I wanted to say to you at the time and I want to say it now that I want to be different. I want to accept it and I really want to ask you for that healing.

Jesus: You are willing to accept the will of God as a blessing and not a curse?

Participant: Yes.

Jesus: As a joy and not a sorrow?

Participant: Yes.

Jesus: As a freedom and not a task?

Participant: Yes.

Jesus: You are willing to be different, even though your family may reject you?

Participant: Yes.

Jesus: Even though they may say, "We cannot let you see the child because you are different?" Do you want it *that* much? Because if that's how much you want it, then so shall it be, but if you allow your fears of not seeing your grandchild, of not being a part of the family, of not being in the House of Abraham, then you will keep your shaking. So you must think deeply, great daughter. You must think, "What is the truth of my being and am I willing to *have* that truth and let go of *anything* else that I treasure?

Remember one thing: Whatever you ask of God, God gives you, and He asks only that you are willing to steadfastly commit to your desires. And then you will find that even the things that you *think* you must give up, that you think you *might* lose, are returned to you a thousand fold and in truth, nothing is taken from you that you treasure.

Participant: Then do I understand you to say that by giving up certain things, I won't be giving them up at all by truly believing in and trusting God?

Jesus: That is true. However, in the interim between the giving up and the receiving back again, there will be a time in which it will seem to you that you are indeed in a lonely place, that you are truly wandering as Moses did. If you can hold to your faith through that interim and recognize that the blessing of God doesn't always appear to be the way *you* think it should appear, then you will find you are healed indeed.

Participant: Will that be within this lifetime?

Jesus: You only have one lifetime. (Laughter)

Participant: It goes from beginning to end.

Jesus: If you desire to be healed, then so be it by the will of God that this child, this fear-filled child, be released of her bondage and in the light of truth and love be free indeed. So it is.

Participant: Thank you.

Jesus: Do we take... Tinkerbell is telling me to get out. (Laughter) Can you hold your question?

***

Lesson

Jesus: I was listening to some of the thoughts that you were having concerning the lesson this morning, and I was listening to some of the ways in which you were *fitting it* into yourselves, into your lives. And most of you are doing pretty good with that, much better than before. So many times words of a language change the meaning of something. My friend asked me before if I would come up and tell the things I said the way I really said them as opposed to how they were recorded. And I gave thought to that and I would have to, I believe you have a term, "paraphrase" many things because of the language difference because I spoke Aramaic and your language is not that.

One of the things that was greatly misinterpreted was when I said, **"Blessed are the meek, for they shall inherit the earth."** That has never been fully understood and I desire to explain that. When I said, "Blessed are the meek," I did not mean blessed are those who are walked upon—and what is your term?...doorways, doormats—or anything of that sort. I was referring to those who are meek before God, those who recognize the power and the majesty and the glory of God and who are humble in that recognition of that, who are meek in the receiving of the love of God, who are not...your modern term, I guess, would be "egotistical" or so into the personality that they do not recognize the touch of God into the Spirit of them.

"Inheriting the earth"—that has been greatly misunderstood as well. The earth is a holy place. It is a very special place, for it is the *form,* solid form, that the ideas of humankind can work out upon in form. The earth is a living thing and to "inherit the earth" means to be able to bring up the blessings from the earth, the vibrations from the earth, the *connectedness* that makes you able to be *whole,* to be *on* the earth but not *of* the earth, to be so centered in your Spiritual Self and yet able to be touched into the earth and act upon the earth in form.

Now when one is "meek" before the power of God, when one recognizes the divinity and the holiness therein and incorporates that so strongly in their consciousness, they "inherit" naturally the blessings of the earth, the power that is in the earth to give life to form and to support the form of life.

So to say, "Blessed are the meek, for they shall inherit the earth," simply means that in your humbleness before God and your recognition of the sustaining power and the love—the divine love, ever the love of God—you inherit the blessings thereof. Now people have always taken that to mean that people who are meek and mild and never speak up for themselves, they're going to end up with the earth, and I've often wondered, what they will do with it? (Laughter)

So it doesn't have that meaning but rather to use and be *aware* of the use of the vibrations that is given from the earth and to be thankful for it and to recognize the *holiness* of that connection because it is a holy connection, very much so a holy connection.

"Blessed are they that mourn, for they shall be comforted." That would sound like one would expect that you should be sad. I was the last person in the world to advocate sadness. Laughter, joy...that's life, so why would I have said, "Blessed are they who mourn"?

Now let us think... When one is growing, evolving spiritually, that means that an aspect of you, like a plant reaching for the sun, is constantly reaching *past what is* to something more. Just as a plant begins as a little sprout and then more—and then yet another, and yet another, and so forth—so that it constantly reaches higher and higher and higher, that is the evolution of the human consciousness, is to constantly to reach higher.

Now in doing so, you have chosen arduous ways. You have chosen to walk through trial by fire, as it were. Do you not think, when you look back over your lives, do you not see how you have created situations that were very difficult and you made your way *through* them? You grew *past* them as a plant grows past its seeming limitations to become more, to bring forth a flower. You grew *past* that, but in the process of going that way, when you were in the middle of your trials, were you not mournful? Did you not sorrow at the pain and the discomfort, the disappointment, the fear? There was a great mourning in you, was there not? There was this longing to be free of it, and while you were in that mourning state, you didn't always see the blessing of where you were, did you?

When you were in the depths of your sorrow, if someone had said to you, "Oh, be thankful. This is a great blessing," you would have thought them cruel and unkind in every way, would you not? So, in looking back and seeing the progress and you recognize that you *did* mourn, indeed you were sorrowful, as a mother giving birth sorrows in the birth pain and yet rejoices greatly at the child she holds afterward and soon forgets the sorrow.

So my words were, "Blessed are you when you grow *past* your sadness, past your mourning, past your trials. Blessed are you, for then you are comforted." When your trials are over and there is peace, then you are in a state of comfort, are you not? Then you are comforted. So "Blessed are those who mourn, for they shall be comforted" is an encouragement to continue on, to keep on trying, to keep on going, to... [To Tinkerbell] I can't use the word "try"? Who sets these rules here? (Laughter)

Audience: Gabriel.

Jesus: Oh. She just said to me, *"He will be upset!"* (Laughter) Ah, angels...no respecter of persons. (Laughter)

You keep growing—is that acceptable?...that is acceptable, alright—you keep growing and you release the mourning, you let go of the sorrow, you let go of the pain, and you go on and you progress.

"Blessed are the merciful, for they shall obtain mercy." This goes hand in hand with "Judge not, lest ye be judged, for with the same measure that you measure, so shall it be measured unto you." When you are merciful, it is a form of compassion, and compassion is very non-judgmental. It is one of the feelings that the human heart can bestow upon another that truly *lifts* the spirit out of the dredges, is to be compassionate, to be merciful.

We are all in need of mercy from time to time. We are all in the need of forgiveness, of being released from the bondage of an error perception. So to be merciful, indeed, does draw to you mercy for yourself.

What would be the mercy of God? The mercy of God is in that He sees no wrong in anyone, not in anyone. If I had brought before his face those who put me on that cross and said to Him, "These are the people who did me in," He would have gathered them to His bosom, loved them, and invited me to join in the embrace. That is the mercy of God—to not *see* what we perceive to be a wrongdoing, to be so full of love that it is impossible not to love.

"Blessed are the pure in heart, for they shall see God." Oh, yes, "the pure in heart"—those who bear no malice toward anyone; those who see the good in even a seeming act of wrong; those whose love is great enough to forgive *at the moment* some slight, some insult, some wrong thought; those who can look upon a wretched situation and say, "Somewhere in this there is a blessing. Somewhere in this there is joy. Something good must come from this." Those are the pure in heart and they *do* see God because they see with the eyes of love and they see and they *know* that it's all an illusion and that in truth, everything is as it should be within the human Spirit.

"Blessed are the peacemakers, for they shall be called the Sons of God." [To Tinkerbell] Can't say "Sons"? Oh...people...children. What is your term, "politically correct"? I don't know that term. (Laughter) This is what she's telling me.

Participant: Something that is acceptable to the masses, being acceptable in the sense of this present moment.

Jesus: I encountered the masses many times. I never found them acceptable. (Laughter)

The "peacemakers"—those who have the ability to be totally non-judgmental in any situation, to see both sides of the story and to believe that both parties are right, to be able to *balance* the extremes, to bring them into balance, and to bring about a peacefulness.

Now that begins within. Before one can be a peacemaker outside of one's self, one must first be at peace *within* one's self, must be willing to relinquish the attitude of war or differences or conquering. They are indeed the Sons...the Children of God.

[To Tinkerbell] Yes, it is a good thing you're here. (Laughter) Angels have such a sense of self. (Laughter) They truly do have such a sense of self. They were created to do one thing and they do it down to a gnat's eyelash (laughter) and there is no aspect of it that is left undone.

The Child of God. What is the Child of God? The Child of God is one who knows his Sonship. The Child of God is one who is so intricately connected to the Father that all things whatsoever they are doing involve God.

When I was a child, I didn't understand people who did not know God because to me, God was such an ever-present force in my life that whatever game—it didn't matter whether I was playing with other children or whether I was by myself or what I was playing at doing— I felt that God was playing *with* me, that there was a joyousness in it.

A *Child* of God. Think of those words...a *Child of God*. To become as a child, absolutely trusting, absolutely without guile, with no hidden purposes, innocent of the thoughts of wrongdoing or evil, as you call it. A child in that there is this knowing that the parent is available, absolutely constant, never failing, never not giving forth of the highest and best.

To be a Child of God in consciousness, one is intimate with God in thought, in feeling. In whatever is being outpictured, there is a sense of the presence of God.

When one is walking through the wilderness with nothing to eat and you are greatly hungered and a thirst, that presence of God can so fill you as to take away your hunger and to quench your thirst. When I said to the Samaritan woman at the well, "This water that you drink of, later you will be thirsty, but the water that I can give you, you will never thirst again." And that is knowing the constancy of God, to being aware in any moment, in any situation, at any point, that indeed, you are *not* alone, that there is that abiding, sustaining, ever-loving presence with you.

You have to practice that every day—ah, every moment—because if you don't, you can get swept away in the earth, in the vibrations, in the mass consciousness, and you can feel that you *can* be alone and you *can* be abandoned and that is not so. So to practice to be the Child of God means to be aware.

"But what if I get angry?" he's thinking. You have to watch yourself because I know your thoughts. (Laughter) I got angry. I lost my patience many times, especially with the twelve who followed me. They tried my patience greatly and it was good. It was good that they did because it kept me from getting arrogant. You know, when you can do anything you want and do it like that, you have to be careful of arrogance. You really do.

You have to be grounded in the Spirit. And when you get angry, that's when you've lost your grounding. That's when you've lost the grounding and you're into the situation and you haven't kept that perspective that "This is what I asked for, this is an illusion, and I can go through this. I can go through this because the God in me is the balance and I will stay balanced and centered in that."

People judge quickly with the five senses. The woman who was brought before me for adultery, the man who wanted her killed was her partner. The reason he wanted her killed was because he was afraid that his wives—*wives*—would find out about it. He had his own wife, but his brother dies so therefore he took his brother's wife because it was believed back then that a man had a right to do that. And then his other brother was killed in the wilderness so then he had three wives. It never entered his mind that the first wife wasn't too happy with this situation, and she frequently was rather terse with him. But this woman that he was with, one of the wives saw him and was going back to the first wife. The first wife always had the final say in the household. Any wife that followed after that was under the dominion of the first wife, and some first wives were not pleasant.

How many of you here are wives? Would you be happy with your husband bringing home two or three others to share his bed? Not too many women are like that. And so he purposefully brought this woman before these others and he accused her of adultery. The interesting thing was that he brought all men; he didn't bring any of the women. He just brought men because he knew every single one of them there was in the same boat, more or less, and so to get *rid* of their sin, they had to get rid of the woman.

When she came, she was so full of fear. You could see it in her eyes this unspeakable fear. This question of, "What have I done that I deserve to die?"

And I looked at these men, who were equally full of fear. "She's going to talk. She's going to tell somebody. She's going to open her mouth and she's going to blab. We have to silence her permanently."

So I knelt down and I wrote the names of all of the men there and the date in which they were with this woman or another woman (laughter) and I invited them to look at what I had written. And they all came and they looked. "Oh."

And I said, "Which one of you would like to cast the first stone?"

And they couldn't. They *could not* because they saw in the writing on the ground their own faces, their own guilt, and they walked away.

And she sat there on the ground for quite a few minutes looking around and then finally she said to me, "Are you going to stone me?"

I said, "No." I said, "But you know, you'd better watch what you do after this. Keep in mind that this was a great lesson for you. Do not be so free with your favors."

And she said, "My lord, I have no other way to live, for my husband divorced me."

Now you have to remember that back then, a divorced woman had two choices: she could go home and live with her parents or a brother if she had any, and if she did not, her only other recourse to earning a living was prostitution. Women didn't have jobs back then.

I said to her, "Go see Mary Magdalene because she can give you work that is not prostitution." And so she did and she became one of the followers. She turned out to be a wonderful cook! A lovely person, a sweet, warm, loving person.

But if you were to bring before yourselves the scapegoat of who you feel is the cause of your anguish, your sorrow, or whatever you're going through, if you were to bring before the eyes of your soul and you were to say, "This must be destroyed or I will be condemned," there is where mercy and compassion come in, because you all have a tendency to blame someone or something else for where you're at and you need *not* to do that, to recognize everybody makes mistakes, and when you get angry, be patient with yourself. Say, "Alright, I lost my grounding for a moment but I'm getting back into it now and I will not be angry."

What about when someone tries your patience over and over and over again? How many times do you forgive them? As many times as they try your patience, because you know why they are trying your patience? Because you invited them to.

Oh, Peter had a terrible time with that. Because Peter's values and his standards by *his* thinking were so narrow and strict and just...it had to be just this way— couldn't be this way or this way—it had to be this way. Peter had a lot of trouble with forgiveness and yet ultimately, the only one Peter ever condemned was himself. And you all have a lot of Peter in you. You condemn yourselves through your condemning of others. Whatever you project out to someone else is the mirror for yourself.

Is there any other part of what I said that you are questioning or I'm not clear on?

Participant: No.

Jesus: Is there any part of anything I said that *any* of you are not clear on? You are familiar with my words, brother. Have you anything to ask of me?

Questions

Participant: I'm a little confused because as I've listened to the Gabriel tapes and tapes of other times when you've been here, I began to believe that God's love was totally unconditional...

Jesus: Oh, it is.

Participant: ...non-judgmental...

Jesus: It is.

Participant: ...and abundance—all abundance is there for our asking if we just let go of our fears and destroy the illusions. Yet today, in response to some of the individuals' questions, I thought I heard you say specifically to one person that as she lets go of her fears...there's some very serious fears there like the loss of a loved one, a child, and you go through a transitional phase, and that goes against what I thought was the understanding, which is if you just let go, the love is there. You're not going to be feeling alone or scared because you've let go of everything and the love is there and nothing matters.

Jesus: That is true, the love is there, but a lot of people call back the old feelings and they have to let go of them again, and then they go a little ways and they let go of more and more. And each time they let go of something more, it comes back less and less until finally they are totally free. Other people are able to let go of everything all at once. It depends upon the individual.

Participant: But when you let go, whether you let go a little or all, there should be no sadness...

Jesus: That's right.

Participant: ...or loneliness...

Jesus: That's right.

Participant: ...because you're really basking in God's love and you understand that you and He are one.

Jesus: That is true but not everyone is able to grasp and hold on to that. Some people can and those are the ones that are healed instantly and their condition never comes back. But then there are those who have that element of doubt, and while they can do it at the moment, they get to thinking afterward about how it used to be and then is when they begin to pull into themselves again the old way of thinking.

Participant: Now when you say, "how it used to be," is it...I mean, you're not giving up anything, right? So...

Jesus: Have you ever noticed that when someone has been through a very terrible time and the time is over and everything is alright now, and they meet a friend and then the friend says, "Oh, how are you?" "Oh, I'm fine now." "Well, how have things been with you?" "Oh, you don't know what I've been through." And they go right back through the old... It's that kind of thinking, beloved woman, that brings back all of the old.

But when you just say, "I'm fine. How have you been?" "I have been well, thank you," and you don't reiterate over and over what has been finished. Do you understand, now?

Participant: Yes, thank you.

Participant: Beloved Master, so good for you to be here with us.

Jesus: It's my pleasure.

Participant: To continue on with that question, if you are having a conversation with someone and you see them...you hear them doing that and you don't want to support them in going back through the past, the story, but yet you are to be accepting of them and realize it's their journey, how would you say...? The question that came to my mind is how can you cut them off but do it so in a loving way where you're not enabling them?

Jesus: One might say, "I know about your trials and I think now you are alright. Why don't we concentrate on that?" and not allow them to go back to the old. If you don't participate, they won't try it.

Participant: Okay. So in the same way, if someone tells you that they are very angry about something and now...

Jesus: They *are* angry at the present, or they *were* angry?

Participant: No, they say, "I'm feeling angry at someone or that type of thing."

Jesus: Listen. Listen to them. Let them talk it out. Sometimes a person will get rid of their anger just by expressing it to someone else. Just let them talk and when it is over, say, "Well, it's over now. Why don't we just bless them and let them be?" They have gotten it out. Now don't take it back. Just let it be.

Participant: Thank you.

Jesus: Are you feeling better?

Participant: Much better, thank you so much. One of the questions I have is when you go through, when you choose our life experiences and you're in a teaching position, is the reason why maybe... You had talked earlier to answer one of the previous questions about compassion and many of the times when we experience things, don't you think if you can go to the depths of feeling it, living through it, experiencing it, and going on, that many times that makes you a more effective teacher? Or do I have that...

Jesus: No, those who teach best teach from a point of experience.

Participant: Right.

Jesus: It's difficult to teach with understanding something you've never been through. But by the same token, don't hold onto *old things*. Don't feel you have to constantly wear the sorrow of yesterday if you are to always be compassionate tomorrow. Once having learned it, then you can leave the experience behind. You know what it feels like; you don't need to go back there. Does that make sense to you?

Participant: Yes, it does. That makes a lot of sense. Thank you.

Participant: Sometimes we, out of fear, act in patterns that are so self-destructive—hurts our health, our relationships—and I think...I know for myself, we lose sight of what the underlining fear is. Can you give us some guidance, how we identify what this belief is, what the illusion is, so that we don't have to go through these patterns?

Jesus: Illusion will give you only momentary comfort. It will give you regret. Illusion gives you a false sense of well-being that quickly dissipates in the face of any challenge. When you feel unsure, when you feel afraid, then you can know you are in an illusion. When you have a sense that I'm not well or I'm not safe, then you know you are in an illusion.

But when you feel the joy of God and when you feel secure, when you can say, "God's walking with me through this; I'm not alone and I'm okay and this is going to turn out alright," then you know you are in your connectedness. You can judge by the fruits of your labors.

Is there joy in your life? Are you content? Do you feel a sense of beingness that brings you an aliveness that is beyond the physical? Or are you just going from day to day?

Participant: Do you think we have to be able to label what the underlining fear is or belief is to change it? Because sometimes I think I'm not conscious of it.

Jesus: No. No, I don't... Fear is fear, and it doesn't matter what *form* it takes; it is fear. So to eliminate the fear, you don't necessary *have* to know why you have it. Always knowing why of something isn't always the answer. There is the rock of faith, the sureness of knowing that "No matter what is happening, I'm alright and I'm going to come out of this okay." You have to believe that wherever you are, you are truly alright.

Participant: I was wondering when you were gathering your disciples around you, particularly the twelve who were closest to you, with all the people around you, why those twelve?

Jesus: What about those twelve that drew them together? First of all, before we even came to Earth, we all agreed—that's the higher level—everyone agreed what they would do. I knew each man had something in him that *when* it was awakened and when he would *live* it, he would be a power upon the earth to bring people out of the past and into the present moment.

I knew that each had a wonderful gift. They didn't know it, but they had a wonderful gift. And there was that *in* them... They all had something that each part of what they had—what each gift was—coming together, made a wholeness. Plus, they chose to have the experience.

Participant: You also mentioned that in your life at that time, you spoke a language called Aramaic, which is no longer spoken. And I'm wondering, was it similar to what is known as Hebrew today? Was Hebrew also spoken at the time?

Jesus: Oh, yes. Yes, very much so...Hebrew, Aramaic, Greek. The Aramaic language has changed considerably, but there is some of what the way I spoke it at that time, there is still some of it upon the earth in mountainous areas and remote places. As your earth grows smaller, it becomes lesser so. But old languages have a tendency to be transformed and transformed and transformed until finally the original seems to have been lost. But there are still people in the hills who speak the original.

Participant: So is Aramaic then considered a regional dialect?

Jesus: Yes, there's many dialects among the Aramaic language, depending on what section you're in as to what dialect you get.

Participant: Okay. Is it related at all to Hebrew or is it separate from Hebrew?

Jesus: There are root words that are the same. There is the guttural sounds that are very similar. I would think, even in your modern day, that anyone who spoke Aramaic would also be able to understand, if not speak, Hebrew.

Participant: Thank you.

Participant: Did the *Course in Miracles* come from you?

Jesus: Oh, absolutely! She was a tough customer, you know. She didn't believe in me.

Participant: I know.

Jesus: That's what made her so good because she never got into the emotional part of it. She never got, "Ahh, Jesus is coming to me. Oh, this is so wonderful. Wait until I tell my neighbors." It was like, "You're who?" (laughter) and that was wonderful. That was wonderful.

Participant: Thank you.

Participant: If we're supposed to be in the present moment and suppose somebody says, "Well, how are you?" and you're not feeling so great, are you supposed to answer, "I am well," if it doesn't come from your...?

Jesus: A good way to say is, "In truth, I am quite well. However, at this time, it appears that I have a headache or I have this or that, but in truth, I am really quite well."

Participant: Alright.

Jesus: Don't get truth confused with reality. They're not the same. (Laughter)

Participant: Right.

Jesus: Truth is truth. Truth is you are the Child of God, you are Spirit wearing a body—that is the truth. Reality is this body is going about, the personality is taking it here and there, and it's mixed up with the illusion. So reality is what *appears to be happening at the moment,* when truth is *not* what's happening at the moment. Do you understand that?

Participant: Yes.

Jesus: Sort of...

Participant: No, I understand it. It's sometimes...I mean if you have a splitting headache and a thousand people coming after you and screaming and wanting your attention...

Jesus: Children can be like that.

Participant: Yeah. Or needy people in general who need of your energy.

Jesus: Like your sister? (Laughter)

Participant: (Laughing) Actually, I never even thought of her...perhaps. (Laughter) Well, sometimes you do kind of lose a little bit of that focus of...your body starts kicking up and you're aching and old conditions start coming back.

Jesus: Then find a place, a little corner by yourself, and you go and you curl up there and you say to your body, "I truly love you. You are the vehicle that God has given me to use and I bless you, and I'm going to let you rest here and just be still and heal." And you say to your mind, "You don't have to answer anybody's questions. You don't have to answer anything. You just can bask in the knowingness that you are an instrument of God, and I'm going into my Spirit Self where all is truly well and I'm going to let the two of you just rest."

Participant: Thank you. I have one more question: Gabriel said he learned his English in England and that was pretty obvious to me the first time I heard him because he has an accent and Penny doesn't have an accent, at least not that kind of an accent. Where did you learn your English?

Jesus: Here.

Participant: That's what I thought.

Jesus: I connected to her many years before she even knew that this was going to happen and I worked with her a lot in her sleep state. I became familiar with how she thinks, how she feels, how her brain works. And therefore, I was able to make the transitional a lot more easily than Gabriel.

Plus, the fact, she's human...I'm human. Gabriel's an angel. There is a difference, such a difference. Gabriel had to adjust to human vibration. He had to learn to manipulate a body. I never had a problem moving her body because I know how to move a body; I had one. Gabriel has never had a body. He's borrowed them from time to time, as he says, but for him to work in the human element required an extreme amount of adjustment on his part—much more so on his part than on hers.

She could be worked *upon*. She did not know how to work; she only knew how to allow the work to be. I didn't have that problem because I knew how to commun... Gabriel would communicate with thought so *words* to him were a whole different thing. He had to learn how to manipulate her mouth to make words. He had to learn the *meaning* of words. As you all know, he didn't always have a clear idea of words. I didn't have that problem because I knew how to speak from my own experience. Gabriel did not.

The learning process was extremely different. His was much more difficult than mine because he was working with a non-angelic form. Now the vibrations of angels are very different than the vibrations of people, and their method of communication, their method of doing everything, is just very different. It would be like comparing vegetables and fish. You're not going to plant a fish in the ground and grow more fish. So, his work with her took much longer and he had to work much more ardently with her than I did. And I am used to her; I've known her a long time.

Participant: Did you speak other languages too? She did at that time. Okay, so you've been with her for more than one lifetime.

Jesus: (Chuckling) Oh, yes. (Laughter)
Participant: Okay, that's all. Thank you.

Jesus: Oh, here she comes with the list.
Participant: Yes. Okay, here we go. Number one: How did you heal? What process did you use?
Jesus: How did I heal? What process did I use? I used whatever process was particular to the individual and some methods, some ways, I healed by working with them in their mental process, especially with a person who had a lot of tangled thoughts, was unclear. I worked with people who had severe illnesses through their soul, through their willingness to go into their soul and recognize that they didn't have to suffer.

It depended on what I was doing with who as to what I actually did at the time. Some people could respond by simply laying my hands on them and they were open to whatever…"Here I am, heal me," and anything I did with them worked because they didn't have any preconceived idea of what I should be doing.
Participant: The second one you answered earlier. What was your biggest disappointment?
Jesus: People.
Participant: Okay. What was your greatest joy?
Jesus: People. (Laughter)
Participant: How do you answer so many prayers at the same time?
Jesus: Oh, I don't. I'd never get any free time.
Participant: Sounds like somebody else I know.
Jesus: Prayer is answered the moment it is expressed. People have this idea that you have to wait a long time for prayer to answer. Actually, prayer is self-answering. When you generate a *need,* the supply is instantaneously

created. As the need is expressed, the answer to the need is there. You don't need anything in the middle. A sincere prayer to God, "Dear God, please help me"—instantly, the help is there. Then it is a matter of the human consciousness taking *in* that help and recognizing it in whatever form it comes...in whatever form it comes. And recognizing this is the help, this is alright; I shall not judge the help that comes. A lot of people judge away the answer to their prayer. Because it doesn't *look* or *seem* or *feel* like what they thought it should, they discount it as not being...as the answer to their prayer.

Participant: If you could summarize in one sentence your best advice to us who are still in physical form, what would that advice be?

Jesus: Love God, love yourselves, love each other, and be joyful.

Participant: If you had to do it all over again, what things would you have changed about your life on Earth?

Jesus: The Crucifixion. It was totally unnecessary.

Participant: When people pass over to spirit and desire to meet with you, do they get to meet you soon?

Jesus: Yes. Yes.

Participant: That's the end of the list. (Laughter)

Jesus: That's the end of her list?

Participant: Thank you.

Participant: Hello. It's very nice to be in your presence. We hear a lot about the twelve male disciples. I'd love to hear about the women who were your followers.

Jesus: Oh, there were a lot of women who followed, a lot of women who learned, a lot of women who went forth and taught, many of them as powerfully and as influentially as the men, but they were written out of your Scriptures by a male-dominant world.

There was Mary Magdalene, who went forth throughout Europe. There was Joanna, who looked faithfully after my mother until her time of transition and also taught. There was my mother, who went forth... You know, my mother was a very determined woman. And she went forth and she taught in places that other people would not have gone, especially other women would not have gone. But her whole attitude was, "He is my son and *he* can do anything and therefore *I* can do anything." And she had that authority; my mother was a very strong authority figure. She even made *me* toe the line.

And there was several Mary's. There was Miriam— Miriam with the music, Miriam who had the voice of an angel that could sing and often brought to people who would not listen to a spoken word the truth in her songs. There was Marguerite—small, dark, so full of fear when she first came and yet so full of truth and courage. She went forth into the darker continents and taught there. Oh, there were many. There were many.

Participant: Thank you.

Participant: Beloved Master.

Jesus: You and the other gentleman bow. Is there a reason that you...?

Participant: The microphone.

Jesus: Oh, I see. Alright. Alright.

Participant: After your time when you were on Earth, there started the forms of religion and all that have carried on to this time. In this current time now, thinking of the groups we have here and what we've taught, are there any suggestions on the best way to carry on or to teach today?

Jesus: Live it. Live it. That is the best way to teach, is to *live* it. You can get up and you can preach, you can heal, you can form prayer groups, you can do anything, but *living* it, therein is where the reality of it comes through. Therein is where the *truth* of it will manifest, is in the individual *living* of what you're doing—living it. And not letting anything distract you or take you from that. Always be absolutely *confident* in *who* you are—the Child of God—and go with that kind of courage…just living it.

Participant: Thank you.

Participant: Beloved Master, I have a question about love. I know we're all one and while I have an innate respect for all life, I perceive that there are differences in the types of love that we experience. And I know I love my children…

Jesus: Even the one who gives you all the problem?

Participant: Yes, because she's been my greatest teacher.

Jesus: Ah, yes! Yes. (Laughter)

Participant: But I do have difficulty when I look at a person—and I realize this is being judgmental—who does not appear to be on the path. I know they're learning lessons but if they are using words and talking about robbing and beating people up and that sort of thing, I look at them and I say to myself, "This person is a Child of God," and I don't feel that love here. I have respect for them in their process but I can't say that I really feel…I certainly don't feel the type of love that I have for my children, but what do we need to come *to* in that process of loving everyone?

Jesus: Love is always filtered...love from your Spirit is always filtered through your personality. When you say you love your children, you love them because they are your children in this lifetime.

Participant: Right.

Jesus: But in other lifetime experiences they were not your children and yet you interacted with them just the same. Some of them you loved; some of them you despised. Now they are your children. You brought them forth from your own body so they are your creation, in a sense, and one always protects one's creation, whether it be a child or a better creature trap or whatever you call those things. One reaches out and collects to one's self that which you feel is a product of your own doing.

The people who...the person you just described is not a product of *your* own doing at all. They are a Child of God, as you are, but they are not connected to...they are outside of your tribe, so you are harkening back to the old way of thinking, "Not of my tribe. Get away from me. You are not a part of us."

Now, that has gone from the actual tribal delineation, broadened out into judgmental attitudes toward people who are different. This person is very different then you. You wouldn't go and plot to rob and kill. They can plot and rob and kill so therefore, they are out of your tribe of what is acceptable to you. So therefore, they are not acceptable because they don't belong to your tribe.

In this instance, you would have to, first of all, recognize you are using the old tribal thing. Secondly, recognize that as a Child of God, that's the past. That has no part of you any longer. And there must come from you an inclusiveness. Now this doesn't mean you say to yourself, "Well, I just love that murderous bank robber," (laughter) but you do say to yourself, "Within that murderous bank robber is the Child of God who is as holy and as pure as the day God breathed it forth, and from the God Self of *me* to the God Self of them, I offer love. My personality cannot love their personality and that's alright because the God of me loves the God of them."

Participant: So that is like a type of respect for the inner God?

Jesus: Yes.

Participant: Okay, I have one more question. While I realize the disciples chose and you chose on some level their method of death, was the suffering that they chose...for instance, Peter, did that serve a purpose other than something in his own process?

Jesus: Suffering serves no purpose in the sight of God. However, the human consciousness feels it must suffer to atone. The disciples who chose martyrdom, as you call it—and there were many of them who did, even Judas who was murdered chose that ending—chose it because *I* set the example. Unwittingly so, but I set the example. And they felt in order to truly *follow* me, they had to make the ultimate sacrifice of being crucified or beheaded or burned alive.

It was their process of...part of their concept of the process of becoming. Like myself, they recognized afterwards that it wasn't necessary, but at the time they felt vindicated of any wrongdoing they may have ever done by the way they died. In other words, it was their sacrificial lamb upon the altar.

Participant: So it was part of the consciousness of that time?

Jesus: Of that time and of that individual.

Participant: And Gabriel has told us that we can always learn our lesson with joy and if it is our intent to do that, does that sort of come about or...?

Jesus: If it is your intent to suffer or to be joyous?

Participant: To be joyous, consciously in this mind right here.

Jesus: You practice being joyous. You practice it. How?

Participant: Is that different from living it or...?

Jesus: No, because you begin practicing and as you practice, you find you're living it. But you have to make a concentrated effort at first to be joyful and then, as you do, you recognize...even times when you're too tired. When you're too tired to be joyful... [Referring to a participant] When you're too tired to be joyful, you can say, "My physical body is weary but the *soul* of me sings the praises of God and I am *joyous,* even though I'm going to go take a nap." So while you're napping, be joyful in God. Oh, that works for you too! You love to nap. One of your favorite things is napping. That's true of both of you.

Participant: I don't get it.

Jesus: No, but you love to nap.

Participant: Yes, I do love to nap.

Jesus: And so does this beloved one. I'm glad you asked that question. (Laughter)

Participant: One more quick question. I often, in my prayers, ask for blessings for Gabriel.

Jesus: Oh, Gabriel is richly blessed!

Participant: Well, I mean is that not a moot point? I mean, how would God bless an angel?

Jesus: I would think rather than asking for blessings for Gab... [To Tinkerbell] I know what I'm saying. She's saying, "Watch what you're saying!" (Laughter) Rather than asking for... Gabriel is already filled with blessings because he is what he is. He is such...so filled with love. Rather to say to God, "I *thank* you for Gabriel. I appreciate him so much." That would affect Gabriel. That would be like a warm caress to Gabriel.

Participant: Okay, thank you.

Participant: Beloved Master, I'd like to ask a question about the ten lepers who you healed, and one came back to thank you and the other nine, you said, "It would return to them." And you said that not because they weren't coming back in gratitude but because you knew that their thinking was...

Jesus: Would revert back to the old.

Participant: ...would revert back to it. And the one you did heal sustained the healing so that he remained healed.

Jesus: Yes, he did.

Participant: The other question I have is the Apostle's Creed, originally written—I read the other day and I just wanted to know if this is true—that the original Apostle's Creed did *not* say anything about descending into Hell. Is that true?

Jesus: I don't know; I didn't write it. (Laughter) I believe...on the ethers is the essence of what your question would be. To descend into Hell is to descend into form because form is limiting. This is the only hell there is, is what you're in right now. This is it. There is nothing over there that at all comes anywhere near close to what is here upon the earth.

The limitation of the body, the limitation of activity, the limitations that the body represents in any way is confinement and confinement is hell to a Spirit that was born in absolute freedom. It would be like taking a great bird—[to Tinkerbell] thank you—a great eagle and putting it in a little tiny cage and making it live its life there when it *knew* it could fly but it had no *way* of flying. And this is what the human body does—it cages the free Spirit of you.

However, the body is also a servant and allows you experiences that you could never have without it.

Participant: Okay, thank you.

Participant: Master, the story that has me always to remember...it's the healing part where the woman touched your robe and you said, "WHO TOUCHED ME!?" and they said, "Master, what are you getting so excited about?" And you said, "Never mind. Who touched me?" And the woman had to come forth. Now, that to me, that story, when I live in this world, I don't know if anyone else in this room they know what I'm talking about... That's real, it happened to you, and it's true.

Jesus: It happened but not in that way.

Participant: Oh well, this is how *I* had gotten it, from the Bible.

Jesus: When I was preparing to do a healing, I had to do internal work and I was doing internal work for a child I was going to see. As I was in the crowd, we were walking along and they were chatting and going on and I was very much within myself, preparing to approach this little child, and this woman, whose presence I was aware of...I was aware of her need but I knew at this moment I had to go first to the child. That was where I was bound. Then I could come, turn, and deal with her, but I was headed...but she reached in... Now, you know about auras?

Participant: Yes.

Jesus: She reached into the aura, into my aura, and it wasn't my garment that did the healing, it was the aura that did the healing. She reached into my aura and she took from me part of that healing, which was no big deal because I just pulled in more, but I knew it went out of me from behind and I turned and I said, "Who touched me?" I didn't say, "WHO TOUCHED ME!?" (Laughter)

Participant: I love it, I love it, I love it!

Jesus: I just said, "Who touched me?" because I knew that in the touching there had to be a follow up, there had to be a closure to that.

Participant: Alright. Okay.

Jesus: And Peter said, "What? In this crowd? Who touched you? What, are you crazy? Could have been anybody!"

Participant: That's the real thing too. Okay.

Jesus: And I stopped and I said, "No, I need to know who touched me," and she stood there and she said, "It was I." And I went over and I lay my hand upon her and I made a closure to the healing and then I went on my way.

Participant: Alright.

Jesus: Taken out of context, it's not the same.

Participant: I know. That's why we're so lucky that you're here and I thank you so much that we can be able to have this with you.

Jesus: You're very welcome.

Participant: I don't want to take too much time away from other people. Thank you again. I love you.

Jesus: I love you.

Participant: Beloved Master, I have another question about...now you're telling us the best way we can teach is through the example of who we are. Does that same thing hold true in little children?

Jesus: Oh, yes.

Participant: A little child that is very loving, very kind, very giving of himself...

Jesus: Your son?

Participant: A child of disease, can he...can he...?

Jesus: He is not diseased; he is distressed. From other lifetimes he brought with him much distress, much distress. As he grows, his distress will decrease and he will be well. You think he will not survive?

Participant: I never had that feeling when I met the child. We're not talking of my son.

Jesus: No.

Participant: We're talking of the other child. Can...?

Jesus: This other child is distressed, greatly distressed. Affirm always to this child how it is loved and needed. But the child only must make its decision whether to stay or to go, but it needs to be assured that its environment is a safe place to be. It doesn't always feel safe.

Participant: Thank you.

Jesus: Can you understand that?

Participant: Very much so. Is there another way that we can help with the whole situation or it just again through teaching by example?

Jesus: Teaching by example and when you are with the child or when you are not with the child, each time you think of the child, affirm its environment is a safe place to be and it will become so.

Participant: Thank you.

Participant: I want to take this opportunity to resolve a debate, a theological debate, that has gone on for several centuries in my former country, India, to do with your disciple, Thomas, the doubter. Because I belong to an old Christian community that has its origins with—we think, according to legends—with Thomas coming, but they say it's legend and there isn't any real factual information.

Jesus: What is the legend that...?

Participant: Thomas, the doubter...

Jesus: Yes.

Participant: ...came on a trade ship from Syria to the state of which is now Kerala, the kingdom of Malabar, and...

Jesus: In India?

Participant: In India and was invited to preach in the king's court...

Jesus: Yes.

Participant: ...and ten of his ministers...

Jesus: Yes.

Participant: ...became converted and married and formed what was called the Syrian Christian Community.

Jesus: Yes.

Participant: But there is no factual information so it's always discussed and presented as legend, and it is a theological debate...

Jesus: No, it is not legend; it is truth. Thomas did do that.

Participant: And then did he go to Madras and...

Jesus: Yes.

Participant: ...die a martyr's death in Madras?

Jesus: Yes, he did. Yes, he did.

Participant: Thank you.

Jesus: Thomas's concept... Thomas was a very physical person. Thomas had to believe through his five senses. He believed in the miracles he witnessed only because he could *see* them. He totally missed the concept behind the miracle and it wasn't until later that he began to realize the truth behind what *appeared*. He began to see the truth behind that and as he began to see that, it filled him with great joy because all the while Thomas was with me, he would sit back and he would watch and he would think, "He'll never do that. He *did* do that! Oh!" And he would sit with me quietly and he would question, "How did you do that? But if you did that, then why didn't this?"

He had an extremely analytical mind. It all had to be where A went to B and B went to C—is that your word?—and so forth, where the others, what they couldn't comprehend, they believed on faith. Thomas found it difficult to believe with faith. It had to be concrete. He had to see it. So when his internal Self began to open and he began to see with faith, he was joyous, extremely joyous, and the first thing he wanted to do was go out and tell everybody. And so he traveled forth and he did that. Yes, he did go to your country.

Participant: I thank you for being here today. I've learned a lot.

Jesus: I'm glad.

Participant: My question is, and it's probably a simple answer, but how do you make amends to someone whose rejection you have felt for a lifetime?

Jesus: The person that you are referring to is using that as a sense of power. Do you understand what I'm saying? If you do not feel it necessary to have their approval, they will lose their sense of power and they will find that they do not really reject you after all, but in your *need* to be accepted by them, you place yourself in a position to be abused, as it were, psychologically.

The way to end this is, first of all, to recognize that you are valid *without* their approval. You don't need it. It isn't important. Their approval is only their and your opinion of what is necessary to make you a whole person, and their approval isn't required for that. Then you go the next step and you say, "I love them and somewhere in the recesses of their beingness, they love me and when they are ready to accept that, I will know it and it will be well."

Participant: So is the forgiveness, the amend, necessary to make?

Jesus: No. They will forgive you only when they are... First of all, understand forgiveness. Forgiveness is not for the person you are forgiving; forgiveness is for yourself. So, their lack of forgiveness of you has nothing to do with you, absolutely nothing. That's *their* concept of who and what they are. You already are forgiven, if there was even any reason to be forgiven in the first place. It has already happened.

Participant: Thank you very much.

Participant: Good day, Master. My question involves the cross and how you said the Source comes in, Mother Earth comes from below—that I can understand. When you're trying to sustain...I think we all have the problem of sustaining. I know you're telling us truth will help us sustain. Are there any easy, practical things we can do to sustain?

Jesus: It's all easy. In the sustain... First of all, recognize that the sustaining aspect comes from the God Self of you. It is *your* energy that you are pouring forth to sustain whatever it is you are sustaining, and your idea of who you are is going to greatly affect the kind of energy you put forth into anything.

So when you feel a weakening, when you feel that you are putting little chips of wood instead of the beams underneath it, then is when you need to say, "Father, help me to maintain that which is truth." That's all you have to say because the truth of your being is the beam, not the splinter. Just say that prayer.

Participant: Thank you.

Participant: I have a question about the Atonement, as related to the Course in Miracles and/or consciously getting home. What is the Atonement?

Jesus: The true Atonement is when you recognize that there is nothing to be forgiven for, nor is there any ill that has been done *to* you. It's when you recognize that *all* of it was just an *illusion* and that in truth, you never left home to begin with and no one has ever done anything to you, nor you to them, that requires forgiveness. That is the *ultimate* forgiveness, is when you recognize that there is no reason to forgive.

Participant: Okay. Also, I realize that there is a lot of people behind me with questions and things like that, but is there any more of a message that you want to give us above and beyond the questions that maybe we're keeping you from because of all of our questions?

Jesus: No.

Participant: Thank you.

Participant: I'm so touched by that story of the woman who touched you, into your field, and I experienced that in my life now with my students, that they reach in and they touch this place and because I'm new to this sensation, I feel that it's almost like I've been violated by a few and there has been some betrayal. But my friend beautifully says, "There's an open wound there and that has to be cauterized," and when you just said that, he said to me...he just spoke about that closure. That's what we were talking about.

Jesus: Yes.

Participant: So if somebody has, in our perception, betrayed us... You went and you put your hands on this woman, but what if that's not the appropriate thing to do? In other words, there has been a parting. So how does one come to that closure?

Jesus: When you cannot physically touch for whatever reason, you can still spiritually touch from heart to heart. To make a closure with someone you are not physically close to or in a way able to go and touch, you simply go within yourself and you envision two beams of energy, yours and theirs, coming together and meeting and as they meet, they form a perfect heart, which is symbolic of love. And that's all you need to do.

Participant: And what can one do in order to avoid that from happening? In other words, this person reached into your aura...is there anything that one can do to avoid...?

Jesus: You can close your aura, close it down and pull it in to you.

Participant: And that doesn't stop you from offering your love?

Jesus: No.

Participant: Okay, thank you so much.

Participant: Greetings, and thank you for the touch. I've been asked to come up and ask you about Pope Joan, regarding the book, and to ask if we could have some more definite dates or something that we could research on that subject?

Jesus: Pope Joan was only a Pope for about two years. They couldn't bear the thought of a woman being in the...well, they just couldn't bear the thought of a female Pope. You know, she didn't go in there as a female; they all thought she was a man.

Participant: I wondered about that.

Jesus: Oh, yes. She shaved her head and she was of a rather masculine appearance. She was a rather large-framed woman for the day and time and rather brusque in her manner—very commanding, very commanding presence—so she simply shaved her head, which women would not have done, and presented herself as a man.

Participant: Who did she succeed?

Jesus: I don't know. I don't keep track.

Participant: Okay.

Jesus: You know that whole Pope thing... [To Tinkerbell] I can say what I want! (Laughter) That whole Pope thing was a great misunderstanding. It all started with the idea that I said to Peter, "You are a rock and upon this, I will build my church." I never said any such thing. I did say to Peter, "You are rather hard-headed!" (Laughter) No, this is true! I said, "You are rather hard-headed and upon this stubbornness, you will build for yourself an edifice that you may one day regret."

Participant: Ah, the regret part didn't come through.

Jesus: Peter...I loved Peter deeply, but Peter and I had a constant conflict because while on the one hand, he loved me, on the other hand, he was one of my biggest challenges. But Peter...Peter was a powerful man, very powerful man, and his power was sometimes misconstrued as wisdom. It took Peter a long time to become wise. But when Peter said to me, "Thou art the Christ,"—he said that, he recognized that...yes, he did—but he knew it with his head and not with his heart.

And I said to Peter, "You must learn to love."

"I do love."

I said, "Peter...*love*."

"I do love."

Many times I confronted Peter. You know, Peter would throw every woman he met out of the synagogue. When we would hold...when people would come, he would be the first one...he's out there..."You get back, you get back. No, no, no...you come up front. You get back." I mean he had all the women in the periphery around the back.

Then I would come along and say, "You, you, and you, come up here," and Peter would take issue with me.

And I said to him, "Peter, why are you so hard-headed? Why don't you see?" but it was picked up as being, "Peter, thou art a rock." He *was* a rock. He truly was. He *meant* well. His intentions were as pure as the driven snow. He just couldn't get it all together.

Going back to Pope Joan, I am told that it was somewhere around in the thirteenth century.

Participant: Okay. Okay. We'd like to do some more research on that, which was why we were asking.

Jesus: Well, good luck. (Laughter)

Participant: Okay, thank you.

Jesus: You really should get into the archives beneath the Vatican. You could find out all kinds of things. The only thing you would have to learn is to read Greek,

Hebrew...things like that. Nothing's written there in English, excepting of later times.

Someone: Do they let people in?

Jesus: I don't know that they would *let* you in. (Laughter)

Someone: So how *do* we get in?

Jesus: I'm not going to publicly declare that. (Laughter) I would have this beloved person in jail.

Participant: Beloved Master, thank you for being here. It is truly a joy for me to be here today. My question is a simple one. Would you consider coming back and doing a lesson for children?

Jesus: Coming back in the flesh you mean?

Participant: No.

Jesus: Or coming back to channel?

Participant: Yes...or both.

Jesus: I will think on that on how that might be worked. I'm not sure they would understand who I was.

Participant: Okay. My son has listened to Gabriel and I know he would be thrilled. Thank you.

Participant: Beloved Master. I'm wondering about... you said a moment ago that, you know, you have free time where you are that isn't here right now?

Jesus: (Laughs) There is no time. I'm free whenever I choose!

Participant: That was my question. And since we are, at this juncture, living the illusion that time is, and in our reality verses our truth, it seems that certain things in our time available in our day are certain requirements—to make a living and to take care of our bodies and take care of our abodes, as you call them. How in your day and time was that handled by you because you had several responsibilities, many of which I'm sure we can't even fathom now? You didn't have to drive a car anywhere or anything like that.

Jesus: I walked.

Participant: I understand.

Jesus: Except for my little stint on the donkey. (Laughter)

Participant: Oh! I was going to ask because I thought you showed up on other continents sometimes. You didn't do that? That was a...?

Jesus: I showed up what?

Participant: I was lead to believe that sometime you...

Jesus: I just appeared?

Participant: You just appeared?

Jesus: Oh yes, I did that.

Participant: So that was a different kind of a vehicle to get there, I assume? You just sort of showed up?

Jesus: So your question is, "How did people deal with time?"

Participant: Yes.

Jesus: For one thing, they didn't live at the fast pace that you live at today. Their day began when the sun rose and it ended when the sun went down. And very few stayed up after sunset because the only light they had was candles and candles were sometimes at a premium. It depended where you were and what their work day were. They worked very hard, they did everything by hand, so there was no such thing as spare time back then.

Participant: Is there something you might suggest that we eliminate? You just mentioned our fast-paced time.

Jesus: Oh, all your stuff—your *attachment* to stuff, to schedules, to having things. You could all live much simpler than you do and be quite happy.

Participant: And in order to do that, it appears to my temporal mind right now that we'd have to get in agreement with everybody else to agree to that because we interact with other people, you know, in our day because of the society we've created.

Jesus: But when one begins to live simply, those around them begin to live simply, and then those around them begin to live simply, and the first thing you know, you've got...

Participant: It's contagious, huh?

Jesus: Its contagious, yes.

Participant: Thank you.

Jesus: But the key is to live *simply joyously*.

Participant: Yes, without begrudging what you're doing without.

Jesus: If you live simply with the idea that it is a drudgery, it's not going to catch on. (Laughter)

Participant: It's important to humankind that there be joy in their living?

Jesus: Absolutely! It's as important to you as food.

Participant: Yes, and vital at the same time.

Jesus: Absolutely!

Participant: Because it brings forth an aliveness...

Jesus: Indeed. Living simply doesn't mean you *deny* yourself *anything*. Living simply means to detach yourself from *things*. In other words, you all are attached to *things*. You all have things you have to have—your creature comforts, I guess, is the term—and when you come to realize you don't need anything like that to be truly happy...but it has to come from your recognition of what joy is *to you* and realizing that whether you have whatever or not isn't the source of your joy.

Participant: I lost you on that one. Joy comes from within.

Jesus: Joy comes from within. If you have a new—what do you call those things?—if you have a new car...

Participant: Yes.

Jesus: Some people, they have to have a new car. The car isn't the source of their joy, nor is the possession of it, nor is it *wrong* to want a new car or to possess one, but the source of your joy is from the God Self of you, it's from the Spirit of you, it's from your own ability to recognize that you were created in *such joy*. We *all* were created in such joy and to *tap back into* that joy.

Participant: So joy is actually beyond instinct then?

Jesus: Joy is beyond anything. Joy is beyond things. Some people are not happy unless they have a partner.

Participant: Right.

Jesus: The partner isn't going to bring them joy. If they don't have joy within themselves, no partner in the world will bring them joy.

Participant: Because that's when people live...until I get this, I won't be happy; until I get this, I won't...

Jesus: Exactly. Exactly. But when you recognize that the *surroundings* in your world are joyful to you only in as much as you have joy within yourself, then you will recognize that the *things* don't bring you joy. They may make you *happy,* but they don't bring you joy. And I'm not saying you shouldn't have things. Don't misunderstand me. You should have whatever you desire, but the... It isn't in the possessing of anything that is wrong; it is in the complete dedication to owning or having or something like that. That's wherein the problem lies. Then you are separating yourself from your source.

Participant: Thank you.

Participant: Hi. First of all, thank you for being here. It's hard for me to put into words sometimes but I have a question and I know you said we can...to teach today, to live it, and preach and heal and truth will manifest. A lot of us are being surrounded now by people that live with the Bible as being *the* word from God, not as being...

Jesus: Ohhh...the born-agains.

Participant: Yes, in fact there are many that would say it would be wrong for me just to be here today. How can we respond?

Jesus: There were many who said to me it was wrong for me to get up in the synagogue and teach.

Participant: Right

Jesus: Didn't stop me.

Participant: Right. How can we live this on a daily basis? What I've tried to do is point the similarities out and how praising God and being...

Jesus: And you're finding it doesn't work.

Participant: Not always.

Jesus: People of that attitude, and it *is* an attitude—a "I have the truth and you don't have it. I am right and you will *never* be. I know God and you haven't got a clue." Those kinds of people never know God. Why? Oh, I mean never in that particular lifetime. Because they are tribal. They are in the tribe of "They are right and everybody else is wrong." If you don't belong to their church or their synagogue, then you are not in that tribe so therefore, you are excluded. Now, instead of killing you, which they once did—take it from one who knows—now they try to convert you. They try to force-feed their belief system down your spiritual throat.

Bless them in their dimness. (Laughter) They mean well. They mean well. I would not engage with them in any kind of debate. You do not have to justify your eternal soul or your belief system to them. I would simply say, "You have your way and I have mine, and God is happy with both of us."

Participant: Thank you. I'm seeing a reactionary word in that. Okay, with the Promise Keepers, you have the men-dominated society. Even though they are respecting women, trying to treat women better, it's still that men need to be in control.

Jesus: Well, I would suggest that you maintain firmly, "I have my belief. I have my path to God. You have yours. I do not expect you to change for me and I do not expect to change for you."

Participant: Okay. And for those that are looking forward to the second coming and how they will be taken up and the rest of us will be left to...

Jesus: Ah, poor souls. The second coming is within the bosom of mankind...humankind. I'm sorry, I stand corrected. The second coming is when the Christ awakens within the individual's *soul* and is *lived*. That's the second coming.

Participant: Wonderful.

Jesus: They *mean* well. Please know that they love God ardently, although erroneously, but they have this...they go back to the Israelites, who expected God to send a Messiah with an army to overthrow Rome. They're still back there in that thinking. The Messiah is outside. The Savior is out there and he will come. You notice they never say, "*she* will come"?

Participant: Oh, absolutely.

Jesus: *He* will come through the clouds and he will take all those who believe as *they* believe to him. The rest of you are…well, you've had it. Now the thing is, this second coming they will see only when they are willing to *in*clude and not *ex*clude. You can't say that to him because he wouldn't understand it.

Participant: I know.

Jesus: And he has an army behind him in the church in which he goes.

Participant: Yes.

Jesus: And you and God stand against him.

Participant: Oh, I don't want to stand against him. I would love to stand with him.

Jesus: I don't mean against him in the sense that as to make war. Against him… You have the right to be *who you are* and to believe as you choose, just as he does. You may have to make choices.

Participant: Granted.

Jesus: Hold to your own truth.

Participant: Thank you.

Jesus: Beloved woman, do not leave your truth just to keep peace, for that kind of peace is not true and it will be brief and it will bring you sorrow. Giving in to another's way of dominance just to bring peace *never* brings peace. Remember that.

Jesus: Beloved woman.

Participant: Greetings Master. Your information about Thomas resonated and I'm sure there are many people out there who have doubted—not me, of course (laughter)—and when we were in Catholic school, we were taught that if we have something that we're grappling with to pray to the patron saint of dada-dada, and I'm wondering if, that those of us who...

Jesus: I don't think I know that one. (Laughter)

Participant: Is there any value, power, speed, in, say, talking to Thomas, to say, "Gee, I have this enormous doubt and I know you've mastered it"? Is there any value to doing something like that versus all the other tools that you've taught us about Angel of Destruction, Holy Spirit, etc.?

Jesus: Saints are made by people, not by God. The idea of a saint goes back a long, long time, back to old pre-Christian—*way* before Christianity—to a belief system in which a dead ancestor had power and could help. It goes back to a belief system in which alms and offerings were brought to the gravesite or to the altar, or sometimes they would take the head of a loved one and place it on an altar, and they would bring alms to that person, asking that person to bless them with some particular favor. And it was believed by the people back then that these deceased ones had a special power, and especially within the family, within the clan, within the tribe. So the idea of a saint is a concept of that brought into more acceptable terms. There still is a belief that if you find a finger bone or something of a saint that it will heal you.

Participant: Alright.

Jesus: All of these things are brought about only through the concepts of the human mind. These are good people, but they are just people. They are the Children of God, as you are, and whatever power they may have is something they acquired through their own evolution upward. They can help you in the same way that others help you, in the same way that a loved one would certainly grant a favor if they could because they love you. But they are not God in that sense that they have that kind of divine power any more than it is in you as much as it is in them, is the point I'm trying to make. Is it of a benefit? Only inasmuch as if you were to go to a loved one and say, "I need a great favor. Could you grant it?" and they say, "Yes." In that wise, it is of a benefit.

Participant: Okay. Next question is... I really want to thank everybody for their wonderful questions because I thought I didn't have to get up and ask a question today. But I do have one and that is: We've been taught to trust to that point of just trusting and knowing, practice knowing to the point where we just *know* it. We just *know* it. Therefore, that being true, we could possibly then ask the question ourselves, get the answer, and know that that's the answer, know that that's the truth. That's possible. I know that. I also know that the ego comes in and does its thing and muddies up the water and then I start—I, people—start wondering, "Gee, is this really the answer?" Is there some way to neutralize the effect of the ego speaking so that the knowingness stays clear and present?

Jesus: Listen to me well. "Father, here is the question. I know that Thou only are the answer. As I have asked, so have I received and I accept that blessing. Bring it to my consciousness and I will live it. And so it is."

Participant: Yeah, that resonates. Thank you. One more question. It's about being in balance between being and doing. Everything that we've been taught, from all the different seminars and the Friday meetings with Gabriel, has said, "Know thyself. Know the God within thy self. Nurture, serve, volunteer for one's self verses volunteering, if you had to make that choice.

And *balance*. There's something about *balance*, about doing for one's self and doing for another...that's one question. There's also, on that same vein, the question of doing internally and manifesting externally. An example of manifesting externally—trivial example— is manifesting a parking space. Now I think a lot of us have practiced that and manifested a parking space for automobiles. So the balance between doing for one's self and doing for others...the balance between doing *internal* verses doing *external,* okay? Would you like me to say more to clarify the question?

Jesus: No.

Participant: Okay.

Jesus: I was just watching you struggle with that because you already know the answer but you keep pushing the answer from you. Think. If you are happy, is it not easier to do for another? If you are not happy, isn't it more arduous to do for another? So, who should you do for? You should do for you—internally, do for you. When you do for you internally, then externally you can do for others with joy and not with a feeling of obligation or regret.

Participant: Okay.

Jesus: And you knew that.

Participant: Gee, thanks. (Laughter)

Jesus: You knew that but a guilty conscience said to you, "But you can't do for yourself when someone else needs you, so I will do for him or her or them rather than for myself." But within you is that feeling of, "Oh well, I'll do this, alright. This one last time, I will do this." Am I correct?

Participant: And I feel guilty if I do it for me, so I spend lots of time doing the guilt thing.

Jesus: Now, when you do for you, you go into the highest part of your consciousness that you can reach and you can say... What is your name?

Participant: Mary.

Jesus: You can... That's a lovely name. (Laughter) You can say, "I, as this Child of God, desire to do this—whatever it is—this for Mary because Mary is the personality that I am using as a Child of God, and Mary needs to be comforted, Mary needs to be made joyous, and so because I love Mary and what she does for me, I want to do this for her because I love her."

Participant: Okay.

Jesus: Okay?

Participant: Yup. Now the balance between the...okay, so the...okay. (Laughs) The doing for myself, I got that, verses doing for others...that's people. And then the practicing the manifesting of external physical things...sometimes I think that maybe we should be practicing because you and Gabriel talked about flexing our muscles. As we learn internally here, that the other just manifests.

Jesus: It just takes care of itself.

Participant: Right, but it also takes practice.

Jesus: Oh, absolutely!

Participant: It also takes practice to *do* that other thing.

Jesus: It does take practice.

Participant: So...

Jesus: So you practice on yourself first. You learn to manifest by manifesting small things for yourself, and you begin by manifesting an attitude of trust.

Participant: Okay, so we practice manifesting the things that are intrinsic, the things that are internal. Okay?

Jesus: The esoteric.

Participant: Okay, and then what I'm hearing you say then is, "As I become more comfortable with that, as that becomes more natural to me, familiar to me, then the... [Gap in recording]

Jesus: ...with that, you will find that you do it automatically, that you don't have to give it a whole lot of thought beforehand; it's something that becomes second nature to you and you don't have to belabor yourself over whether you should do for you or them first.

Participant: Okay, or whether I should be practicing manifesting physical things out there.

Jesus: Why manifest physical things? Learn to manifest the internal things first and the physical things will follow on their own. That's the law.

Participant: Oh, good. Then I was being lazy about practicing those other things...

Jesus: No, you're in a state of denial. When you want to manifest *things* without manifesting the spirit of the truth *in* you first, you are not taking responsibility for yourself. You are looking out here for the Messiah. Look within.

Participant: Okay, thank you.

Participant: I won't take too much time. I have one question and I didn't want to leave before I asked you. Thank you. It was wonderful today and I'm very thankful because my prayers this last Christmas were accepted. And I want to ask you, it's no coincidence today that I am here. I've been trying...I've been talking to you and I want to know before I leave today, was there anything, among all the messages I got today, anything that before you were trying to tell me that I didn't get, that I couldn't get?

I've been trying to get a message. I just want to know. I'm sorry it's a personal question.

Jesus: Don't worry about the little things. You worry a lot about little things. Have faith, trust God. Little things are easily taken care of.

Participant: Thank you. And...

Jesus: Do you understand why I said that to you?

Participant: Everything seems too little and insignificant sometimes, including myself.

Jesus: You are not insignificant.

Participant: But I feel better when I pray.

Jesus: The one thing that you worry about is that you don't matter, and you do. You matter very much. Keep connected to God and you will someday see how much you matter. You will come to realize how dearly you are loved and how important you are. You need to know that.

Participant: Thank you. One more question I have quickly: Can I help two people in my life and to be able to forgive? Can I do anything for them because I cannot tell them? I cannot help by talking to them.

Jesus: Pray for them. Pray that their internal...that the Child of God of them will wake up. It sleeps. Pray that that God Self in them is awakened and made aware and they will learn to forgive.

Participant: Thank you.

Participant: Hello. I had a question concerning the Book of Mormon and the Doctrine and Covenants, especially concerning initiation into the church and everything that's involved with that, the necessity of it. I understand but I don't understand...a little confused maybe.

Jesus: Any church or synagogue that requires initiation is harking back to the old... When one wanted to become important or to become accepted in an important place, they had to pass a certain test. Now, the original process of that was to assure their faithfulness, their commitment to that which they wished to be a part of. In other words, are they going to stand *with* us against our foes.

That has been refined down through the ages but it still is a question of commitment. How committed is this person who applies? None of that is necessary. If your heart is with God, then who do you need to prove to man? What do you need to prove man?

Participant: Are they...not baiting, but are they—for lack of a better word...I had one organized in my thoughts but I lost it—but do they bait God into giving them specific instruction in saying, "I am God and I have this for you"? Is it their vibration, their only way of understanding?

Jesus: It is their only way of feeling a sense of God-power, is to say that. How can I put this? The God-power within the human being does not need an organized religion to manifest itself. At the risk of offending pastors and ministers here, you don't have to go to church to know God. In fact, very few churches have God really there. They have committees for the committees for the committees and they have rules and regulations that are sometimes impossible to keep. They are extremely critical and judgmental. Behind all of this is *their* idea of what God is.

Groups of people gathered together to listen to someone speak of God originally as a kind of a support thing, as a kind of a community *love* thing, to be reminded how God loved them, to be reminded to follow the spiritual path. But that went greatly astray. How many... [Seeing someone from the clergy in the audience] Ah, beloved brother, how many would you say of the churches truly follow the concepts of Christ?

Clergy: How much trouble will I get in? (Laughter)

Jesus: This is very important. Here is a man of the cloth for forty years. Is this...?

Clergy: The church is like Noah's Ark. If it weren't for the storm on the outside, you couldn't stand the smell on the inside. (Laughter) And one of the things which the church does in order to try to overcome the difficulty is to teach all of its members how to grow mushrooms in the stuff in the hold. (Laughter)

What I hear you saying is that the church, in fact, should be the community of those people who are open to the Presence and to share it with one another. A church is not nice people being nice to other nice people and to those that agree with them. The church is filled with beggars who know where they have found food and share that information.

Jesus: Indeed.

Clergy: And how do you do this? And that is why we're here. I haven't...I agreed that I would talk to a group of people during the period of Lent about the faces of Jesus. Today has been very, very helpful. I see Jesus as teacher, Jesus as healer, and what you said and did is very important. I see the feminine face of Jesus, which has gotten lost in the grinder, and I shall be open in thinking because Lent isn't very far off. (Laughter)

Jesus: I thank you very much.

Clergy: Thank you.

Jesus: Has that answered your question?

Participant: That's what I felt deep down. One other question, and I don't want to put you on the spot, but the very specific instructions given to the Prophet Joseph Smith...it concerns me and I wanted to do the right thing.

Jesus: Joseph Smith was a very sincere, open young man who listened and then weighed what he heard with what would be acceptable and what would not get him run out of town. He softened, changed, modulated whatever he needed to do to bring what he received without offending. So much of what he received was changed by him—and later on, by others—and part of what it was changed to do was to give absolute authority to the church.

Participant: How do we help them?

Jesus: Pray for them. Again, let me say, they *mean* well. They act with loving ignorance and they mean well.

Participant: Thank you so much.

Jesus: You are so welcome. I guess we have to stop. She [Tinkerbell] keeps poking me. Have you learned this day?

Audience: Yes, thank you. May we have a prayer?

Jesus: Yes.

Prayer

My Father,
O Thou Whose voice speaks to the hearts of humankind
in sweet whisperings,
Who pours the cooling waters of healing and truth
into the burning hearts of those who long to know,
O Thou, Whose strength created the earth and caused
the mountains to rise,
Whose power molded the heavens
and brought into being Life,
O Thou, Who art the love that we express and know,
the peace that we seek, and the joy that we are,
O Thou, most wondrous,

I give You thanks for this that has transpired this day.
I thank You for my brethren and sisters
who have come to listen, to learn, and to grow.
I thank You for this beloved instrument
who is an example of perfect trust in You and in me.
I thank you for her loving arms
that brought me comfort
and for her trust that teaches me Your love,
even now.
I thank you that I AM and that we are in You, ever.

And so it is.

I will see you again, as will Gabriel.

Index

Index

Index

Index

Index

Index

About the Author

Reverend Penny Donovan, a natural medium since childhood, was ordained in 1960 at the John Carlson Memorial Institute in Buffalo, NY. She obtained her Doctor of Divinity degree from the Fellowship of the Spirit in Buffalo, NY. In 1964 Rev. Penny founded the Trinity Temple of the Holy Spirit Church in Albany, NY, and served as the pastor there for thirty years. In 1994 she retired from that position to devote full time to spreading the teachings of Archangel Gabriel (whom she had channeled from 1987 to 1999) and other master teachers. Since Gabriel's departure, Rev. Penny has continued teach and conduct spiritual healing sessions in classes and retreats through Sacred Garden Fellowship.

About Sacred Garden Fellowship

Sacred Garden Fellowship (SGF) offers workshops, retreats, and publications that teach practical spiritual tools to help people successfully transform life's challenges. Indeed, the first point in its mission is to "encourage all to become aware of and live from their God Self." SGF, founded in 2009 by Rev. Penny Donovan and Donald Gilbert, is a nondenominational 501(c)(3) nonprofit organization located in the Capitol region of New York. For more information about the organization and its offerings, see www.sacredgardenfellowship.org.